Dannie Abse:
A Sourcebook

Dannie Abse:
A Sourcebook

edited by Cary Archard

SEREN

Seren is the book imprint of
Poetry Wales Press Ltd.
57 Nolton Street, Bridgend, Wales, CF31 3AE
www.seren-books.com

Editorial and Introduction © Cary Archard, 2009
Writings in sections 1-5 © Dannie Abse

ISBN 978-1-85411-507-2

A CIP record for this title is available from the British Library.

The publisher acknowledges the financial assistance of the
Welsh Books Council.

Printed in Plantin Light by Cromwell Press Group.

Mixed Sources
Product group from well-managed
forests and other controlled sources
www.fsc.org Cert no. TT-COC-2082
© 1996 Forest Stewardship Council
FSC

Contents

Section A: Writings by Dannie Abse

Section B: Writings on Dannie Abse

Introduction

Dannie Abse: Finding His Voice

Dannie Abse is a very popular poet; his books have sold well. Single volumes in the past have sold 10,000 copies, more recent volumes 5000 copies. He has had three Collected Poems, the first over 30 years ago in 1977, the most recent in 2003. He has had three Selected Poems (1970, 1994 and 2009). It is sixty years since his first book was published. He is also a very popular reader of his work – a consummate performer whose poetry readings are always well attended. His readers are naturally interested in how a poet whose mature work they read with such pleasure arrived at this position.

When readers praise young poets they frequently talk of the poet having already achieved their own voice. Clearly, all speaking voices are distinctive: we easily recognise someone by their voice. The distinction is so common it's not thought noteworthy. But, for a poet, developing a distinctive voice is seen as the beginning of success. Often poets serve an apprenticeship in which they try out their voice/s. Dannie Abse is a poet who has written many times about his search for his own voice. And what is striking about his development as a poet is how different were the voices he spoke in when he was young. In his teens he was influenced by rhetorical political poetry. In his early twenties the overriding influence was Dylan Thomas. The change between his first book, *After Every Green Thing*, (published in 1948, though the poems were written by 1946 when it was accepted by his publisher, Hutchinson), and his third, *Tenants of the House* (1957), is extraordinary. It is a change he recognises himself: he includes only one poem from the first book in his *Collected Poems*, five from his second book, *Walking Under Water* (1952), but twenty-one from his third. The latter collection includes, and it is clearly no accident, an 'Elegy for Dylan Thomas' and a poem about the Movement poets, 'Enter the Movement', (originally called 'Tenants of the House') which is not a particularly warm welcome.

This Introduction examines the formative years between 1940 (when Abse was seventeen) and 1955, and explores briefly the influences which led to the achievement of Abse's distinctive voice, so familiar to hundreds of poetry lovers – the one he himself usually characterises as conversational and direct, given to paradox, metaphysical, economical in language, prone to inclusion of classical/ Jewish/Welsh allusions, historically aware. It starts with the important family influences on his voice, for, as he was growing up in Cardiff in South Wales in the Thirties, poetry, mostly of a political nature, was all around him; poetry of a kind that was meant to be *heard* and meant to stir, and to which he was introduced by his brother, Leo, the future Labour M.P.. In 1940 he was given the yellow-jacketed *Poems for Spain* in which he read Miguel Hernandez's poem 'Singing I defend myself' and John Cornford's 'Huesca' – poems he can still recite from memory. The rhetorical tone of so much of his early writing – 'hortatory' is the word he uses to describe the most declamatory of it – was already rooted in him before he came across the inescapable influence of Dylan Thomas; it was in the air in his home. In his autobiography, *Goodbye, Twentieth Century*, Abse describes how at this time, before his brother was called up, Leo used to expound his strong socialist views in public in Cardiff from a soapbox. The ear as judge of language was part of family behaviour. It is also significant that his Welsh and Yiddish speaking mother was given to reciting Longfellow around the house. From his earliest days poetry was linked to the ear but also linked to socialism and communism; Leo had a portrait of Lenin on his wall.

The problem for Dannie Abse as he developed as a poet was how to include the moral and metaphysical aspects of his life-view in a poetry that wasn't declamatory. The later Forties, the post-war period, the early Fifties, the beginnings of the Cold War, saw very different attitudes to Communism, to Lenin, to political/committed poetry than had prevailed in his adolescence and early twenties. What he felt about his own voice and the direction poetry itself should go in led him to his argument with the Cold War Movement poets. The collision course was set from the beginning.

Abse's early writing was extraordinarily experimental and especially open to Modernist influences. It is difficult to over emphasize the sheer range and variety of verse forms, the variety of voices/masks he adopts throughout his twenties. This is a poet who is constantly searching, constantly rewriting, constantly reading. His making of himself into a poet is very conscious indeed. He is very aware of what he is doing. He writes and listens to what he is writing. Then something significant happens: as he moves through his twenties, he begins to think he is listening for the wrong things.

Dannie Abse has always been a poet very conscious of the voices around him. He is a poet who had and has a remarkable ear for the voice that suits him. Being the only Jew in a Catholic secondary school helped to hone his ear, as his career as a doctor in a chest clinic taught him to listen. His Jewish and Welsh background did not so much put him outside English traditions and influences as widen and add to those traditions. The consequence is that his voice is more 'European' than other poets of his generation and that this quality has a lot to do with his being a Welsh Jew. He found in European and Hebrew voices forms that enabled him to speak as himself.

Abse's early books indicate just how much poetry he was writing in his early twenties. Most of the poems in his first book had been written by the time he was twenty-three. We have to see the young Dannie as a very committed writer indeed. He was writing before he went to London, but going there to study medicine during the war had a very stimulating effect on him. He has written many times about meeting great European figures such as Elias Canetti, who won the Nobel Prize in 1981, for example. He was also affected by meeting the many German and Jewish refugees who frequented the cafés of Camden and Swiss Cottage, discussing art, music and literature with them. He didn't come from a background in Wales that could in any way be called deprived – far from it – but in London he became involved in a cosmopolitan city life that had been enriched by the war. This was better than going to university to study an arts course. It is not surprising that later in his career he edited books which related poetry to art and music. For a young man his awareness of the wider world of poetry itself was remarkable. It's interesting to look at the acknowledgements pages for the first two books: besides the usual 'Poetry Quarterly', 'Poetry Review' and 'Outposts', there are a disproportionate number of overseas magazines, American – such as 'Poetry Chicago', 'Commentary', and 'Glass Hill' – but also the 'Canadian Poetry' magazine, 'Arena' (New Zealand), 'Rann' (Ireland), and 'Bottege Oscure' of Rome. By the early Fifties, American magazines were especially keen to publish his work, among them many of the best known – such as 'Kenyon Review', 'Sewanee Review', 'Partisan Review', 'Harper's Bazaar' and 'Midstream'.

His first book, *After Every Green Thing*, is prefaced by an old Chinese proverb: 'If you have two pennies to spend, spend one penny on bread that you may live; spend the other penny on a flower that you may have a reason for living'. This introduces us to the author's fondness for proverbs and aphorisms, and parables; a fondness for emblematic writing that includes some wider significance, some relevance outside the poem. It's also a summary of the essence of the book. Abse went to London, aged nineteen, before the end of the war. He was studying medicine and working in hospitals. He was very young, away from home; he was handsome and excited by women. He met many refugees where he was staying; during the war, bus conductors often referred to Swiss Cottage as Tel Aviv. Ugliness and suffering were not theoretical to him: 'I too, am tired of calamities. I too have seen / their salt faces torn apart like red silk... I have seen what none should ever see. I also awake from dreams the colour of skin.' London was a place of air raid warnings and blackout dark. When he moved to Swiss Cottage from Wandsworth in January, 1943, he walked down a Finchley Road, one side of which consisted of mostly bombed houses, the result of the Blitz.

When Abse looks back at his first two books, *After Every Green Thing* (1948) and *Walking Under Water* (1952) he sees the influence of Neo-Romanticism and Dylan Thomas. What strikes the reader of these poems now is the tendency to allegorise experience. It is surprising how little of the broken London around him or of his medical life appears in the poems. More evident, alongside the poet's absorption in his own feelings, is the attention to the musical qualities of language. So many poetic forms are tried out: couplets, long unrhyming lines, quatrains of various rhyming schemes or none. Probably the sheer variety of forms and free verse tells us these are the poems of a young man.

Walking Under Water includes 'The Odour of Nothing' written in 1949, a long poem part philosophical, part autobiography, in which Abse looks over his youth, his self as poet. In his notebooks he labels it, 'Argument with Myself'. He convicts himself of too much music: 'This music justification of a habit long since begun.' Sees too much superficiality and regrets the uncertain, troubled romantic poet persona of the first book. This very dedicated, diligent young poet, consciously looking for a poetic voice in which he can hear his own speaking voice – and which also acknowledges the 'ghosts' – Jewish and Welsh – under his voice, (a poem in *After Every Green Thing* speaks of 'Forever seeking the ghosts beneath / my speaking voice') – recognises he needs a plainer style.

'Odour of Nothing' is significant for another reason. Abse's notebooks show us that parts of it started off in a poem called simply 'Rilke', later 'Rilke, the man', which he was working on late in 1949. Rilke, to whose work he was introduced in 1946 by Rudi Nassauer, a Swiss Cottage refugee and poet who married the Cardiff novelist Bernice Rubens, was hugely important to Abse. He says Rilke taught him to listen. It is highly significant that a quote from Rilke's *Letters To A Young Poet* prefaces his autobiography. He read the *Book of Hours* and *Duino Elegies* in translation and his poem about Rilke is actually a debate with him, with this powerful influence.

I see my own faults in him, and so would forsake
My silent tryst with the appointed agonies,
Even, yes, the gentle exultation of daffodils in the mind
But would gather them as flowers not as yellow images.

His movement towards a plainer style, towards greater objectification (called here 'nearer realities'), develops through this debate:

Rilke also forgot to embrace the true, only saying 'I will',
And dissipated the humane, in letters and in poetry
That could never kill the ever-arriving Angel,
The ever Invisible Bride that denied nearer realities
Which as surely and gorgeously as a sunset in the distance
With painful wires, worked his long suicide.'

Generally *Walking Under Water* is still written in the old styles of *After Every Green Thing*, but with more self-questioning. It was one thing to debate the need for plainness but another to write in this way. Does the volume include any moves towards plainness? Towards gathering the daffodils as flowers? There are more of what Abse calls 'portraits' in this collection. Abse's mature poetry is very peopled and that sociableness starts here. Titles include 'Two Portraits', 'Portrait of a Marriage', 'Albert' and 'Letter to Alex Comfort'. Three of these poems are among the very few poems from this book which have always been included in the *Collecteds*. These poems are certainly plainer, in the sense that they use fewer words; and there's less solitude too. The poet is replaced by a character or by economical narratives – parables. 'Albert', one of the best known, has these qualities and also reveals T.S. Eliot's influence on the young poet's reading. There's humour here too – a note missing in the first book.

The notebook history of 'Albert' is interesting. It was first called 'Animals' which was then crossed out and replaced by 'Love Story'. There was no Albert to begin with but 'he' which was then changed to 'Prufrock', crossed out and replaced with 'Alfred' before being changed again to Albert. The final poem echoes the loneliness and melancholy of Eliot's famous poem.

There's also strong Jewish influence evident in this book. In his 'Poem on my Birthday' (his 26th) 1949, Dannie refers to himself as 'that small Jewish boy', asks not to 'forget the jewries of the future-less'. There's also a 1948 poem which speaks specifically of Israel but not in any political way. The state of Israel had just come into existence. In the book the poem is simply called 'Song': and it is a very patterned, very economical poem, one that expresses hope for Israel in terms of fruitfulness. Sometime later – around 1970 – the poem's title was changed to 'Song for Dov Shamir'. The origin of this title is described in a humorous story in his autobiography. In 1948, Abse was commissioned to write an article of 3000 words on contemporary Hebrew poetry. To spice up his piece, he decided to invent an Israeli poet of his own, Dov Shamir. Of course, to convince the reader that such a poet existed he had to make up a poem by this lyrical young poet, so 'Song' was composed. A while later, he included the poem amongst others he sent to Eliot who wrote back picking out 'Song' for praise and advising Dannie to attempt more translations of this interesting poet. Eliot recognised something genuine in this fake translation. Through arguing with Rilke, Abse saw his own weaknesses. He also tested the influence of Eliot's poetry but discovered a more appropriate voice in his imaginary Hebrew poet.

Abse's third book, *Tenants of the House*, is a book of engagement, a manifesto for the future. The poems were written between 1952 and 1958 when he was in his early thirties. That 21 of the 32 poems in this collection appear in his most recent *Collected* shows that the poet himself feels that in this book he had found a voice. In his first two books the young poet was consciously experimenting; in his third, the period of apprenticeship comes to an end and the more mature poet takes his stand. This is a book which sets directions and makes clear the poet's position in relation to the poetry debate of the early Fifties.

The fashion of the time was for a poetry not of Abse's liking. One manifesto poem is 'Tenants of the House', in which 'the famous tenant' in the poem is clearly Dylan Thomas 'whose song was true, no mere ranting shout'. 'He sang the great passion others lacked.' The new tenants are portrayed as paltry, cowardly figures, bloodless, about as passionate as the suited men who work in the city. It is a funny and angry poem celebrating the larger than life figure of Thomas in comparison to Larkin, Amis, Conquest, Wain and Davie – the Movement poets. The last stanza of this very formal (perhaps deliberate movement-style) poem in neat rhyming quatrains caricatures the Movement beautifully:

> The new choir that moves in is neat and sane
> And dare not whistle in the dark again.
> In bowler hats they sing with sharp, flat voices
> But no one dances, nobody rejoices.

In a version revised sometime later, perhaps 1970s, the famous tenant is made obvious, more visible, by changing the 'strange house' to the 'Boat House' and the 'great passion' becomes the 'Welsh passion', making an episode in the history of poetry clearer for latecomers, making it also a Welsh v English contest – the sort of contest with which Abse, the Cardiff City football fan season ticket-holder, is very familiar. Abse's own celebration of Thomas, 'Elegy for Dylan Thomas', comes immediately before this poem making clear his debt and his allegiance. And that things had changed. Abse was objecting, in his quarrel with the Movement poets, to their rejection of modernism and, in particular, to that aspect of modernism which embraced metaphysics and wider European cultures.

'The Game' is important because it's about his beloved football team and because symbols and allusions develop out of the description of what is recognisably a football match at a football ground; the poet is not thinking in metaphor from the start. And because the poet uses actual names: Saturday, Ninian Park, Canton. It is unusual for an Abse poem this early to be rooted in such particulars. In his notebook, where the poem is first called 'Sports Page', the introduction of particularities is very clear: 'when first we traipsed' becomes 'Saturday afternoon has come' and 'Leslie Jones, Bryn Jones, in their Welsh red shirts' is changed to 'Fred Keenor, Hardy, in a royal blue shirt'. It would be fair to say that 'The Game' is also a parable poem; it becomes a story of courage, and of good and evil. In relation to parables and poetry, the American poet Jorie Graham has written:

'Just learning to read a parable invites a very different and very precious, and very accurate notion of what we mean by 'reading' – as well as a trust that larger quotients of 'not-knowing' are involved in that sensation we call 'understanding' – as well as pleasure in that sensation'. Here we have a post-modernist poet echoing Abse's own credo that poetry should discover 'the invisible in the visible'. Wallace Stevens said something similar in 'The poem must resist the intelligence / almost successfully'.

The last poem in *Tenants of the House*, 'Go Home the Act is Over', implies the poet is a performer, in this case, a trapeze artist performing a magical balancing act, if diverted likely to fall. The poem reminds us that Dannie Abse has always been a superb reader/performer of his poetry. His poems work on the page and in the hall. The sound of the poem has always been important to him. He reads his lines aloud when writing. Corrects them by ear. The metaphor of poet as singer never disappears from his work. The notion of performer is also linked to his career as a dramatist; during the Fifties, he was successfully writing plays which were published and performed. Language in the ear is the key to his achieving his tone. Soon after *Tenants*, in 1961, he became involved in the poetry and jazz concerts organised by Jeremy Robson and performed with Spike Milligan, Laurie Lee, Jon Silkin, Stevie Smith, Vernon Scannell amongst others throughout the decade.

Another influence hovering over Abse throughout the Forties was Pound. He first read Pound when he was seventeen, finding his poetry in Cardiff Central Library. He was disturbed by Pound's anti-Semitism but taken by the poetry. At the same time as his debate with Rilke, around the end of 1949, early 1950, he was grappling with Pound's influence. His notebooks show him working on a poem called 'First of Ten Cantos', with the sub-heading 'Against Ezra Pound'. What was driving him was Pound's support for Italy in the war. In places, Abse's poem sounds like a parody of Pound:

Touch the lamp and it shall break to dust in the mirror,
And how then shall the fishermen return home?

It rains: it is evening
The lights of a car follow the coast road
The paws of the sea are white

> Stretching themselves up the beach
> The back of the sea is grey
> Pricked by the rain, soundlessly.

The broken lines, the fragments – the writing has the look of Pound on the page.

The poem ends with a reference to Pound's imprisonment in 1945-6 in Italy:

> Listen: you, in your mad dungeon, in Italy,
> With your luminous cursing visions,
> Whereto the springtime moths fly.
> Come you say, let us speak of religion.
>
> Be silent, you swine – I speak in religion
> I say forgive noone, lest they know what they do.
> Hear O Israel and you juries of the futureless
> I speak in religion, before I ride into the desert.

Pound's politics drew him closer to 'half the dead of Europe'. Perhaps we can see in Pound – 'that beautiful poet' (from 'Release of Ezra Pound' 1958) – why Abse could not avoid arguing against the Movement, against the nationalistic, the parochial, the 'English', against the poetry which has no place for history or politics, for the 'nearness' of those 'realities'. By the late Fifties, in his thirties now, three books of poetry published, he has argued with the influential voices of his youth – Dylan Thomas, Rilke, Eliot and Pound – and reconciled them with family influences, Welsh, Jewish and social, and in this process found a voice that can accommodate the moral and the musical. His search is over for the poetic voice that can speak for the ghosts beneath his speaking voice.

CARY ARCHARD

Chronology

1923   September 22nd, born Whitchurch Road, Cardiff, youngest of four children, Huldah, Wilfred and Leo – (claims he was conceived in Ogmore-by-Sea). Attends Marlborough Road Elementary School and St Illtyd's College (Catholic secondary school) in Cardiff.

1938   early political position, against Franco.

1940   reads *Poems for Spain* (eds. Spender & Lehmann) and *Left Review* and memorises Cornford's poem 'Huesca'. Begins writing poetry, encouraged by his older brothers Wilfred and Leo.
Moves to Windermere Avenue, Roath, Cardiff, setting for much of *Ash on a Young Man's Sleeve*

1942   first year medical studies at Welsh National School of Medicine, Cardiff.

1943   continues medical studies at King's College and Westminster Hospital, London.

1946   September: Hutchinson accept first book - not published for two years.

1947   first meeting with Joan Mercer.

1949   edits *Poetry and Poverty* No1.

1950   qualifies as a doctor.

1951   called up for National Service in May; August 4th marries Joan Mercer.

1952   *Poetry and Poverty* No 2.

1953   daughter, Keren born.

1954   joins Central Medical Establishment Chest Clinic – till 1989.

1957   moves to Golders Green. Daughter, Susanna born.

1959   *Tenants of the House*, first book to be published in USA. Son, David born.

1960   Charles Henry Foyle Trust Award for drama, for *House of Cowards*.

1961   joins Poetry and Jazz concerts – which continue till 1967.

1962   *Poems, Golders Green* made Poetry Book Society Choice.

1963   *House of Cowards* performed at The Prince of Wales Theatre, Cardiff.

1964   first poetry reading tour to USA.

1969	*The Dogs of Pavlov* performed at The Questors Theatre, Ealing.
1970	Jewish Chronicle Book Award; Arts Council of Wales Literature Award.
1971	British Council tour of Israel with Ted Hughes.
1972	purchases Green Hollows in Ogmore-by-Sea.
1973-4	made Senior Fellow of Humanities, Princeton University, USA.
1976	*Pythagoras* performed at Birmingham Repertory Theatre.
1977	*Gone* in January performed at The Young Vic.
1978-92	President of the Poetry Society.
1979	receives Arts Council of Wales Literature Award.
1982	contributes to *Authors Take Sides on the Falklands*.
1983	made Fellow, Royal Society.
1985	receives Cholmondeley Award from Society of Authors.
1989	awarded Honorary Doctorate, University of Wales.
1992	made Fellow of Welsh Academy.
1995	becomes President of Welsh Academy.
1997	awarded Honorary Doctorate, University of Glamorgan.
1999	made Honorary Fellow of Wales College of Medicine.
2002	*The Strange Case of Dr Simmonds & Dr Glas* longlisted for Booker Prize.
2005	June 13th, Joan Abse killed in car crash.
2007	receives Roland Mathias Prize.
2008	wins Wales Book of the Year for *The Presence*.
2009	made Honorary Fellow of King's College, London.
2009	receives Wilfred Owen Association Poetry Award.

Section A: Writings by Dannie Abse

Preface

The emphasis in this section, as in the book as a whole, is on Abse the poet.
His articles on poetry therefore predominate: the extracts from his prose
writings, especially his fiction and journals, illustrate his diversity as a
writer and have mostly been selected to throw light on his poetry, its
themes and concerns. His career as a dramatist has also been covered. As
with his prose, it deserves much more space than it has been given here.

Dannie Abse has always had an interest in the relationship between
poetry and the reading public. He has also been an enthusiastic
supporter of other poets, especially young poets and poets from
Wales. In his twenties he was involved in the setting up of poetry
magazines and throughout his life he has edited important anthologies and taken leading roles in institutions like The Poetry Society,
the Society of Authors and the Welsh Academy of which he is now
the President. His Editorial Note to *Poetry and Poverty* characteristically cautions against extreme positions and outlines a view of poetry
which closely aligns it to parable: the essence of poetry, he believes,
is to be found under the surface, as though the nature of poetry itself
can only be expressed in metaphor. The pieces in this section outline
Abse's view of the history of British poetry post-1930 very clearly. In
1952, he described the recent history of poetry, from the social
realism and political commitment of the Thirties poets, such as
Auden, Day-Lewis and Spender, to the 'Neo-Romanticism' of poets
such as Dylan Thomas which he considered to be a reaction to the
effects of the war's 'mass comradeship'. The emphasis in poetry
shifted to 'romantic vision', 'myth' and to a stronger focus on the
individual. Then in the early 1950s, the emphasis shifted again: Neo-
Romanticism was replaced by a poetry lacking in ambition; poems
that read as exercises and reportage, in which form triumphed over
content. His concern was that a justifiable reaction to the excesses of
Romanticism was leading to a sterile formalism.

A few years later this concern had grown into a conviction that
something needed to be done. Dylan Thomas died in 1953 and, as
though to mark a new direction in poetry, Larkin published *The Less
Deceived* in 1955 which was consolidated in 1956 by Robert
Conquest's anthology, *New Lines*. The Movement, Oxbridge's attempt
to dominate the nature and direction of British poetry in the Cold

War, had arrived. Abse saw little to suggest that this group of nine poets had very much in common. His own very individualistic view of poetry meant that he couldn't believe that poets would ever be so clubbable. His 'Letter Introduction' to *Mavericks*, the anthology he edited with Howard Sergeant, developed ideas he had outlined in 1952. He characterised the Movement poets as timid, afraid of mystery and of what might lie beneath the surface and saw them as specifically anti-Dylan Thomas. He instantly recognised Larkin as the best of them – an admiration which has remained constant. It is possible that Larkin, himself, might have agreed with some of Abse's criticisms of the Movement. Writing to Conquest at the time of the anthology (in which Conquest included nine of Larkin's poems), Larkin argued that there was something significant missing from Movement poetry: the poets had 'got the method right – plain language, absence of posturings, sense of proportion, humour, abandonment of the dithyrambic ideal' but were 'wanting for the matter: a full and more sensitive response to life as it appears from day to day' (*Selected Letters of Philip Larkin 1940-1985* ed. Thwaite; 28/5/1955). When Conquest claimed that Movement poetry was 'written by and for the whole man', Larkin could not agree. There was always something of the romantic about Larkin. In his younger days, he was certainly more of a romantic than Abse. When he was a student at Oxford, he admired Yeats, Blake and Shelley, and even compared some of his early work to Rupert Brooke's. For many years, he thought Lawrence the most important English writer of the twentieth century. In a letter in 1940 he offered a romantic view of poetry: 'Poetry (at any rate in my case) is like trying to remember a tune you've forgotten... A poem is written because the poet gets a sudden vision – lasting one second or less – and he attempts to express the whole of which the vision is the part.' (Letter 20 Dec 1940 J.B. Sutton). Later, Larkin admired Betjeman largely, it seems, for his accessibility but he had a very different attitude to readers in 1940: '...a poet never thinks of his reader. Why should he? The reader doesn't come into the poem at all'. Larkin was not always a critic of Thomas. When he heard Dylan Thomas read at Oxford in 1940, he was very impressed. But some years after, he came to see Thomas as a dangerous influence; 'I agree he is a shocking influence: I had him for a while but not for very long or very badly' (Letter 11/1/47 Amis). Thomas's remarkably strong influence was one that Abse also had to struggle against.

Looking back now on the Fifties what is striking is how fragile the notion of 'The Movement' has become. The nine poets seem to have had very little in common, the notion of a group largely incoherent. Abse's *Mavericks* anthology appears more appropriately named. There has been a tendency, especially amongst institutionalised critics, most based at universities, to find clear threads, distinctive schools in British poetry, and an unwillingness to accept the maverick nature of poets generally. Larkin, similar to Abse, during his career did his best to challenge such manufactured histories, hence perhaps his advocacy of Betjeman as the finest poet of the late twentieth century. Abse, in *Mavericks* and later anthologies, performed the same service, reminding readers of the variety and energy of poetry. If 'The Movement' was a movement then its inchoate nature was evident from the beginning. The same year as *Mavericks* was published saw Ted Hughes's first collection, *The Hawk in the Rain* which offered a very different direction for English poetry. Just two years earlier a Welsh 'country priest', R.S. Thomas, had published *Song at the Year's Turning* in which the final poem turned away from 'wild creatures', concluding 'nature's simple equations / In the mind's precincts do not apply'. R.S. Thomas's book had an introduction by Betjeman (Larkin's idol), who had also been a subscriber to *Mavericks*. Dividing 'Lines' in poetry tend not to be very clear or particularly 'New'.

Abse developed his interest in European poetry in his teens influenced by the Jewish socialism of his brother Leo (who became a Labour MP), a strong anti-Fascist and supporter of the Republican side in the Spanish Civil War. When he read *Poems For Spain* (eds. Spender and Lehmann) he was immediately impressed by the writing of the young Spanish poet Miguel Hernandez. When he went to London to study medicine, he was introduced to Rilke for the first time; 'He became a passion for me' he writes in 'Under the Influence'. Hernandez and Rilke both appear in *Modern European Verse*, one of a popular and influential series of 'Pocket Poets' published in the 1960s. Other volumes in the series included *Beat Poets, Jazz Poems, Negro Verse*; the series also included a selection of Abse's own work amongst other single author selections of Burns, Betjeman, Lawrence, Keats, Edward Thomas and Donne. With this volume, Abse was once again reacting to what he saw as the insularity of much English poetry in the post-war period. His selection included sixteen poets from eight different languages, namely Spanish, Russian, Italian, Polish, French, Greek, German and Yiddish.

In the Sixties, Abse also frequently took part in the popular Poetry and Jazz concerts organised by Jeremy Robson. In 'Under the Influence of...', he writes amusingly about performing with, among others, Spike Milligan and Stevie Smith.

Poetry Dimension, an annual of 'The Best of the Poetry Year', ran from 1973 to 1980, and, all but the first, which was edited by Jeremy Robson, were edited by Abse. From the start, this was a very eclectic enterprise. In the first volume, Robson included Abse and Larkin, Heaney and Pound, and the Movement poets Donald Davie, D.J. Enright and Elizabeth Jennings. Abse's own first issue included Larkin's essay on Betjeman, and poems by Davie and Gunn. But there was also space for five Mavericks. Clearly the earlier debate had had little effect on Abse's choice of poems. Yet, as the introduction included here suggests, Abse's concern for the relationship between poet and reader was a factor in his choice of poems. The early link in his thinking between poetry and social issues, poetry and politics, that poetry should contribute to something beyond itself does affect his choices, hence his hostility to 'instant poems' and 'cross-word puzzle academic verse'. If there is a bias in his selection it is towards the Celtic countries, the 'margins' as they were considered then. Scottish and Irish poets and poets from Wales feature prominently in every issue. A significant absence is poems by women which rather reflects the relatively small number of women poets being published in the Seventies.

Many of the contributions in this section make clear the seminal importance of the war and post-war years on Abse's poetry. Also striking is the influence of members of his family, especially his brother, Leo. Parable-like stories about his family constantly appear in these essays illustrating how that intimate conversational style so distinctive in the poetry is also a characteristic of his prose. In these pieces he discusses in detail the early influences on his poetry of Thomas and, in particular, Rilke and of how his voice changed its tone from 'singing' to 'conversational'. The pieces offer many insights into the development of his poetry. He links his poems to parables in the way that he wants them to only appear to be translucent. They should arise from 'experiences' rather than 'naked ideas'.

In his talk to the Institute of Psychoanalysis, he explores the relationship between imitation and originality (another way of writing about the poet's struggle to develop his own voice) and offers the insight that the poet is like the trapeze artist or the racing driver – individuals who enjoy living dangerously, hence 'martyr-poets' such as Dylan Thomas, Wilfred Owen and Sylvia Plath. There's also a fascinating exploration of the Jewish and Welsh influences in his writing, what he calls the 'relationship of David and Dafydd'.

The pieces in part 2 of this Section are taken from two of the five novels Abse has written over a period of fifty years. *Ash on a Young Man's Sleeve*, his first novel, from which the two extracts are taken, was published in 1954, though parts of the novel had already appeared in magazines a year or two previously. The other two pieces are self-contained stories which were included in *There was a Young Man from Cardiff*, published in 1991. The titles of both novels suggest autobiography, the mention of 'young man' in both for example, but also there is that hint of the literary – in the quotation from Eliot in the first and in the suggested fairy tale opening of the other. Abse calls them 'autobiographical fiction', aware that many readers have taken them for actual autobiographies. In his 'Author's Note' to *There was a Young Man from Cardiff*, Abse points out that when Penguin reprinted *Ash on a Young Man's Sleeve* in 1982 they 'mistakenly printed Autobiography on the cover'. In his 'Note' he is at pains to point out that in this novel as in his first one 'I have attempted to write autobiographical fiction; that once more I have deleted my past and, despite approximate resemblances, substituted it with artifice. If I am disbelieved so much the better'. The distinction between autobiography and the novel has never been straightforward; some of the earliest novels, *Robinson Crusoe*, *Moll Flanders*, for example, were offered to the public as memoirs. What is striking about Abse's novels is the degree of attention given to Dannie and his family, and to family places such as Cardiff and Ogmore-by-Sea, and the way in which they are always seen in relation to actual key historical events and people. These are novels imbued with history. Like his poetry, Abse's prose is experimental. Each of his novels is formally different.

Abse's Journals (part 3) cover a twelve year period, 1981-1993, and many of the entries were written for publication in his local paper, *The Hampstead and Highgate Express*. They contain so much humour and wisdom that making a selection is not easy. Some extracts have been chosen because of the light they throw on Abse's own poetry and the poetry of others, especially Larkin's. Other extracts because they reveal so much about his life as a doctor and the influence of his family, his love for Cardiff City football team and Ogmore-by-Sea, the village where the family stayed when he was a boy and where, since the Seventies, he has made his home in Wales. The clarity and control of these passages remind us of his versatility as a writer as does the extract from his article about his play-writing (part 4). Many readers of Abse's poetry may be unaware of his career as a dramatist. He enjoyed visiting the theatre when he was at school and this interest grew when he was at medical school and reviewed plays for a theatrical magazine. He wrote plays for the stage from the early Fifties and one of his most successful, *House of Cowards*, won the Charles Henry Foyle Award in 1960 and was included in *Plays of the Year*. During the Sixties, he wrote many radio plays for the BBC. Abse continued writing dramas into the 1980s but unfortunately none of his plays ever transferred to the West End. The allegorical and conversational qualities of his poetry and the experimentalism of his prose are echoed in the surrealism and eccentricity of his plays. (See James A. Davies's essay in section 7 for a detailed and perceptive account of Abse's writing for the stage.)

1. On Poetry – Essays and Introductions

Editorial Note – *The Second Phase of Neo-Romanticism* (1952)

In England, in recent times, the character of modern poetry appears to change roughly every ten years. The socio-political poetry of the thirties, which had as its protagonists the talented Auden-Day Lewis-Spender triumvirate with their concern for humanism, contemporary reality and direct communication, itself superseded a less socially aware decade. The war came, however, to drive the younger generation into regiments of mass behaviour and plural boredom, making the individual amongst that Vera Lynn clamour all the more singular, all the more lonely. And the new poets of the Forties were unable to exchange their individuation for a mass comradeship. With the changing conditions of daily habit, the manner and climate of poetry altered also, and not unnaturally the poetry of the forties began with a manifesto. Inspired by Henry Treece and J.F. Hendry, *The New Apocalypse*, as the resultant 'movement' was called, began with an emphasis on a romantic vision, eternal rather than contemporary subject matter, importance of myth and an aggressive personalism. The mood of poets writing at that time was exhibited in the publication by Herbert Read of the Routledge Series of poets, amongst whom could be numbered John Heath-Stubbs, Sidney Keyes, Alan Rook, Emanuel Litvinoff and J.F. Hendry himself. This general tendency of writing characteristically came to be known as Neo-Romanticism.

Like succeeding governments, each new school of poetry has denied the virtues of its predecessors. The Neo-Romantics attacked the poets of the thirties for their crude insistence on contemporaneity, on propaganda, on slick journalism, just as now the Neo-Romantics in their turn are being flailed by the young critics of this decade for their floridity, rhetoric, lack of intelligence and wilful obscurity due to an excessive private vision. Paradoxically the psychologist Jung, doubtful hero of the Neo-Romantics has been quoted against them: 'The personal aspect is a limitation – and even a sin – in the realism of art. When a form of 'art' is primarily personal it deserves to be treated as if it were a neurosis'. Geoffrey Grigson, too, the Poetry Headmaster of the thirties, delightedly remarked in 'Polemic': 'The romance we are drifting back to is a romance without reason: it is altogether self-indulgent and liquescent. An Ink Cap mushroom grows up white and firm and then flops down into a mess of ink – which is our new romance'. For the body of the work produced in the last decade this was a fair enough assessment. But just as the judgement of the verse of the thirties does not take account of the true virtues of the Auden group, so those who now discredit the romantic writers fail to recognise the true achievement that a good anthology could well exemplify.

Some of the more self-conscious quarterly periodicals (there is no dearth of them whatever the popular press might suggest) – quarterlies like *Nine* and *Colonnade* – belligerently criticise the sagging weaknesses in much of the adipose poetry of the last decade and would replace this subjective Neo-Romanticism with a sterile and dull Neo-Classicism. More important, this present fashion of discrediting the romantic movement and replacing it with a calibre of poems that read as futile exercises, with poems that seem to have no urgency, or even necessity, would on the whole appear to be reflected in the back pages of the influential *New Statesman and Nation*. The danger is toward a new cultural journalism, snobbish and anti-humanistic. At best these sorts of poems can be exquisite reportage with roots in the worst aspects of seventeenth century standards of taste. There is the old insistence on 'conceits' and artifice, on that which Crashaw described as 'fair and flagrant things'. Without the rapture of the seventeenth century poets, the present manner of so much of the work printed in magazines like *Nine* or *The New Statesman* deserves to be labelled as 'The New Exercise'. In *Nine* for example, Iain Fletcher wrote in an editorial: 'Most contemporary readers have become insensitive altogether to style and structure: the only critical question which they ask is: "how much of a jolt or kick does this poem give me?"' But these remarks are tantamount to a plea for 'style and structure' as an end in themselves. Mr. Fletcher should know that the poem which in effect jolts and kicks the imagination has done so in part through its craft – or to put it another way – through its 'style and structure'. But craft is a means not an end. Those poems in *Nine* or *The New Statesman* that conform to what appears to be the editorial ideal are neither memorable nor even entertaining. They are simply boring. Communicability need not only fail through a too romantic vision. Communicability can be stifled in a yawn.

It is not, then, in this over-compensated reaction to Neo-Romanticism that the poetry of the fifties has hope of importance or readability, but rather, I believe, in the modification and development of the romantic vision of the poets of the last decade. Nobody wants to save the corpse of *The New Apocalypse*, or indeed even attempt to keep it breathing with an iron lung; rather the time has come for poetry to move into a new and second phase of Neo-Romanticism. What should be discarded are its faults alone: there is no need to throw the whole apparatus of Romantic expression overboard, particularly as the present alternative mode of writing appears to be so trivial and precious.

The work of the Neo-Romantics is that sort of poetry that we should 'enter sober and leave drunk'. What happens too often is that one enters sober and, because of its rich exuberance and lack of proper organisation, one leaves not drunk but merely nauseated, sick. Where, though, organisation and discipline of Idea bind the poem into a formal whole, so that the whole pattern of music, image and meaning marches in harmony toward an inevitability of communicative conclusion, the romantic ideal of poetic impact is realised. The validity of a poet like Sidney Keyes, young as he was, can be immediately recognised for he was always aware of the necessity for the poem to be informed with a basic conceptual power. Again Dylan Thomas is one romantic poet who at his best level touches the sublime and at worst appears bogus and dull. It is commonly agreed that amongst the most memorable of his poems are 'Fern Hill', 'The Hand that Signed the Paper', 'After the Funeral', 'In my Craft and Sullen Art' etc. Each of these poems is organised by a central theme or idea. Without such a constraining influence he can write nonsense like:

Now
Say nay
Man dry man
Dry lover mine
The deadrock base and blow the flowered anchor,
Should he, for centre sake, hop in the dust
Forsake, the fool, the hardiness of anger.

One can almost hear Mr. Dylan Thomas whispering: 'When in doubt, fox 'em'. The same sort of fault appears to be indigenous in the mass of neo-romantic work. A New Apocalypse anthology like 'The Crown and the Sickle' may be opened at random to find:

I take four devils with me when I ride
My animal of muscle and of love,
To match the demons grinning in my steed,
Who thumb their noses when I make a move
Who prick my body with their little pins
To make me bleed who finger all my sins.

Or another anthology again taken down from the shelf of the Forties and opened fortuitously gives us these lines to read:

Hound me the comet lashing with
    Groans of desire
Upon the aching lips of the blood-bath
    On the wheeling mount;
For you caressed the eucharist
    In systems of Venus.
And after the muttering of the thigh
    The word of the Saviour....

One could quote *ad nauseam* lengths of this visceral 'poetry'. What is clear is that the power of the word alone is not magical unless used as the vehicle of the Poetic Idea. Certainly it is not enough to have a fury of images, or a devotion to musical patterns or eccentric typography. A disciplined romantic texture must be insisted upon. Romanticism must be tempered with an organic concept in its substance so that the concept at least on one level (preferably on more) may be fairly and honestly communicable. It is important though to understand that a poetic intelligence should correlate the wedding of aural and visual elements, not a prose one. For obviously poetic thought is not the same as prose thought so that even where a clear idea illuminates the poetry it should not lend itself to entire paraphrasing. Again the Poetic Idea may be no more than a symbol breathed from beginning to the end of the poem, or it may be expressed in fragmented terms of a poet's 'weltanschauung', through parable perhaps, myth or theme. It may be even directed toward a Contemporary Event as long as the poet does not descend into mere reportage and this should not occur if that event is adequately and subjectively universalised. Either way the magical or poetic Idea must become the sinews of the poem so that the romantic equipment of urgency and power of word does not dissolve into a 'mess of ink'.

This magazine has attempted to print poems which conform to these standards. In *Poetry and Poverty* No. 1, G.A. Wagner's 'Threnody for a Ruined Landscape' or Louis Adeane's 'Poem for Three Persons' can be cited as examples. In No. 2, Kathleen Raine's 'The Instrument' or John Smith's 'Walking on Stilts' are only two poems which illustrate this second phase of Neo-Romanticism. In No. 3, Peter Viereck and Paul Engle show that America has poets combining a romantic vision with a new lyricism, all controlled by the discipline of a central communicable idea.

These remarks have been made only to indicate the sort of poem we are looking for (but too rarely find) and also perhaps to point a direction different from the way of the New Exercise.

From: *Poetry and Poverty*, no. 4, London, 1952

Introduction *Two Letters* (1957)

Dear Howard,

Thank you for sending me the Philip Larkin and the Price Turner books, both of which I like. Larkin seems to me to be the best of the Movement poets, though what he has in common with the others, or, indeed, what they have in common with each other, is difficult to define. Except perhaps their antagonism towards sensibility and sentiment and their corresponding emphasis on being "tough".

Language, The Movement believes, should be straight and unadorned. It would be all right if they were just anti-rhetorical. But the Lucky Jim attitude is – apart from anything else – fundamentally *anti-poetic*. So it's not surprising that they distrust the image and seem to fear primary Dionysian excitement: it is as if they're afraid of the mystery conversing with the mystery – or to put it into contemporary jargon – the depth mind talking to the depth mind. One is reminded of Browning's: "Oh my dove, let us be unashamed of soul." But there are other young poets writing from the centre of inner experience: who allow the argument at the centre to become audible in the grace, decorum and discipline of poetry. The poem, in fact, that is symbol of the centre and which is, therefore, not only *about* something but *is* something at the same time.

With the Movement poets the reader hardly ever receives the impression that the poem has seized the poet and that a struggle has ensued between the poem and the poet, between the nameless, amorphous, Dionysian material and the conscious, law abiding, articulating craftsman. Still it will be interesting to see the anthology, *New Lines* which Macmillan are publishing soon. I understand that that anthology will draw on nine Movement poets: Larkin, Holloway, Enright, Amis, Gunn, Davie, Elizabeth Jennings, Wain and Conquest. Some of them interesting enough but how did all this "grouping" arise? The truth is that poets can hardly ever be put into real groups. One can subdivide and subdivide until each poet is a group on his own. Every poet, in one sense, is a Movement. Fashions, in any case, change so quickly. The word "romantic" now has an ugly connotation, associated as it is, in poetry, with a preposterous ornamentation. (Hence the Movement is anti-Dylan Thomas.) But what seems to one generation ugly and untidy may appear to others, at a later date, to assume the dignity of noble line and grandeur. I suppose I am equating the romantic with the Dionysian and the Dionysian with that mysterious, permanent element in poetry that irradiates and moves us and endures down the centuries. But if, for this reason, I am anti-Movement, I'm certainly not opposed to discipline and form and style. For these qualities make those disturbing Dionysian elements acceptable to oneself and to others.

So it would be nice – even if only as an antidote – to publish another anthology of less fashionable young poets – say all born after 1920 – though they shouldn't form a school for that would be false from the start. To choose poets unafraid of sensibility and sentiment, who are neither arid nor lush. I can think of a number of young poets who are not writing mere exercises but working from the heat of personal predicament and common experience; who remember perhaps Dryden's "Errors like straws upon the surface flow; He who would search for pearls must dive below."
What do you think?

DANNIE ABSE

From: *Mavericks* eds. Dannie Abse and Howard Sergeant, Editions *Poetry and Poverty*, London, 1957

Introduction – *Modern European Verse* (1964)

Twenty-five years ago, the work of European poets such as Rilke and Lorca was read in England with great avidity. Not only were poetry readers internationally minded but the English poets themselves seemed to be engaged emotionally and polemically with the political happenings in Europe. Such writers reacted unequivocally, like litmus paper to acid, to European conflict – to the civil war in Spain, for example. They were hostile in their writings, and in their ancillary activities, to the rise of Nazism in Germany and Fascism in Italy. But fashions change, so that not long after World War II had ended, if an English poet proclaimed in his work a similar, engaged interest in the social upheavals of distant countries he would, undoubtedly, have been labelled a political romantic – and, by then, the very word 'romantic', in critical parlance, had become almost a dirty word.

Indeed, by the 1950s, critical opinion in England had ventured to the opposite extreme, and the virtues in poetry, primarily praised, were those that could be singled out as distinctively English. Poets like Eliot and Pound whose influences and interest were obviously European in scope were downgraded, and Hardy, Edward Thomas, Robert Graves, achieved a new popularity. Though poets such as Edward Thomas have their own attraction and excellence, many looking back may, nevertheless, come to think that much ephemeral reviewing and criticism in England during this period was marked and limited by a barely conscious chauvinism. In any event, a criticism which countenanced poetry as a kind of genteel, social accomplishment could hardly spotlight favourably the vigorous, and rather differently ordered poetry that was being written abroad.

There are signs, though, that such a parochial critical climate is coming to an end, and this trend is reflected not least in the new revived interest in European poetry generally. Recently, there have been numerous anthologies of translations published, including one of 20th century Polish poetry, another of 20th century Yugoslavian poetry, and yet another of 20th century German poetry, and so on. There have been several public readings of European poetry in translation which have been well attended and kindly received. A book like Robert Lowell's *Imitations* too, with his free versions of European poems has been welcomed and abundantly praised. Poets, critics, and editors, then, are once again encouraging readers to develop more eclectic tastes and so the work of modern European poets is being explored.

Not infrequently, such European poets have been committed to more than their poetry. Unlike English poets they have not, after all, been living necessarily in a mild, fortunate, and liberal political ambience. Many have been subjected to grim social pressures which, by and large, English poets have happily escaped. Amongst the contributors to this anthology one has only to think of Lorca murdered, Mayakovsky committing suicide, Hernandez dying in a Franco prison, Celan surviving a Nazi concentration camp, Brecht exiled, and so on. It is not surprising therefore, that from Europe we have had much 'platform' poetry – poetry that is missionary, poetry that was not written to delight the reader but to arouse his indignation and, perhaps, move him to action. In the first world war our own Wilfred Owen confessed to a similar intention.

However, many celebrated poems from Hungary, Poland, etc. – e.g. Gyula Illyes' 'One Sentence on Tyranny', or Adam Wazyk's 'Poem for Adults', have not been included in this anthology for, in the opinion of this editor, such work is of more interest to the sociologist and political historian than to the poetry reader. Indeed, though there are several samples of aesthetically satisfying 'platform' poetry to be found here – for example Hernandez's moving 'Hear This Voice' which was written during the Spanish civil war – many inclusions are interiorly composed and directed, and not written at the top of their voices. There are exclusions, too, of poems by European poets, most eminent among them Valéry and Montale, but this is either because of length, or because the English versions, in my view, are not faithful enough or, if faithful, not satisfactory enough as poetry. There is, I hope, nothing to apologise for in this anthology – only for what, because of such reasons, had to be regretfully left out.

From: *Modern European Verse*, Vista Books, London, 1964

Introductory Note – *Poetry Dimension* Annual 5 (1978)

Four years or so ago, Anthony Thwaite discussed in *The Two Poetries* the common reader's response to verse being written now in Britain. He remarked, with sad resignation, on the popularity of that oral poetry cradled in Liverpool, and more importantly, he drew attention to the revulsion of many University graduates towards verse that had academic sanction simply because of its complexity. This revulsion stemmed, he suggested, from the aridities of their Eng. Lit. education. 'They (the students) had been through the mill,' Thwaite wrote, 'and had come out as chaff. Years of 'Tradition and the Individual Talent', *Principles of Literary Criticism*, *Seven Types of Ambiguity*, and *Revaluation* (with all the derivatives and by-products of these) had made them incapable of looking at literature with other than an over-subtlety, an ingenuity, as fatigued as it was detachable. *Criticism* stank in their nostrils.'

Recently, Philip Larkin, in an address in Hamburg on accepting the 1976 Shakespeare Prize (the last poet to receive this prize was John Masefield in 1938!) returned to similar themes: the inadequacies of both the mindless simplicities of oral poetry and the academically structured poems built out of fragmented artifacts of literature rather than life. But instead of focusing on the reader's response to such poems Philip Larkin was concerned with the poets themselves who might be tempted unconsciously, because of material reward, to write in a certain way so that they might star on the Poetry Circuit or advance on the Campus:

In the Seventies it has become possible... to make a living, if not by poetry, then at least by being a poet. Take poetry readings, for example: what Dylan Thomas called 'travelling 200 miles just to recite, in my fruity voice, poems that would not be appreciated and could, anyway, be read in books.' If by such readings a poet enables his audience to understand his poems more fully, and so to enjoy them more, this is good. But if doing so tempts him to begin writing the kind of poems that succeed only in front of an audience, he may start to deal in instant emotion, instant opinion, instant sound and fury, and this may not be so good...

The same kind of danger awaits the poet on the campus. If literature is a good thing, then exegesis and analysis can only demonstrate its goodness, and lead to fresh and deeper ways of enjoying it. But if the poet engages in this exegesis and analysis by becoming a university teacher, the danger is that he will begin to assume unconsciously that the more a poem can be analysed – and therefore the more it needs to be analysed – the better poem it is, and he may in consequence, again unconsciously, start to write the kind of poem that is earning him a living.

All this may be obvious but it needs saying loud and often. Fortunately those writers who produce oral pieces for the microphone do not pose any durable threat. They may bamboozle an untutored audience for a while, and this, of course, is to be regretted. But once their poems are visible on the page so too are their limitations. Rather it is the poem that has been wilfully or unconsciously structured so that it may be disentangled by a critic short on feeling but high on invention that is the more pernicious danger. If such critics, despite their erudition, were less naive there would be fewer poems that consisted only of ambiguity and footnote.

Certainly no poems of this kind are to be found in this annual nor, indeed, any of the platform variety. They have all been taken from magazines and books★ published in Britain between March 1976 and March 1977. Despite the usual shortage of interesting criticism, and instant poems and cross-word puzzle academic verse notwithstanding, it seems to me to have been a good year.

D.A.

From: *Poetry Dimension* Annual 5, Robson Books, London, 1978

★ All the books are by British poets. There was not space to include any of the many translations that appeared or poems by those American poets – Daniel Hoffman, Louis Simpson, James Merrill, Anne Sexton, Richard Eberhart, etc. – who had books published in the U.K. during this time period.

Rhyme (1980)

I

As you read this prose-note your expectancy will be that I shall not rely on words that regularly or irregularly rhyme. On the contrary, as I write, should a word here or there inadvertently and frankly rhyme it may interfere with the clear progress of the sentence, and I, aware of the sound words make (as all writers are whether of prose or verse), will accordingly substitute another word for the rhyme-obstruction.

Of course, there are occasions when the writer of prose will deliberately borrow devices that are commonly associated with poetry: false rhymes, pararhymes, assonance, alliteration, parallelism and so on. I take down a book from the nearest shelf. Because it happens to be *The Oxford Book of Welsh Verse in English* edited by Gwyn Jones and I wish for the moment to dwell on prose I turn to the introduction. Almost at once I discover what I am looking for:

> The two centuries ran their course, fashions rose or were adopted; fashions fell or were adapted; by 1800 the poetic landscape showed a visible shortage of tall trees, and the ninth wave had ceased to roll and thunder...

It is perhaps amusing to note that Gwyn Jones's reliance on such poetic devices as parallelism and pararhyme – 'fashions rose or were adopted; fashions fell or were adapted' – prompted him, probably unconsciously, to borrow immediately a second property of poetry, namely metaphor. The ostentatious *aural* pattern is followed by *visual* metaphors, albeit mixed! I am not, need it be said, criticising the quality of Gwyn Jones's prose. What I am endeavouring to point out now, no doubt laboriously, is how often any writer of prose with half an ear deliberately uses – pick up any book from any shelf – all the devices associated with verse *except true, frank rhyme*.

There are, of course, many living poets who follow prose writers in this and just as stringently eschew rhyme in their verse. It is not because they, like Milton, recall with reverence the non-rhyming parings of the Latin or Greek tongue or the august high seriousness in the non-rhyming poetry of the ancient Hebrews. Rather it is because they feel rhyme is too obviously an artificial device and that such transparent artifice contradicts Wordsworth's still modern

41

proposition that poets should keep as far as possible to a selection of language really used by men. In addition, some small number mistakenly feel that, with the advent of the modern movement more than half a century ago, rhyme became dated, old-hat – and this despite the example of the best poets writing since T.S. Eliot.

What has *genuinely* become dated though are those limitations on the use of rhyme that once governed poets in their employment of it. My father, soon after the First World War, bought a set of encyclopaedias from a travelling salesman. These encyclopaedias, published by the defunct Gresham publishing company, at present adorn my bookshelves, and I confess that before beginning this note I took down volume IX, PHO-ROM, to look up *Rhyme*. I discovered much prejudice about rhyme that no longer endures. For instance:

> English writers have allowed themselves certain licences and we find in the best English poets rhymes which strike an accurate ear as incorrect. In some instances such as *sky* and *liberty*, *hand* and *command*, *gone* and *alone*, the correspondence in the letters makes what may be called a rhyme to the eye which supplies, in some measure, the want of correspondence in sound. In other instances, however, this is not the case, as in *revenge* and *change*, *remote* and *thought*. Such rhymes may be tolerated if they only occur at rare inter-vals, but they must certainly be regarded as blemishes, and are carefully avoided by all who wish to write harmoniously.

Autres temps, autres moeurs. The fact is, whatever may be the case in prose, there are no immutable laws of when and where not to use rhyme in poetry or what kind of rhyme is legitimate and acceptable.

When I look back at my own work I discover that sometimes I have used regular rhyme, sometimes irregular rhyme, sometimes internal rhyme, and sometimes no rhyme at all. I should like now to refer to two poems I wrote more than a decade ago which have cooled in that distance allowing me some measure of objectivity. Both poems have an autobiographical basis; both indeed arose from harrowing experi-ences, though of a different kind; both were informed with a more than ordinary emotional charge. One of anger, one of grief. Neither were poems that resulted from emotion remembered in tranquillity.

One poem was called 'In Llandough Hospital' and was written in rhymed quatrains, the other 'A Night Out' consisted of three unrhymed, eleven-lined paragraphs or stanzas. Both poems can be found in my *Collected Poems* so I shall not reprint them here. I would like, though, to say why I felt it necessary to use rhyme in one poem and no rhyme at all in the other.

'A Night Out' relates the experience of going to a cinema and being surprised by a too lifelike Polish film about a concentration camp in Hitler's Germany. The film assaulted me as a matter of fact. I quit that cinema in London's Oxford Street in an undefined rage and needed, soon after, to write a poem about the experience. Such was the charge of my emotion that rightly or wrongly I felt that I did not wish to make any pretty artifice out of it. I did not want to be lyrical about such a theme. I wanted to be as truthful as possible, to avoid all kinds of artificiality, to say what I felt and to say it plainly. I wanted the *verisimilitude of prose* – and so wanting that I used rhythms associated with prose and of course, as prose writers do, I eschewed rhyme.

'In Llandough Hospital' is a poem about the death of my own father when I, as a doctor, also happened to be in attendance some of the time at his deathbed. I have written a little elsewhere about that poem – in my autobiography *A Poet in the Family* – and perhaps I may be allowed to quote from that book here:

I started to write a poem about that recent experience in Llandough Hospital. Then I put my pen down listlessly. To convert that raw finale into a mere wordy resemblance of it seemed wrong. Why should I allow myself to pull back the curtain on a scene so intimate to me? Yet since poetry was my raison d'être – my ambition, I had said often enough, was to write the next poem – then surely not to try and make a poem about that urgent eye-brimming experience would be to admit that poetry-making was a trivial act, a silly useless fiddle with words, and that my own life, its direction and centre, was silly and useless too? I began to feel I must write a poem called 'In Llandough Hospital', I had written poems about a stunted tree, about a railway shunter, about a piece of chalk even, about the halls of houses, about odours, about a hundred things, hundreds of things, so not to write about my father's death would be an insult to my father's memory...

What I did not go on to say was that when I began the poem I was oppressed by the need – as much as one may be at a funeral – for some ceremony in the diction, for the poem itself to own the formality of ceremony. Nothing too elaborate. A simple form and simple rhymes. Not the intricacies of the *cywydd* or any English approximation of it. No, a quatrain say, with line-endings *abca*. What could be more simple, appropriate? (And more difficult!) Not a choir then, but one voice, and that single voice on this occasion not too colloquial.

Ridiculous pressures, feelings? Maybe. Perhaps another poet experiencing that Polish film in the way I had done or the trauma of a father's death may have made poems of and about these experiences with the discipline of a contrary technique? No rhyme in this poem but in the other. Or no rhyme in either. Or rhyme in both. It is all subjective, is it not? There are no laws. And what seems, in the end, inevitable, was at one time probably not so.

II

Looking back at the poems I have written during 1978 I observe once again that some depend on regular rhyme, some on irregular and internal rhyming, and some eschew rhyme altogether. The poem I choose to print here, 'In the Gallery', was finished but a month ago. It is irregularly rhymed and I select this poem rather than another because its genesis is eccentric for me in that it is rooted in a rhymed couplet, or to be exact two rhymed couplets of a sort.

A little while back in writing an introduction to my *Collected Poems* I remarked, 'For some time now my ambition has been to write poems which appear translucent but are in fact deceptions. I would have a reader enter them, be deceived he could see through them like sea-water and be puzzled when he cannot quite touch bottom.' This comment has provoked a number of people, to ask me to elaborate on it. On one occasion I was called upon to do so after a poetry reading and perhaps too succinctly I replied, 'Think blue, say green.' My response doubtless did not satisfy my interlocutor but I liked my own suddenly made-up phrase. Indeed, later, going home, it occurred to me that *Think Blue, Say Green* might well be a good title for my next book of poems! The trouble was soon another line occurred to me: 'Squeeze apple-pips from a tangerine.' So there I was now stuck with two lines of a poem:

> Think blue, say green,
> squeeze apple-pips from a tangerine.

At regular intervals these two lines came into my head and were as regularly dismissed because I did not know what lines could follow or precede them. More recently, while watching a programme on BBC television about Schubert, I saw a shot of birds flying up from a waste of snow. The commentator spoke of snows and crows, unintentionally presenting a rhyme, and almost at once I thought:

> Four hoofmarks in the snows
> flew away. They must have been four crows.

Like 'Think blue, say green...' these two lines also focused on deception, a visual deception. Perhaps each of these 'couplets' though rhythmically different, had something to do with each other? Now I have long believed that poems should arise out of experience, true or imagined, rather than from naked ideas. An image itself or a musical phrase can be a kind of experience but to set lines authentically ticking and onward I needed a further and more concrete experience and this was given to me when I accepted an invitation to a party at an art gallery.

I do not propose to talk about the meaning of 'In the Gallery' for it is about deceptions as any reader could perhaps have predicted from what I have already said. I shall draw attention, though, at any rate briefly, to the rhymes in the poem or rather some of the rhyming problems that exercised me as I worked on the different lines. Certain parts of the initial conception of the poem had to go – including 'Think blue, say green / squeeze apple-pips from a tangerine.' That 'couplet' I eventually discovered did not belong to the poem; as for 'four hoofmarks in the snows' this image became separated from 'they must have been four crows' because I wanted the last two lines of 'In the Gallery' not so much to rhyme as to each end with the same word – that is with *crows*.

I do not know why I wanted such a conclusion. Shakespeare, I can reason, concluded scenes with a rhyming couplet sometimes when he had used no rhymes earlier. But in 'In the Gallery' I had employed irregular rhyme throughout so to finish the poem with a rhyme would hardly have been surprising. On the other hand to repeat the word-sound exactly is a small surprise for that repetition is a variation that could, as it were satisfactorily, snap shut the poem finally.

Any image in a poem should be alive and to be alive it needs to be both surprising and apt. So it is with rhyme though, I think, to a lesser extent since there is something satisfying also in predictability of sound patterns. How then can predictability and surprise both be present in one rhyme? That apparent contradiction can be solved in different ways. For instance, in the lines:

> Outside it is snow snow
> snowing and namelessness is growing

I hope it is accomplished by the placing of *snowing* at the beginning of the second line rather than at the end of the first line where the reader may justly expect it to be. It is a small adjustment and only changes the sound pattern by the briefest of hesitations. In other lines I trust the problem is solved by using hidden, internal and approximate rhymes with a consistency – *chandelier, weather, sculptor, straw, forever, anywhere* – that the authoritative contributor to the old *New Gresham Encyclopaedia* (vol IX) would have baulked at.

Of course, there were temptations to use additional frank rhymes, to write for example, 'Her name is forgot' rather than 'forgotten' so as to allow *forgot* to chime more loudly with *spot, not* and perhaps *bolt*, but that temptation was resisted because *forgot* is an archaic mode and a discerning reader would have sensed that I had merely been ruled by rhyme rather than being the master of it. Besides, I wanted a three-syllable word, *forgotten*, at this point in the context of the lines that immediately followed it, for these also are end-stopped with three-syllable words (namely *disputed* and *forever*), for such a sequence, though short, can set up a pleasing aural pattern. All this may be of small matter to the reader and I wish to avoid becoming tedious. In other words it is time for me to conclude. So please turn to 'In the Gallery' and do read the poem the second time anyway without noting its rhymes if you can. It wasn't written to demonstrate any technique or lack of it.

In The Gallery

I

Outside it is snow snow
but here, under the chandelier,
there's no such thing as weather.
Right wall, a horse (not by Géricault);
left, a still life, mainly apples;
between, on the parquet floor, a box
or a coffin which is being opened.

Through a gold-framed mirror,
the Director, dressed as if for mourning,
observes the bust
of an unknown lady
by an unknown sculptor
being lifted out of the straw
by a man in overalls.

II
The apples do not rot, the horse will not bolt,
the statue of the lady
cannot breathe one spot
of tissue paper on the mirror.

Her name is forgotten,
the sculptor's name is disputed,
they both have disappeared forever.
They could have been born
in the North or the South.
They have no grave anywhere.

III
Outside it is snow snow
snowing and namelessness is growing.

Yesterday four hoofmarks in the snows
rose and flew away.

They must have been four crows.
Or, maybe, three of them were crows.

From: *Poetry Wales* 15.3 (1980)

A Voice of My Own (1980)

At the top of the report my name, *D. Abse*; my address, Mayim, Windermere Avenue, Roath, Cardiff; my age, 15½. Opposite English Literature, in red ink, the tidy handwriting of our English master, Mr. Graber: *He has a voice of his own.* My parents would be puzzled by that remark. 'He means,' I would tell them uselessly, 'that I have a style of my own.' I recalled how, some years earlier, my brother Leo had brought home his school report and that next to his Latin mark of 25 (out of 100) a master had written, *He is in a class of his own.* Leo's oratorical and persuasive gifts were such that he had managed to convince my innocent parents that Latin was not his worst subject but his best, that the Latin master's comment had not been derogatory but a startling and honoured compliment. Only quite recently I heard my mother declare, when a neighbour was discussing the Latin temperament, 'Our Leo was always excellent at Latin.'

Reading my report my father's lips moved silently before he finally lifted his face from the page to blindingly search mine, 'Everybody's got a voice of his own,' he grumbled. 'Everybody's face is distinctive. I don't see that your English master's comment is particularly praiseworthy.'

I fumbled until, inspired, I said, 'It takes time even to grow into your own face.'

Ever since I had been *so high*, cheek-pinching fussy visitors with strong thumbs had pondered, 'Who does he look like?' The Shepherd side of the family, round-headed Sumerians, said with an 'Alas' that I resembled an Abse; the Abse side, though, insisted that I, poor boy, looked like a Shepherd. That kind of luminous conversation would always conclude with my mother reminding everybody that she had once been the prettiest girl in the Swansea valley and that when she had married my father the neighbours had called the newly-wed couple Beauty and the Beast.

One wry aunt, not listening to this true but worn story, and staring at me as if I were in a cage pronounced that I looked like nobody in particular. This was a most fearful and scandalous metaphysical judgement. Yet she was right. My face was not then, nor yet at 15½, my own. Similarly my English master was wrong: I did not yet have a voice of my own. All I had was an accent. And when I started to write my schoolboy poetry, in 1941, even that suggestion of individuality was soon submerged as I caught, like a happy infection, the intonations of the poets I had read at school and at home.

I had become interested in poetry after reading one of Leo's books, *Poems for Spain*. Stephen Spender in the Introduction to that book declared, 'This collection of poems about the Spanish War written and translated by English writers is a document of our times... The fact that these poems should have been written at all has a literary significance parallel to the existence of the International Brigade. For some of these poems, and many more which we have not been able to publish, were written by men for whom poetry scarcely existed before this Spanish War.' Until I read that book, poetry scarcely existed for me. For matriculation I had studied and liked Tennyson's 'Lotus Eaters', Keats's 'St Agnes Eve', Wordsworth's 'Lines at Tintern Abbey'. Earlier, at home, sometimes in the corners of an evening, Leo would also read me poems. I particularly enjoyed hearing him recite Browning. And when I played tennis, and was losing, I would rouse myself into a proper aggressive stance by mouthing lines from 'The Lost Leader'. Wordsworth had sold out, Leo had told me years earlier – become Poet Laureate. Wordsworth, it seemed, was a turncoat like Ramsay MacDonald. So as I endeavoured to serve an ace I would mumble to myself, 'Just for a handful of silver he left us.' *Smash...* OUT. 'Just for a riband to stick in his coat.' *Smash...* DOUBLE FAULT. 'Blot out his name, then, record one lost soul more.' – *Smash...* OUT.

Poetry, then, had its uses but it moved into the centre of my preoccupations gradually, and that movement only commenced after I had read my contemporaries in the urgent, yellow-jacketed anthology, *Poems for Spain*. Here I read for the first time poets whose adult moral concerns and protestations engaged my own wrath and imagination. Their voices had a passionate immediacy and their language was fresh, of the twentieth century. The raw political poems of the Spanish peasant poet, Miguel Hernandez, moved me to express my own indignation about the horrors of war in verse. I had begun to write verse voluntarily, not as an exercise for school. I hardly thought about technique at first or worried about owning a voice of my own. Looking back, now, I realise that, as I wrote, I was beginning to exchange the collective tone of the nineteenth century – Wordsworth, Keats, Tennyson, Browning – for that of the twentieth – Hernandez, Auden, Spender. And, naïvely, I wanted to make political statements.

Recently, my *Collected Poems 1948–1976* was published. A reader lingering over these poems would discover occasional references to the most important public events of our time – events in Nazi Germany, or war in Vietnam, or man landing on the moon. For instance, a first visit to Germany in 1970 prompted lines like these:

> Can't sleep for Mozart,
> and on the winter glass
> a shilling's worth of glitter.

> The German streets tonight
> are soaped in moonlight.
> The streets of Germany are clean
> like the hands of Lady Macbeth.

(From: 'No More Mozart')

A few years earlier, lying on a foreign beach, after reading an English newspaper with its news of Vietnam I looked up at a single cloud in a blue sky and thought how Euripides had made Helen say, 'I never went to Troy. Only a phantom went.' To which the messenger, according to Euripides, replied, 'What's this? All that suffering for nothing, simply for a cloud?' And soon, still thinking of such things as Vietnamese women newly-widowed, I wrote:

> Later, I walk back to the hotel thinking:
> wherever women crouch beside their dead,
> as Hecuba did, as Andromache,
> motionless as sculpture till they raise their head,
> with mouths wildly open to howl and curse,
> now they call that cloud not Helen, no,
> but a thousand names, and each one still untrue.

(From: 'On the Beach')

As for man landing on the moon, the news that those computer-speaking astronauts – bleep bleep bleep, over – had brought back some moon material to be examined by scientists made me write a poem called 'Moon Object'. You could pronounce that title as Moon Ob*ject*, if you wish. Addressing a scientist examining samples of moon-rock I continued:

Blue eyes, observe it again. See its dull appearance
and be careful: it could be cursed, it could be sleeping.

Awake, it might change colour like a lampshade
turned on, seething – suddenly moon-plugged.

Scientist, something rum has happened to you.
Your right and left eyes have been switched around.

Back home, if you dialled your own number now,
a shameless voice would reply, 'Who? Who?'

(From: 'Moon Object')

So, over the years, I have managed to write lines like these, poems such as these; but I've never managed to make an overt political poem of the platform variety such as Hernandez once so passionately wrote. For that early resolve to write direct political verse dissolved after a year or two – long before I served my long apprenticeship in learning how to write. Perhaps I realised even then that a voice shouting loses its distinctive quality. The voice of, say, John Smith speaking is his own but John Smith shouting becomes the raised voice of anonymous humanity.

But I see that I am immodestly suggesting that by not shouting I have at last achieved what Mr Graber once falsely claimed – a distinctive style, a voice of my own. Style, though, is something more unconscious than deliberate. Poetry depends upon unconscious engenderings and proliferations. Poetry is written in the brain but the brain is bathed in blood. So a writer intent on recognising what distinguishes his own poetry from that of his contemporaries is confronting a dilemma. He looks into the mirror but sees no-one there. To put it another way: style is like an odour in a room he has lived in for so long that it is not recognisable to himself – only to visitors.

That is why someone with the integrity, for instance, of Victoria Sackville-West could happen on a typescript of a poem among her papers called 'St Augustine at 32' and could believe that it was one of her own discarded efforts – not a poem by Clifford Dyment who, as a young poet twenty-two years younger than she, had sent it to her for appraisal many years before. Not knowing her own style she read it as if it were her own – critically, yes, but with that especial tolerance proper and common to authors examining their own work!

With cosmetic changes, she decided, this neglected draft could be rendered into serviceable verse. Soon the poem bore a new title, 'The Novice to her Lover' and some months later a puzzled and irate Clifford Dyment read it in *The New Statesman*.

But if style is truly unconscious how, in another issue of *The New Statesman*, could one of those competitions which directs its readers to write a paragraph in the style of Graham Greene be won by Graham Greene, himself, when he entered under a pseudonym? I think a writer while not able to apprehend the matrix of his own style can become aware of its superficial elements – the audible mannerisms and visible devices – and it was these that Mr Greene supplied. I would now, therefore, like to change my metaphor of a writer in search of his own style being one who looking into the mirror sees no-one there, to one who because of mannerisms and devices looking into the mirror sees clothes with no-one in them – clothes without an Emperor!

Every writer, some time or another, is likely to ponder the question of literary influence: of who has influenced him and whom he has influenced; what are just and proper borrowings and what is a too overt imitation. Perhaps writers generally feel sympathy with the Lacedomians who used not to punish theft so much as the inability to conceal it. But it is better to sin than to be sinned against. For imitations debilitate, somehow, the power of the original; they cheapen the original. True, when fashion changes, and changes again, the original work of art discharges once more its old energy, whereas the imitations seem poor, inert reproductions with only as much resemblance to the original as handwriting has to its rough reflection on blotting paper.

When I look back at my earliest published work of the late 1940s I discern not only the then fashionable manner of Neo-Romanticism, but the unpremeditated influences, too dominant, of Dylan Thomas and Rainer Maria Rilke. Whatever individual voice I owned had to make itself heard above such noisy echoes. It seems to me, now, what is probably obvious to everybody else, that a poet's progress towards discovering his own voice is marked by the shuffling off of all discernible individual influences. In his youth, a poet reading this or that poem with admiration may often murmur, as I did, 'I wish I had written that'. Later he will never articulate such a wish for he will realise that only one man can write one particular poem, that the style of that poem cannot satisfactorily be borrowed, and that without that style the poem cannot exist. This man's gift, that man's scope, may continue to be admired, but the mature poet will know it is better to be that ill-defined thing, himself, rather than the second Rainer Maria Rilke or the second Dylan Thomas. A true poet may envy another poet's material success, the winning of awards, the adulation of critics, but he cannot envy the other poet's poetry. To put it another way, as Eliot would have said, and indeed to quote Eliot, there are 'men whom one cannot hope to emulate, *but there is no competition*'.

Those poems of mine marred by the too intrusive accents of Rilke and Dylan Thomas I left out of my *Collected Poems*. And if some of the earliest poems in that volume seem to me half-successful it is not because I now find my own individual voice in them. On the contrary, it is because they imitate everybody and in doing so sound like nobody in particular. That is to say they belong to an anonymous tradition. Here, for instance on Page 2 of my *Collected Poems* (the poems in this volume are arranged more or less chronologically) is a poem called 'Epithalamion' which belongs, I think, to the central English lyrical tradition:

Singing, today I married my white girl
beautiful in a barley field.
Green on thy finger a grass blade curled,
so with this ring I thee wed, I thee wed,
and send our love to the loveless world
of all the living and all the dead.

Now, no more than vulnerable human,
we, more than one, less than two,
are nearly ourselves in a barley field –
and only love is the rent that's due
though the bailiffs of time return anew
to all the living but not the dead.

Shipwrecked, the sun sinks down harbours
of a sky, unloads its liquid cargoes
of marigolds, and I and my white girl
lie still in the barley – who else wishes
to speak, what more can be said
by all the living against all the dead?

Come then all you wedding guests:
green ghost of trees, gold of barley,
you blackbird priests in the field,
you wind that shakes the pansy head
fluttering on a stalk like a butterfly;
come the living and come the dead.

Listen flowers, birds, winds, worlds,
tell all today that I married
more than a white girl in the barley –
for today I took to my human bed
flower and bird and wind and world,
and all the living and all the dead.

I was trying to say earlier that a shout becomes less particular in character than a level speaking voice. The voice of John Smith talking is his own, but John Smith shouting is the raised voice of anonymous humanity. That direction towards anonymity is also evident, is it not, in the singing voice? I think it no accident that as the years pass by I use more and more a conversational tone rather than a singing one. Could it be, incidentally, that the poet's general tendency to be more lyrical in youth is related to his own existential doubt, his own falterings about his immature and unstable identity?

I find a letter addressed to me by T.S. Eliot, when I was a medical student and publishing poems for the first time, more enlightening now than I once did. I had sent him a number of poems including one by an imaginary Israeli poet. In 1948, the State of Israel had come into existence and I wrote a song which I purported was by a young Israeli called Dov Shamir. Eliot who did not know about my impersonation liked my 'Dov Shamir' poem and he wrote to me more or less saying that I should do more Dov Shamir translations because they were better than my own work! I still think that judgement ironic and amusing, but I realise now that Eliot was at least right about the song for Dov Shamir, it was better than the others I had sent him. The others had unintentional bits of Dylan Thomas and Rainer Maria Rilke in them, whereas the Dov Shamir song could have been written by anyone – even by Dov Shamir himself! For that is the point I am trying to make. A pure song has no particular voice in it. It merely waits for a particular voice to sing it.

A Voice of My Own (1980)

So if I have found eventually my own voice it would be more evident in the later rather than the earlier pages of the *Collected Poems*, in those poems conversationally directed. I stare now at these pages and try to assess the poems on them rather like some frowning critic. I see they are rooted to the time and the country and the tradition in which the author works. I note certain recurring preoccupations and evidence to confirm the autobiographical facts that the poet is a married man practising as a doctor in a city in the twentieth century. I might even be able to guess (as if I didn't know) that one of the author's favourite precepts about aesthetics is that of Han Fei who, in the third century B.C., maintained that it was too easy to paint a ghost but most difficult to paint horses or dogs! Playing the part of a sympathetic critic all this and much more I can apprehend. Further, I hear no particular alien voice in them – those intonations of Dylan Thomas and Rainer Maria Rilke having faded entirely. I hear no voice at all that sounds particularly like someone else's. Only in this negative way can I conceive that I have, in fact, a voice of my own. And the only other confirmation I have in this is when others tell me they can recognise my way of saying things or when, occasionally, I am confronted by imitations of my own work. Then I think, 'Why, that's damn it all, like me.'

But, of course, it's not for me to make any judgement about such a matter. Strangers less prejudiced in my favour, must arrive at their own conclusions. It seems sensible, then, to help them in this by ending with a poem. The last one in my *Collected Poems* should do as well as any other. It does not seem eccentric compared with many of those that precede it, nor do I think it better or worse than them. It's called 'The Stethoscope'.

    Through it,
over young women's abdomens tense
I have heard the sound of creation
and, in a dead man's chest, the silence
    before creation began.

    Should I
pray therefore? Hold this instrument in awe
and aloft a procession of banners?
Hang this thing in the interior
    of a cold, mushroom-dark church?

Should I
kneel before it, chant an apophthegm
from a small text? Mimic priest or rabbi,
the swaying noises of religious men?
Never! Yet I could praise it.

I should
by doing so celebrate my own ears,
by praising them praise speech at midnight
when men become philosophers;
laughter of the sane and insane:

night cries
of injured creatures, wide-eyed or blind;
moonlight sonatas on a needle;
lovers with doves in their throats; the wind
travelling from where it began.

(B.B.C. Radio 3 and 4)

From: *Poetry Dimension* Annual 7, Robson Books, London, 1980

From: 'Pegasus and the Rocking Horse' – Notes on Originality and Imitation in Poetry (1981)

(...) But why is a distinctive voice in *poetry* so important to us in the enjoyment of it; or why, conversely, are recognisable imitations so irritating? The same criteria apply as in painting, not least the territorial claims of primacy. Consider for a moment those majestic lines of *English* poetry in Ecclesiastes that many of us may have known and valued for years – valued as literature, I mean.

> ... Or ever the silver cord be loosed, or the golden bowl be broken, or the pitcher be broken at the fountain, or the wheel broken at the cistern. Then shall the dust return to the earth as it was and the spirit shall return unto God who gave it. Vanity of vanity, saith the Preacher, all is vanity.

In the New English Bible of 1972 we find a different translation from the Hebrew which the editors believe to be clearer, more readable, more accurate:

> ... before the silver cord is snapped and the golden bowl is broken, before the pitcher is shattered at the spring and the wheel broken at the well, before the dust returns to the earth as it began and the spring returns to God who gave it. Emptiness, emptiness, says the Speaker, all is empty.

It is not possible for those of us attached to the older version to accept the recent rendering as anything but a paste copy of less value. Apart from its sense, 'Emptiness, emptiness' has a passable sound relationship to 'Vanity, vanity' but the final 'all is empty' seems faintly ridiculous because we hear a distinct aural error as we, reflexly, echo what we already know and admire. Only those totally new to both versions are able to make a more objective judgement about which is the better poetry; they, unlike us, have not to contend with the power of primacy. Translations, like original poems, if they are really fine, can inhabit us and, once accepted, all other versions, all other translations, whether objectively better or not, are dismissed by us as imposters.

Sir Joshua Reynolds's advice to apprentice-painters was complex: he warned them of the dangers of imitation though he recommended the practice of it. In poetry these dangers are even more acute. The power of primacy and therefore the importance of originality remain paramount. Certainly no metamorphosis of the wooden rocking horse can occur unless a new-made poem is active with originality, and paradoxically this originality can only subsist where there have first been models.

It is obvious that the work of some poets appears to be more original than that of others. Some, by being least imitative of the fashionable modes of the period – poets absorb generic modes as much as individual models – seem eccentric when they first attract the public's eye. They have been more rebellious, have adopted a more confident, pugnacious posture towards the dominant literary tradition than most of their colleagues. I recall Freud believed that 'a man who has been the indisputable favourite of his mother keeps for life the feeling of a conqueror, the confidence of success that often induces real success'. The aetiology of artistic confidence, a poet's risk-taking and adventurousness in technique, may indeed reside in early developmental entanglements.

I dare say a number of you would consider that some of, if not all, the hidden roots of a poet's technical rebelliousness – his overturning of models, his striving for marked originality – may find nourishment in the darkness of his Oedipus complex. Be that as it may, the general reader's initial response to blatant originality is one of hostility, a degree of hostility of greater moment than that directed against blatant acts of imitation which I commented on earlier. Poets who remark metre in an original way are particularly likely to irritate most poetry readers. What Robert Bridges declared about metre still obtains: 'It offers a form which the hearers recognise and desire, and by its recurrence keeps it steadily in view. Its practical working may be seen in the unpopularity of poems that are written in an unrecognised metre and the favour shown to well established forms by the average reader.'

It may be that Bridges privately, with a too complacent satisfaction, was thinking of his own fame – he was Poet Laureate – and of the contrasting neglect of his innovative friend Gerard Manley Hopkins. The irony, of course, is that with the passage of time it is Manley Hopkins who has found favour with poetry readers rather than Bridges whose diction, if not metre, seems stale to us. Yes, Bridges perhaps was too imitative of the poetic conventions of his day, while we can now see to what end Manley Hopkins confessed, 'The effect of studying masterpieces makes me admire and do otherwise.' In short, it is not a matter only of models becoming part of a poet's natural disposition like his heart that beats and his blood that throbs; he may go further, he may inventively react against such models so that the rocking horse gallops up the mountain and takes wing.

I should like to return to the reasons why some writers feel compelled to be innovative in an extreme way whereas so many others seem content to work within the constraints of a dominant literary convention. It may be that psychoanalysts have news to give us about this enigma other than the old headlines on page one about Oedipus. One text I discovered to be particularly audacious and rewarding is *Thrills and Regressions* (1959) by the analyst Michael Balint. To be sure, he does not concern himself with the nature of originality, that is not his central theme, but I believe his propositions to be relevant to it.

A baby, Dr Balint suggests, may respond to the early traumatic discovery that important objects lie outside himself in one of two ways: (a) he may create a fantasy world where firm objects, though having now an independent existence, are deemed to be still benevolent and reliable; or (b) he may recreate the illusion of the world prior to the trauma – when there were no hazardous, independent objects at all, when there were only free, unobstructed, friendly expanses.

It seems the direction of these early responses persists, to a greater or lesser extent, into adult life. So there are those who, when their security is threatened, would *cling* to objects. These are the so-called ocnophils. Then there are those who are their antithesis – the so-called philobats who, finding objects hazardous, would reach for the free spaces between them. For the extreme philobat, objects are indeed objectionable whereas for the extreme ocnophil they are objectives.

In describing adult behaviour patterns, Michael Balint spotlights the philobat as one who prefers to be solitary, devoid of support, relying on his own resources – indeed, the further he is in distance (and time) from safety, from *mother* earth, the greater the thrill he experiences in proving his independence. That is why, Dr Balint suggests, some find it attractive to undertake solitary crossings of the Atlantic or remain aloft in gliders for long periods. Clearly the philobat, or rather the extreme philobat, for there are all kinds of mixtures and gradations, would be perceived by most of us as having the character of a hero. Such men live dangerously. They are, though, according to Dr Balint, bolstered by their feelings of their own potency by holding on to phallic objects, to a magic penis: the tight-rope walker carries his pole, the lion-tamer his whip, the skier his stick, and yes... the poet his pen!

It is odd that the poet, the true poet, should be conceived to be, like the trapeze artist or lonely mountaineer, or racing motorist, a philobatic hero. Michael Balint infers as much. Other analysts too have done so in the past and will continue to do so in the future. How romantically one such as Jung discusses the Poet with a capital P. 'Art', he writes in *Modern Man in Search of a Soul*, 'is a kind of innate drive that seizes a human being and makes him its instrument. The artist is not a person endowed with free will who seeks his own ends but one who allows art to realise its purposes through him.... To perform this difficult office it is sometimes necessary for him to sacrifice happiness and everything that makes life worth living for the ordinary human being.'

'Tosh,' one might say, but the fact is that this view of the poet as tragic philobatic hero-figure is commonplace and poets themselves have contributed to the making of this myth. 'Why,' asked Yeats, 'should we honour those that die upon the field of battle, a man may show as reckless a courage in entering into the abyss of himself?' And here's Rainer Maria Rilke pronouncing in a letter, 'I feel myself to be an artist, weak and wavering in strength and boldness.... Not as a martyrdom do I regard art – but as a battle the chosen one has to wage with himself and his environment.' As Robert Graves has justly remarked, 'Despite all the charlatans, racketeers, and incompetents who have disgraced the poetic profession an aroma of holiness still clings to the title "poet" as it does to the titles "saint" and "hero", both of which are properly reserved for the dead.' Nor does Mr Graves demur from this popular belief.

It may be inferred from my remarks that I do! I certainly would not subscribe to the notion that the poet is a hero, that the writing of poetry is an heroic act. That notion seems absurd to me; yet when I look back at the poems I myself have written and at the few in particular that have taken as theme the creative process itself, I am surprised to see that my rational belief is contradicted by those very poems. I am even startled to discover that one of them, a poem written some years before the appearance of Michael Balint's *Thrills and Regressions*, actually spotlights the poet as trapeze artist, the very same figure Dr Balint characterises as an extreme philobat.

I called my poem, 'Go Home the Act is Over'. It was written soon after Dylan Thomas died in 1953 and I had Dylan Thomas very much in mind when I wrote it. I subsequently suppressed the poem. I did not, for instance, include it in my *Collected Poems* (1977) because I did not think it good enough. However I should like to read it to you now for it does lucidly define what I am saying:

'Go Home the Act is Over'

Roll up, roll up, the circus has begun
and poets, freaks of multilingual Time, perform.
Fingers, ten dwarfs, beat thunder on a drum
and whizzing spotlights flash as in a storm.

Look, like a trapeze artist he flies with wires
above pedestrians who with iambics freeze.
To those with cold hands he offers fires
and sings the catastrophes.

Play gaudy drums then, let the lions roar,
the circus crowd is ready. You others
is it his death you're waiting for?
Where any poet sings, the vulture hovers.

Electricians above the balcony point the light.
Against the roof his two shadows dance
and somersault. He sings for our delight
but seeing gold he trips and loses balance.

The audience is hushed. The sawdust ring
is empty except where that singer lies.
Still, high in the air, two trapezes swing.
Does that last image leak from his two eyes?

Return now to that place. The grass, instead,
the wind and stars where once the spotlights shone.
His funambulists and jugglers are dead.
The show is over. The big tent gone.

It seems that each generation needs to create a martyr-poet: in the fifties when I wrote 'Go Home the Act is Over', it was Dylan Thomas, a generation earlier Wilfred Owen. More recently, Sylvia Plath has been cast for that role. There are those who feel romantically – common reader, analyst, sometimes, as you see, the artists themselves – that somehow the poet soars to forbidden heights, steals the ambrosia of the gods, illicitly brings heavenly fire to earth. What has been said of the public's attitude, in another context, about drug addicts could equally describe general feelings about the *poète maudit*: 'Prometheus, having illicitly brought the fire to earth, is condemned to a millennium of being eaten alive; Tantalus, having stolen the ambrosia of the gods, suffers a fate that makes his name a symbol of an exquisite form of torture; Icarus, having sought the forbidden heights, suffers the inevitable consequence of plummeting to the depths.'

And so the poet too, receiving merciless justice, becomes sacrificial martyr and then is glamourised: Alec Guinness, incongruously wearing a red wig, a curly red wig, impersonated a libidinous Dylan Thomas on a Broadway stage; Glenda Jackson, of luscious proportions, transformed slight, angular, flat-chested Stevie Smith in a British film; and even as I'm speaking now, they are preparing in Langholm, a small border town in Dumfriesshire, to erect a sculpture-monument to honour their locally born Hugh MacDiarmid. When MacDiarmid was alive, by the way, his poetry was of less consequence to members of the Langholm council who declined to grant him the freedom of the town – instead they honoured Neil Armstrong the astronaut, whose connection with Langholm was somewhat more cosmic. In any event, dead, it seems MacDiarmid has become as philobatic a hero as any astronaut alive.

Indeed it is not unusual that the poet, elevated to a pedestal after his death, may have received scant attention from the public at large during his lifetime, especially if his work has been conspicuously original. The analyst, Phyllis Greenacre, in describing an individual's reactions to strange events – events not poems – wrote, 'Any experience which is so strange that there is little in his life to which he can relate it, is felt as inimical, alien and overwhelming. On the other hand, an experience which is only somewhat or a little bit new is pleasantly exciting.' As with external events, so with poems: if too strange (original) the poems may be felt to be inimical, if 'a little bit new' they may be welcomed as 'pleasantly exciting'. But I should like to qualify Dr Greenacre's proposition: the intensity of the experience, the poem's effect, depends surely not only on the gradation of its strangeness (originality) but on the ocnophilic or philobatic temperament of the individual, the particular reader. A strange experience, whether an event or a poem, may provoke in one person, at first, inordinate hostility or fear; in another it may merely promote curiosity or unease.

Most people have ocnophilic leanings. Accordingly they prefer that the pattern of any new poem be not too strange, the cadences and images and syntax not too strange, the organisation, structure and theme not too strange. The word *ocnophil*, by the way, was suggested to Michael Balint because it stems from the Greek verb meaning to shrink, to hesitate, to cling. So the reader, with his ocnophilic tendencies, *clings* to the nourishing breast of proved traditional modes, to that with which he is most familiar. The avant-garde writer apprehends this: he expects resistance to his way-out inventions. William

Wordsworth in his day, publishing the *Lyrical Ballads*, certain of the marked originality of his poems in style and theme – poems that were so different from those currently receiving general approbation – expected more derision than praise. And he was correct in this assumption. Thirty years after the publication of the *Lyrical Ballads* the common ocnophilic reader in England thought Wordsworth to be a fool who could write forty dull sonnets on one streamlet or go berserk about linnets, red-breasts, larks, cuckoos, daisies and 'the scenery of the English Switzerland'. That was generally the blunt response to a particularly original poet. Later in the nineteenth century, the same reader, or at least his great-nephew, would have been more comfortable with the poems of Robert Bridges than those of Manley Hopkins. The paradox is that though the common reader may hanker for the familiar he also inwardly desires the poet to take heroic creative risks. This conflict is resolved eventually: strangeness endured ceases to be strange. As Dr Greenacre has pointed out in another context, the fear an individual may experience as a result of a strange event may in time give way to the triumph of recognition. It is sad that this recognition, in connection with fresh poetry, is so often postponed until after the poet's death.

Earlier I suggested that we are likely to resent an imitation of an admired model. I spoke of the claims of primacy, I remarked that something in us, prim and primitive, leads us to whisper, 'Copycat, copycat,' derisively. Perhaps at this point I can partially identify that something in us. For if we do, consciously or unconsciously, conceive the artist as hero, as one who takes philobatic risks, we will, with some irritation, discount the efforts of those who merely make replicas and imitations. For these imitators have not truly adventured, have avoided the thrilling risks that we admire, or will in time admire. We recognise that the imitator is no more philobatic than we are and so cannot, must not be acknowledged as poet-hero. On the contrary, he is a pretender and impudent. He is an impostor, and scorn, not honour, should be accorded him!

From: 'Pegasus and the Rocking Horse' – a lecture delivered at the
Institute of Psychoanalysis in London, 1981

Under the Influence of... (1984)

I

I am told by scholarly critics, some of whom are presently anchored not too far from here, that Anglo-Welsh poetry is imbued with certain characteristics. These, it would seem, are derived from the Welsh language literature tradition. No matter that the Anglo-Welsh poet cannot read the old language, that real thing strange; or that he does not even know translations of Welsh poetry despite the efforts of those like Gwyn Jones; the influence of it on his creativity, though he may deny it, is still active. 'Seepage' is the word our scholarly critics bandy about. The seepage 'on all cultural levels between the two language-groups of Wales' as Anthony Conran puts it.

Certainly it is a somewhat mystic notion that allows an Anglo-Welsh poet, ignorant of Welsh literature, to be most marvellously, most miraculously, affected by it. I do not mock. At least I do not mock with conviction because I know things can exist even when they cannot be invulnerably defined – like the concept of Welsh nationality itself.

In the introduction to the recently published *Anglo-Welsh Poetry 1480-1980* Raymond Garlick and Roland Mathias attempt to identify the idioplasm of the poetry they anthologise. The first ingredient they refer to is the 'inborn Welsh feeling... that praise is what poetry should be about.' They argue, for instance, that when Dylan Thomas declared his poems were written 'for the love of Man and in praise of God' he spoke as a Welshman; in the same way, centuries earlier, when George Herbert asserted that a poet should be 'secretary of thy praise,' he was defining the Welsh view of a poet's function.

What Garlick and Mathias do not do is ponder on the relationship of David and Dafydd. After all, the Old Testament poets, when not uttering the poetry of curses, were also secretaries of praise. They extolled the Lord. They heaped praise on praise, image after image. Theirs was a most wondrous and rhetorical propitiation. Almost one thousand and eight hundred years ago the illustrious Rabbi Judah said, 'In our days the harp had seven strings, as the Psalmist has written: "By seven daily did I praise thee."' Or consider the Talmudic blessing of the same century that is still sung over a goblet of wine at present day Jewish weddings: 'Blessed art thou our God, King of the Universe, who created joy and gladness, bridegroom and bride, mirth, song, delight and cheer, love and harmony, and peace and companionship. Soon the Lord our God, may be heard in the cities of Judah and in the streets of Jerusalem, the voice of joy and the voice of gladness, the voice of the bridegroom and the voice of the bride, the jubilant voices of the espoused from their wedding canopy and the young people from their feast of singing. Blessed art thou our Lord who rejoices the bridegroom with the bride.'

Wouldn't that blessing fit nicely in Welsh? Or even uttered in a broader Welsh accent than I own? Doesn't it, come to think of it, sound like Dylan Thomas larking about, setting it up, in one of his prose pieces? When my grandfather, in 1887, was invited to preach in the chapel at Ystalyfera, when he uttered translated Hebrew rhetoric of this kind, David spoke to Dafydd, and the non-conformist congregation found neither the substance nor the manner of his sermon alien.

It can be remarked, cynically, that the praise of God was a somewhat amateur enterprise. The extolling poet had no guarantee of his reward: rain would not fall; nor was he relieved of his scabs and haemorrhoids. The Welsh bards were professional in comparison. Their praises, if laid on beautifully thick, were suitably rewarded by Prince ap Mammon. Sometimes the flattery was directed towards a lady but then, too, the bard looked for and probably received love's honorarium.

The Song of Songs, which is Solomon's, the early theologians suggested, was religious praise-allegory. The 2nd century A.D. rabbis, in order to include it in the canon, maintained that it signified God's love for the people of Israel. The Church Fathers of the same century, also finding the poem lush and alarming, interpreted it as being Christ's declaration of love for the Church. Nobody would imagine the Song of Songs which is Huw Morus's, to be allegorical. 'In praise of a girl' was in praise of a certain seventeenth century girl, praise of 'a slip of loveliness, slim seemly, freshly fashioned. Moon of Wales, your loveliness prevails.' Both poems – Solomon's and Huw's are... lovely; one observes yet again that the literary traditions of David and Dafydd are not separate entities. Simply, the older tradition permeates the younger, there is a dialectic, a development. A seepage!

Raymond Garlick and Roland Mathias suggest that one piece typical of Welsh-flavoured praise poetry is George Herbert's sonnet,

'Prayer'; that it owns, moreover, characteristic devices of bardic craft: compound words and the heaping up of comparisons. Not long before the publication of their Anglo-Welsh anthology, in short well before I read their introduction, it so happened that I wrote a sonnet based on Herbert's poem which I called 'Music'. It, too, consists of consecutive poetic definitions – though not of prayer but of music. Since both are brief I shall read them to you. First, 'Prayer':

Prayer

Prayer, the Church's banquet, Angel's age,
  God's breath in man returning to his birth,
  The soul in paraphrase, heart in pilgrimage,
The Christian plummet sounding heaven and earth;

Engine against th'Almighty, sinner's tower,
  Reversed thunder, Christ-side-piercing spear,
  The six days' world-transposing in an hour,
A kind of tune, which all things hear and fear;

Softness, and peace, and joy, and love, and bliss,
  Exalted Manna, gladness of the best,
  Heaven in ordinary, men well drest,
The Milky Way, the bird of Paradise,

  Church-bells beyond the stars heard, the soul's blood,
  The land of spices, something understood.

Now (excuse the impudence of following George Herbert) my own sonnet, 'Music':

Music

Music in the beginning. Before the word,
  voyaging of the spheres, their falling transport.
Like phoenix utterance, what Pythagoras heard;
  first hallucinogen, ritual's afterthought.

A place on no map. Hubbub behind high walls
of Heaven – its bugged secrets filtering out:
numinous hauntings; sacerdotal mating-calls;
decorous deliriums; an angel's shout.

If God's propaganda, then Devil's disgust,
plainchant or symphony, carol or fugue;
King Saul's solace, St. Cecilia's drug;
silence's hiding place – like sunbeams' dust.

Sorrow's aggrandisements more plangent than sweet;
the soul made audible, Time's other beat.

The question I would like to ask you here is what amalgam of
influences are apparent in 'Music'? Because of its covert praise-
component, its strategy of using a catalogue of analogues, should it
be classed as an Anglo-Welsh poem? Is it of the tradition of David
and Dafydd? Or, simply, is its influence only that of George Herbert
himself?

II

When I was a schoolboy, my elder brothers Wilfred and Leo were
already in their twenties, young adults. They became the most important influences in the direction of my life. Wilfred, when he himself
became a doctor, newly qualified at the Welsh National School of
Medicine here in Cardiff, came home one day to find me uselessly
pushing a saucer of milk towards our sick cat, Merlin. I was a
fourteen year old who wanted to play football for Cardiff City, rugby
for Wales, cricket for Glamorgan.

'Better to become a doctor,' Wilfred suggested. 'I could put your
name down for the new Westminster Hospital they're planning in
London.' 'I wouldn't mind being a vet,' I said, looking at the cat.

I did not fancy shifting to London. I resented even moving the 1½
miles from Sandringham Road, Roath, Cardiff, to Windermere
Avenue, Penylan, Cardiff, as we were to do the following year. For
God's sake, who wanted to travel 160 miles every Saturday to reach
Ninian Park or Cardiff Arms Park? And where, in London, would
you get a better chip shop than the one opposite the Globe Cinema?

By the time we moved to Windermere Avenue, Wilfred, with my

father approving, had responsibly charted my future. He persuaded my parents to put my name down for Westminster Hospital and, at school, I now turned to the science subjects – physics, chemistry and biology – with a more purposeful interest.

If Wilfred set me towards studying Medicine, my brother Leo, inadvertently, faced me towards Poetry. At school, at St. Illtyd's where I was taught by Christian Brothers, I did not enjoy our poetry classes. It was, I thought, cissy stuff. Daffodils, Lesser Celandines, Skylarks, Cuckoos, Jug-jug, pu-we, to-witta-woo! That sort of thing did not seem of moment. There was a war going on in Spain; one of Leo's friends, Sid Hamm, had been killed out there fighting for the International Brigade; Mussolini was puffed out and ranting in Italy; Hitler, eyes thyrotoxic, dangerously maniacal in Germany. There was sloth and unemployment and depression in the Welsh valleys and the Prince of Wales had said poshly, uselessly, 'Something must be done.' But nothing was done, so what relevance, 'Cuckoo, jug-jug, pu-we, to witta-woo'?

At school we still sang, 'Let the prayer re-echo, God bless the Prince of Wales,' though I mistakenly believed that patriotic lyric to be 'Let the prairie echo, God bless the Prince of Wales', and wondered vaguely where the devil those grass-waving prairies were in mountainous Wales. At home, though, I read those left-wing magazines Leo brought back and, in them, I discovered poems of a political nature and of the war in Spain. How moved I was, for instance, when I happened on 'Huesca', the simple, direct poem by John Cornford. Not twenty one, John Cornford had been killed at the battle of Huesca while fighting for the International Brigade. How poignant his melancholy premonition of his own death; how terrible those lines of his, the last lines he ever wrote.

Poetry moved into the centre of my preoccupations gradually and that movement only truly commenced after I had read, in 1940, an anthology, *Poems for Spain*, edited by Stephen Spender. Here I encountered poets whose adult moral concerns and protestations engaged my own schoolboy wrath and indignation. Their voices had a passionate immediacy and their language was fresh, of the twentieth century. The raw, political poems of the Spanish peasant poet, Miguel Hernandez, especially, triggered me to try and express my own indignation about the horrors of the Spanish war in verse. Yes, naïvely, wanting to make political statements, I had begun to write verse voluntarily, not as an exercise for school. I showed my efforts to my elder brothers and Wilfred, particularly, encouraged me.

The war in Spain ended and Hitler was screaming and given thunderous applause. It was not long before we heard our Prime Minister, Neville Chamberlain, utter on the B.B.C., 'I have to tell you that no understanding has been received and that consequently this country is at war with Germany.' My sister had married, had already left home. In 1940 it was Leo's turn to leave Wales. He was called up for the R.A.F. Later, Wilfred joined the Army. Suddenly the house seemed larger. There was only father, mother, me and the dog.

Perhaps it was fortunate for me that my brothers had to go away at this crucial period: at least it allowed me to develop unimpeded in my own tentative way – dreaming most of the time or browsing in Cardiff Central Library or listening to Duke Ellington records or to the war news of the B.B.C., or playing games, or fumbling after girls, or preparing myself for a medical education, or writing a collocation of words that I wrongly called a poem.

III

Medical students, in their pre-clinical years, are allowed long summer vacations. In Cardiff, I spent much of my holidays in the Central Library reading poetry. First I reached for the books on the left hand side top shelf of the Twentieth Century Poetry Section: Richard Aldington, W.H. Auden. Then I worked my way across and downward. I read for pleasure, in this untutored way, alphabetically, not chronologically, without benefit of knowing who was considered by critics to be worthy, who to be scorned! One day I asked a girl called Joyce Herbert who was reading English at Cardiff's University College if she had heard of Dylan Thomas. My question provoked a little chuckle and a contemptuous, 'Of course.'

Dylan Thomas's poems powerfully engaged me – too much so, for a number of my own poems which can be discovered in my first volume, *After Every Green Thing*, are touched by his manner. Certain phrases sound like Dylan's cast-offs: 'harp of sabbaths', 'choir of wounds'. Admiring his work as I did, naturally I became curious about the man who lived not far away from my own home-patch. I was most intrigued when Leo, soon after he was demobbed from the R.A.F., told me that he had met my hero and that, moreover, Dylan Thomas had related to him a remarkable dream.

It seemed that Dylan, in this dream, entered a huge cavern or chamber in which he witnessed a biblical scene being enacted: Job, head bowed in grief, sat on the ground, crosslegged, with his three bearded comforters in silent attendance. Dylan quit this chamber to enter another and here saw Absalom, caught by his long hair, struggling and swinging from the boughs of a great oak. Then the dreamer entered another chamber where frenzied crowds danced around a golden calf. He passed from chamber to chamber, cavern leading into cavern, going back in time, watching Jacob wrestling with the angel or Abraham, in rage, destroying the wooden idols. At last, Dylan came to the ultimate chamber. He entered into almost darkness. He peered. Something was glinting against the rock of the back wall. He approached. Two skeletons became visible: the skeletons of a man and a woman, hand in hand.

That dream was surely a waking vision, rather than one recalled from sleep, and perhaps it owed something to William Blake's memorable fancies in *The Marriage of Heaven and Hell*? No matter, Leo's recounting of it made me pause and wonder. I relished it and, soon enough, back in London, retold it to literary friends in one of the cafés of Swiss Cottage that, in those post-war years, I regularly visited.

I had lodgings in Swiss Cottage. It was a cosmopolitan area with a remarkably vivid café-life because of the refugees, mostly Jews, from Austria and Germany. They had settled in the district. So ubiquitous were they that the bus conductors, approaching Swiss Cottage, would bang the bell and shout out, 'Next stop, Tel Aviv.' In cafés such as The Cosmo or The Cordial loitered theatre and film people such as Peter Berg, Lotte Lenya, Peter Zadek; or writers like Elias Canetti (who insisted on being called Canetti since he loathed his first name) the poet Erich Fried (who happened to have an abnormally thick-boned skull and could thump it, bang bang bang, against a wall for our amusement) and Rudi Nassauer (who had been influenced by Dylan Thomas, even more than I had, so that he thundered out his poems in an arresting but unnatural booming voice that would have delighted Dylan Thomas's elocution teacher).

In this ambience I heard of European poets who had hardly featured in the Poetry Section of Cardiff's Central Library. I read some of these in translation and one, especially, became a passion with me: Rainer Maria Rilke. How exciting to read such praise-poetry lines as:

There is nothing too small but my tenderness paints
it large on a background of gold.

When I read Rilke's *Letters to a Young Poet* I felt he addressed not
merely Herr Kappus but me: 'This before all: ask yourself in the
quietest hour of your night: *must* I write? Dig down into yourself for
a deep answer. And if this should be in the affirmative, if you may
meet this solemn question with a strong and simple, I *must*, then
build your life according to this necessity...' I responded, of course,
with a strenuous, 'I must' and I have, though it may sound somewhat
grand to say so, unconsciously as much as consciously, ordered my
life ever since to allow for this central need.

The eighth letter addressed to Kappus from Sweden in 1904
stimulated me to write a poem called 'The Uninvited'. It is the only
poem I am now willing to acknowledge that appeared in my first
volume, *After Every Green Thing*. Rilke, in that letter, spoke of how
certain sorrowful experiences alter us because of what they may
engender. When we are open to important moments of sorrow,
argued Rilke, then our future 'sets foot in us'. Though we could easily
believe nothing has truly happened, our destiny begins and 'we have
been changed as a house is changed into which a guest has entered'.

Rilke's influence endured and could set me ticking like a wheel of
a bicycle going downhill. In 1954, I wrote a number of poems on
existentialist themes, among them 'Duality' and 'The Trial' as a result
of reading a passage in *The Notebook of Malte Laurids Brigge*. Here
Rilke described an encounter with a woman who was deep in
thought, completely sunk into herself, her head in her hands. 'At the
corner of the Rue Notre-Dame-des-Champs,' wrote Rilke, 'I began
to walk softly as soon as I saw her... The street was too empty; its
emptiness was bored with itself; it caught my step from under my
feet and clattered about with it hither and yon, as with a wooden clog.
The woman took fright and was torn too quickly out of herself, too
violently, so that her face remained in her two hands. I could see it
lying in them, its hollow form. It cost me an indescribable effort to
keep my eyes on those hands and not to look at what had been torn
out of them. I shuddered to see a face thus from the inside, but I was
still more afraid of the naked, flayed, head without a face.'

Rilke not only triggered me to write a number of poems but taught
me lessons which I took to heart. In his first letter to Kappus, for
instance, he averred, 'A work of art is good if it has grown out of

necessity.' I assented to that: so many poems that I admired most had sprung from the stress of a personal predicament or from an active emotion like indignation or rage or love. Had I not been turned on originally to poetry because of the urgent cries of help from some poets in beleaguered Spain – poets like Miguel Hernandez? Had I not been moved by John Cornford's 'Huesca' or going back through the centuries by John Clare's 'I am' and William Cowper's 'The Castaway'?

Again Rilke suggested that one should be committed to difficulty. 'We know little,' he wrote, 'but that we must hold to the difficult...' Poetry, true crafted poetry was scandalously difficult to write. And the practice of medicine, too, at least for me, was hardly an easy ride.

Some poems of Rilke, too, became guru-lessons for me. At a hospital bedside, in a consulting room, I have listened, as a doctor must, purely to patients – never having to silence the clamour that my own senses might make. But discarding the white coat, encountering strangers of interest, I have tended to talk too much, to display, rather than to listen. Then I have reminded myself of these lines by Rilke that I know, in Babette Deutsch's translation, by heart:

> If only there were stillness, full, complete.
> If all the random and approximate
> were muted, with neighbours' laughter, for your sake,
> and if the clamour that my senses make
> did not confound the vigil I would keep –
>
> Then in a thousandfold thought I could think
> you out, even to your utmost brink
> and (while a smile endures) possess you, giving
> you away, as though I were but giving thanks
> to all the living.

There are those who cannot bear Rilke – among them friends of mine, poets, whose opinion I generally value; and indeed there are many occasions when Rilke, in his letters seems too sanctimonious, too high flown, phoney even. I thought this when I first read him. In the margins of my old copy of *Letters to a Young Poet*, years ago, I scrawled, 'Note here his evident insincerity.' Or I remarked on his patronising attitudes and pomposity. I argued in an abbreviated form (with question marks and exclamation marks) against the poetic ideas he proposed about such matters as the attainment of inner solitude, of the need to be alone as one was in childhood when surrounding adults seemed so busy and distant. Yet arguments with a mentor can be valuable in themselves, be productive. I disliked then, as most Welshmen would, the way Rilke, encountering others, thrust out his arm, as it were, to keep them away. His need to distance other people as if other people were vulgarly dangerous. Years later I wrote a poem concerning a lady with these Rilkean attitudes. If the poem that follows, 'Close Up' (N.B. no hyphen) is any good at all then my argument with Rilke was not entirely worthless:

> Often you seem to be listening to a music
> that others cannot hear. Rilke would have loved you:
> you never intrude, you never ask questions
> of those, crying in the dark, who are most near.
>
> You always keep something of yourself to yourself
> in the electric bars, even in bedrooms.
> Rilke would have praised you: your nearness is far,
> and, therefore, your distance like the very stars.
> Yet some things you miss and some things you lose
> by keeping your arm outstretched; and some things
> you'll never know unless one, at least, knows you
> like a close-up, in detail – blow by human blow.

What I could have learnt and should have learnt from Rilke was the value of experiences in making a poem. That I was to learn later when I began to believe poems should not begin with ideas but rather spring from true or imagined experience. One poet whom I met in Swiss Cottage, Denise Levertov, was more percipient than me about this. She has said in *Light Up the Cave* that her first lesson from Rilke was to experience *what you live*. I should have heeded, right from the beginning, how Rilke told the secret that verses amount to little when one begins to write them young. Rilke continues, 'One ought to wait and gather sense and sweetness, a whole life long, and a long life if possible, and then, quite at the end, one might perhaps be able to write ten good lines. For verses are not, as people imagine, simply feelings (we have these soon enough); they are experiences. In order to write a single verse, one must see many cities, and men and things; ... One must be able to return in thought to roads in unknown regions, to unexpected encounters, and to partings that had been long foreseen; to days of childhood that are still indistinct... to days spent in rooms withdrawn and quiet, and to mornings by the sea, to the sea itself, to oceans, to nights of travel that rushed along loftily and flew with all the stars – and still it is not enough to be able to think of all this. There must be memories of many nights of love, each one unlike the others, of the screams of women in labour, and of women in childbed, light and blanched and sleeping, shutting themselves in. But one must also have been beside the dying, must have sat beside the dead in a room with open windows and with fitful noises.

And still it is not enough yet to have memories. One must be able to forget them when they are many, and one must have the immense patience to wait until they come again. For it is the memories themselves that matter. Only when they have turned to blood within us, to glance and gesture, nameless and no longer to be distinguished from ourselves – only then can it happen that in a most rare hour the first word of a poem arises in their midst and goes forth from them.'

IV

In the structuring of experience into poems I have sometimes drawn on literary texts in a way that I suspect is not visible or audible to others. The texts generally are soluble in the poems. Sometimes they are not soluble and could be discerned if the reader happened on certain sources. For instance, I have, in recent years, drawn on brief Midrashic lesson-stories. Here is one example:

Rabbi Eliezer was sick. Rabbi Yohanan came to visit him. He saw Rabbi Eliezer lying in a dark house. Rabbi Yohanan bared his arm and the room lit up. He saw that Rabbi Eliezer was crying. He said to him, 'Why are you crying? Is it for the Torah in which you have not studied enough? We have learned, do more, do less, it matters not, as long as one's heart is turned to heaven...' Rabbi Eliezer replied, 'I am crying over this beauty of yours which one day will wither in the dust.' Rabbi Yohanan said, 'You are right to cry over that.' And they wept together.

Under the influence of that succinct anecdote I wrote a narrative poem called 'The Silence of Tudor Evans'. I'll repeat the title because it makes an important point: 'The Silence of Tudor Evans'. It goes like this:

Gwen Evans, singer and trainer of singers,
   who, in 1941, warbled
an encore (Trees) at Porthcawl Pavilion
   lay in bed, not half her weight and dying.
Her husband, Tudor, drew the noise of curtains.

Then, in the artificial dark, she whispered,
   'Please send for Professor Mandlebaum.'
She raised her head pleadingly from the pillow,
   her horror-movie eyes thyrotoxic.
'Who?' Tudor asked, remembering, remembering.

Not Mandlebaum, not that renowned professor
   whom Gwen had once met on holiday;
not that lithe ex-Wimbledon tennis player
   and author of *Mediastinal Tumours*;
not that swine Mandlebaum of 1941?

Mandlebaum doodled in his hotel bedroom.
   For years he had been in speechless sloth.
But now for Gwen and old times' sake he, first-class,
   alert, left echoing Paddington for
a darkened sickroom and two large searching eyes.

She sobbed when he gently took her hand in his.
   'But my dear, why are you crying?'
'Because, Max, you're quite unrecognisable.'
   'I can't scold you for crying about that,'
said Mandlebaum and he, too, began to weep.

They wept together (and Tudor closed his eyes)
   Gwen, singer and trainer of singers
because she was dying; and he, Mandlebaum,
   ex-physician and ex-tennis player,
because he had become so ugly and so old.

I have plundered different Midrashic texts to energise other poems, not a few of which have been portrait poems, a genre that has been favoured, according to Garlick and Mathias, for centuries because of 'Welsh curiosity about other people.' To be sure; there are no kept secrets in Wales. All women leak; all men are moles.

Everybody knows Dai, the spy. Or to put it more diplomatically: we gossip so much because we are all so interested in the unfathomable strangeness of other human beings.

If what Garlick and Mathias say about portrait-poems is true, then it would seem, that in an odd way, I may have inadvertently once again tried to make the traditions of David and Dafydd confluent.

V

In February 1961 I became involved with the astonishing Poetry and Jazz concerts that were to take place with regular success in the theatres, town halls, school halls and public libraries of Britain during the rest of the decade. I had received a phone call from a young man called Jeremy Robson inviting me to read at the Hampstead Town Hall along with Jon Silkin and Lydia Slater who would recite her brother's poems in translation. (Lydia Slater was the sister of Boris Pasternak). Jeremy Robson did not inform me that he planned intervals of jazz between the poets' readings nor that he, himself, would read his own poetry especially written for jazz accompaniment. In addition, he omitted to tell me that the comedian of Goon fame, Spike Milligan, would also feature.

I was, I suppose, a literary snob! If I had known the 'pop' nature of the Hampstead Town Hall reading, if I had seen the advertisements, I doubt whether I would have accepted Jeremy Robson's invitation. I set out that evening expecting to participate in a genteel poetry reading with the usual numbers attending and thus I was baffled to discover, at the doors of the Town Hall, a huge crowd demanding entrance while a distraught porter shouted, 'Full up, Full up.' I had difficulty, in fact, in pushing my way through. Inside, hundreds sat on the Town Hall's upright wooden chairs, others sprawled in the aisles, leant on the side walls and back walls while jazz negligently blared. Soon Spike Milligan appeared in dramatic spotlight saying, 'I thought I'd begin with a sonnet by Shakespeare but then I thought why should I? He never reads any of mine.' The concert was not solemn.

Over the next six years Jeremy Robson organised hundreds more of these concerts, inviting a score or so of alternating, different poets to take part. Some, such as Vernon Scannell, John Smith, Jeremy

Robson himself, read their poems to jazz; others such as Ted Hughes, Laurie Lee and myself, read our poems 'straight', unaccompanied, believing as we did that each poem had its own music and, for that matter, its own silences. (Stevie Smith sometimes sang her poems in a peculiarly flat voice.) The enthusiastic, large audiences clapped frequently and seemed to be genuinely entertained. Later they bought books (in the interval) to investigate in private, on the page, the poems they had heard publicly in the auditorium.

We always arrived in one or another provincial town at lighting-up time. I still feel that on entering such places as Nottingham or Leicester somehow the lampposts should all jerk into life, and on quitting them the hands of the clock should turn fast and turn again until the streets are late, deserted, the shops darkened except for the one, lonely, lit Indian restaurant that beckons jazz musicians and poets to eat and unwind.

Over the next six years, did the regular practice of reading poems aloud to large audiences affect, consciously or unconsciously, our strategy in structuring poems? When Dylan Thomas began to read to proliferating mass audiences the idioplasm of his poetry gradually altered. His poems, while growing more complex in their rhythmic orchestration, also became somewhat less dense, less recondite generally. There were seductive dangers in being exposed to large audiences and I daresay some poets sometimes succumbed to them and not in the way Dylan Thomas did. In my case, I know that my poems about this time became more conversationally pitched but I doubt if this was the result of performance and live audience. When I wrote a poem I did not usually consider reader or listener. The exception to that was in writing longer poems. Then, at a certain point in their maturation, I would become aware that I would actually enjoy reading this or that one out loud to receive a public response. When I wrote plays I had to be aware of audience, of allowing the narrative its tensions and relaxations. So, too, with a long poem which otherwise could freeze an audience into lassitude. In writing, for instance, 'The Smile Was', about 1965, after some drafts I knew I would read it out loud at a Poetry and Jazz concert. I became more aware of the problems of pace, density and humour than might otherwise have been the case. And I ensured that the rhythms did not become too monotonous, that the repetitions of sound patterns were appropriately varied. Once Eliot had generously said of a play of mine that it had the virtue of being both for the stage and the study. I would like to think some of my longer poems could be similarly characterised.

VI

Most of us hardly question what influences us and do not observe our barely fathomable metamorphosis steadily. We merely mark how our life situation may have changed or how our interests have been developed; how our children have grown up, how others we loved became much older or died. All authors, though, have visible concrete evidence of their own internal changes: they can turn to their artefacts – in my case, to my plays as well as to my poems – and see how these give witness to altering attitudes, preoccupations, arguments with oneself. They recall debts to other writers, textual influences, transient or repetitive experiences and moods, successes and failures, occasions – and relationships. Poems on the page lie there and do not lie: their own progenitor can scrutinise them as if they were spiritual X-rays.

Certainly my poems relate, in hidden narrative, my true biography. There is hardly an important occasion in my life that is not covertly profiled or overtly re-inhabited in my poems. So when I open my *Collected Poems* and turn, say, to page 107, I suffer almost an abreaction as I hold again my father's hand while he is dying in Llandough Hospital in 1964; or when the book falls open on page 131 I can remember, altogether less painfully, how with my wife and children, I attended a demonstration in Trafalgar Square, in 1968, against the war in Vietnam.

Poems can remind me of such things because they are rooted in my mental life, in my experience, some mundane, some dramatic. I recall the words of Rilke again: 'In order to write a single verse one must be able to return in thought... to unexpected encounters... to days of childhood that are still indistinct... to nights of love... But one must also have been beside the dying, must have sat beside the dead in a room with open windows and with fitful noises.' I have experienced such things as so many others have; and I have done my best to tell of these things in the best way I can, with what gift I have, sometimes going to other men's texts like a sleepwalker and sometimes wideawake.

Nor have I worried about such matters for I agree with Goethe when he remarked... 'We are all collective beings, let us place ourselves as we may. For how little have we, and are we, that we can strictly call our own property? We must all receive and learn both from those who were before us, and from those who are with us. Even the greatest genius would not go far if he tried to owe everything to his own internal self. But many very good men do not comprehend that; and they grope in darkness for half a life, with their dreams of originality. I have known artists who boasted of having followed no master, and of having to thank their own genius for everything. Fools! as if that were possible at all; and as if the world would not force itself upon them at every step, and make something of them in spite of their own stupidity... And, indeed, what is there good in us, if it is not the power and the inclination to appropriate to ourselves the resources of the outward world, and to make them subservient to our higher ends... The main point is to have a great will, and skill and perseverance to carry it out.'

And here's the curious thing: after decades of writing poems, every poet, I believe, if he takes his own work seriously as he should, comes under the influence of it. When a poet begins to write a poem there is no reader; but as he concludes his poem he himself becomes the first reader. Sometimes the last! He receives his own words. Thereafter, in subtle ways, his poems even as they may recede for others, remain for him strangely active. They help to determine not only how he will write but how he will live. Some may argue that poetry is a useless thing. It influences no-one. But whatever else poems do, or do not do, they profoundly alter the man or the woman who wrote them.

Annual Gwyn Jones Lecture, University College Cardiff, 1984

From: Introduction to *The Hutchinson Book of Post-War British Poets* (1989)

The poetry written in the immediate post-war years in Britain has been labelled 'neo-romantic'. It was an hortatory poetry – wordy, ornamental, florid. The young poets of those years concentrated on being textually sensuous and gaudy and there are a few older poets to this day, Peter Redgrove among them, who continue this line. Most of those immediate post-war poets, alas, lapsed into a ludicrous grandezza, if not incoherence. Simply, they were not as gifted as their older models, Dylan Thomas and George Barker, nor as musical. By 1953, the year Dylan Thomas died, a violent reaction to Neo-Romanticism was plainly evident and a new generation of young poets began to claim attention. These poets came to be known as The Movement and eventually Robert Conquest published their work in his interesting dynamic anthology *New Lines* (1956). They favoured a poetry which nurtured rationality, that was inhospitable to myth, that avoided poetic diction, that was conversationally-pitched and in opposition to Neo-Romanticism. It was deliberately formal and lucid and small-gestured, regarding itself as being in the mainstream of the tactful English tradition. One of their number, Kingsley Amis, wrote:

> Let us make at least visions that we need:
> Let mine be pallid, so that it cannot
>   Force a single glance from a single word...
>   Let there be a path leading out of sight
> And at its other end a temperate zone:
>   Woods devoid of beasts, roads that please the foot.

These poems of a temperate zone, of a slower metabolism, became popular because they reflected the attitude of a new post-war intellectual generation of writers who, sometimes nationalistically English, liked to think of themselves as tough, cynical and 'anti-wet' – a literary critical term used then and one which latterly has assumed, without difficulty, political connotations. Nationalistic or not, the Movement could count among its numbers poets genuinely talented, not least Philip Larkin. Others included in this present anthology are Elizabeth Jennings, Donald Davie, D.J. Enright, Thom Gunn and John Wain. While the Movement poetry was ubiquitous during the 1950s other poets, less hostile to romantic modes, unashamed of rhetorical energy, were also at work, among them mavericks such as Thomas Blackburn, David Wright and Jon Silkin; and these soon after were joined by Ted Hughes, a poet also writing a differently ordered poetry from that of the Movement poets. His work, first published in 1957, received immediate acclaim. 'Ted Hughes,' wrote Edwin Muir in the *New Statesman*, 'seems to be quite outside the currents of his time.' Kingsley Amis had called for 'woods devoid of beasts'. Ted Hughes offered beasts without woods.

Nevertheless the pitch, tone, strategy, bias of the Movement poets has predominated, with modifications, to the present day. The majority of poets in this anthology whose first books were published after 1960, various as they are, would, it seems, subscribe to the main theses of the Movement aesthetic for they have appropriated the concern for propriety in the use of language. Was Samuel Johnson right when he wrote in his Preface to Shakespeare: 'If there be, what I believe there is, in every nation, a style which never becomes obsolete, a certain mode of phraseology so consonant and congenial to the analogy and principles of its respective language as to remain settled and unaltered; this style is probably to be sought in the common intercourse of life, among those who speak only to be understood.'? Be that as it may, even poets addicted to a temperate zone do, on occasions, need to speak with a greater precipitation and elegance. Few will not acknowledge, with Anacreon, that it is pleasant to be frenzied at times.

NOTE

In Acumen, April 1988, Michael Hulse remarked, 'the poets we think of as having their place in a central English line – Cowper, Hardy, Edward Thomas, Sir John Betjeman, Philip Larkin'. Other critics would add other names – not least, surely, Wordsworth.

Poetry and Poverty Revisited (1998)

I

Sometimes, during those immediate post-war evenings, I would cast my medical textbooks aside and quit my digs in London's Swiss Cottage to meet a girl or search for company in the chattering cafés of the nearby Finchley Road. That winter of 1946 I would pass the dolorous ruins of bombed buildings where darkness loitered and walk under the occasional functioning lamppost to the lit enticements of the Cosmo or the Cordial or the Winter Garden. Adventures, conversational or otherwise, beckoned.

Many refugees, most of them Jews from Germany and Austria, had come to live in the area. So much so that sometimes the conductors on No. 13 and No. 2 buses approaching Swiss Cottage would shout out with venom, 'Next stop, Tel Aviv.' Big joke.

The refugees brought with them the habits of a continental café life. Not a few were writers such as the poet Erich Fried, or the novelist Elias Canetti. There were musicians, too, like Hans Keller and members of the Amadeus Quartet; theatre people, like the director Peter Zadek and the actress Renee Goddard.

Soon British writers and artists frequented these Swiss Cottage cafés – among them the budding novelists, Peter Vansittart and Bernice Rubens, art critic David Sylvester, sculptor Bill Turnbull. Congenial company then for a young man such as myself who fancied himself as a poet, having had, in September 1946, a book of poems accepted by Hutchinson.

That book, which is so defective that I would now gladly burn all copies, did not appear until December 1948. Not long before its publication you could have discovered me, still neglecting my medical studies, in one or other of those Swiss Cottage cafés, discussing with art student Godfrey Rubens and red-haired Molly Owen the possibility of publishing a poetry magazine. We had no cash to pay a printer but Godfrey and Molly felt confident that they could steal paper and surreptitiously arrange for it to be roneoed and stitched at the firm where Molly worked. It would be called *Poetry and Poverty* – not only because we were broke but also we decided that in each successive issue a contributor would be invited to comment on the poverty of current literature.

'I'll design the magazine,' promised Godfrey 'and you know poets who will contribute.'

A number of the younger British poets occasionally visited Swiss Cottage, among them Emanuel Litvinoff and John Heath-Stubbs. Litvinoff's poem 'To T.S. Eliot', which was to have later reverberations and consequences, appeared in the first issue of *Poetry and Poverty*, as did a now forgotten poem by John Heath-Stubbs called 'Meditation on a Name'.

[...]

II

Amazingly Desmond MacCarthy reviewed that first issue of *Poetry and Poverty* in the *Sunday Times*. It was a warm, generous notice. Indeed, we were encouraged by the general response, but we had no resources to enable us to carry on. Molly Owen disappeared from sight, had left her firm, had left London. The other girl habitués of the Swiss Cottage cafés had no enthusiasm for typing out copy and stealing paper, however intimate we were with them. Besides I had to take my final medical examinations and become a responsible doctor.

One evening, though, soon after I had qualified and had married Joan Mercer, we visited the Cosmo and were collared by a young South African who demanded, 'Where's the second number of *Poetry and Poverty*?' We were happy to meet an admirer but utterly surprised when he offered to finance it for at least a couple of issues. 'Get it decently printed,' he commanded.

Because of my own commitments I could not immediately take advantage of his patronage. As a result, the second issue of *Poetry and Poverty* did not appear until 1952. Among the poems was one of Lawrence Durrell's best, 'Clouds of Glory' and some brilliant translations of Jacques Prévert by Paul Dehn. Peter Viereck wrote about the Ezra Pound Bollingen Prize controversy and Emanuel Litvinoff wrote the *Notes on the Poverty* (Literary) No. 2. Meanwhile, two books I admired had come my way: *The Man Outside*, the prose works of the young German poet Wolfgang Borchert, who died in 1947 at the age of twenty-six, and *Nones* by W.H. Auden. I persuaded Michael Hamburger to review *The Man Outside* and John Heath-Stubbs to pen the notice of *Nones*.

John Heath-Stubbs wrote of Auden:

> Are some of those qualities which so charmed his readers in the nineteen-thirties abated in his later work? And, if so, is his religious re-orientation or his Americanisation to be held responsible? The answer to these questions is, I think, 'Yes, partly.' The wit and the colloquial ease are still there, but the particular Audenesque combination of Angst and Weltschmerz has given place to a rather uneasy resignation to the limitations of the human condition. And the Audenesque mythology – Boy Scouts, Long Legged Scissor men, and the like has been replaced by such images as the rather classical baroque furies, 'with clear and dreadful brow.' But what have been lost, I think, were essentially adolescent and romantic qualities...

Those adolescent and romantic qualities were also being lost in the work of John Heath-Stubbs himself, or, at least, maturely modified. The poems he was writing in 1952 were later to be published in *A Charm Against the Toothache*, a volume I later reviewed in *Poetry and Poverty* in which I claimed that it was Heath-Stubbs's best book to date and that 'the earlier romantic grandeur of diction is now studded with contemporary slang and modern object references... his concessions in relaxing the high tone of his diction allow John Heath-Stubbs to display a humour and humanism that his earlier style forbade and this engagement with the street rather than the study make his poems applicable to others... His poetry, in my view had progressed into the second phase of Neo-Romanticism.'

By 1952 a violent reaction to Neo-Romanticism was in full swing. Another generation of young poets, my own generation, began to claim attention. All of these were graduates of Oxford or Cambridge, most of them having recently accepted academic posts in one or another university. Robert Conquest later was to corral them into a group known as The Movement. They were, ostensibly, anti-romantic. Kingsley Amis attacked Dylan Thomas and outlined the programme of The Movement poets succinctly in a poem he called 'Against Romanticism':

> Let us make at least visions that we need:
> Let mine be pallid, so that it cannot
>   Force a single glance from a single word...
> And at its other end a temperate zone:
>   Woods devoid of beasts, roads that please the foot.

Those in sympathy with Kingsley Amis's views felt not only antagonistic to the work of Dylan Thomas, then the most popular poet in the English-speaking world, but to the New Apocalypse writers of the 1940s inspired by Henry Treece and J.F. Hendry who recognised the importance of myth, preferred eternal rather than contemporary subject matter and a hortatory mode of expression. The mood of these 1940s poets was exhibited in the publication by Herbert Read of the Routledge Series of poets, among whom could be numbered Sidney Keyes, Emanuel Litvinoff, John Heath-Stubbs and J.F. Hendry himself.

Though, in truth I, as editor of *Poetry and Poverty*, personally deplored the worst traits of many of the neo-romantic poets, their formlessness, their fear of writing about the quotidian, their floridity, their wilful obscurity due to a too private vision, I did not welcome replacing the fashion of Neo-Romanticism with a calibre of pallid poems so temperate they would read, at best, as a form of exquisite reportage. I had witnessed how Dylan Thomas's work had developed from the incoherence of much of the verse in his first book, published in 1934, to the communicable richness of poems like 'Fern Hill' and 'Poem in October', 'The Hunchback in the Park' and the villanelle 'Do Not Go Gentle Into That Good Night'. I believed then, as I do now, that Thomas's progression from that obscurity to a necessary degree of rationality resulted, not altogether consciously, from his famous exposure to audiences, and to their expectancy, when giving his poetry readings.

In any event, I wrote in the editorial of *Poetry and Poverty* 4, in 1952:

> It is not then, in this over-compensated reaction to Neo-Romanticism that the poetry of the fifties has hope of importance or readability, but rather, I believe, in the modification and development of the romantic vision of the poets of the last decade. Nobody wants to save the corpse of The New Apocalypse... rather the time has come for poetry to move into a new and second phase of Neo-Romanticism. What should be discarded are its faults alone: there is no need to throw the whole apparatus of Romantic expression overboard, particularly as the present alternative mode of writing appears to be so trivial and precious.

Poetry and Poverty lost its African financial backer early. Our patron suddenly joined the Communist Party and decided that he could have nothing further to do with what he called 'bourgeois formalism'. However, the subscription list was growing and the actress Margaret Rawlings, unsolicited, sent me enough money to print one issue. I should record here, too, the generosity of Edith Sitwell, who put a fiver into the kitty, again unsolicited, though I had in *Poetry and Poverty* No. 1 remarked that I had been 'nauseated by her narcissistic and pretentious comments upon her own work' when she had been allowed to broadcast on the Third Programme.

Poetry and Poverty continued for seven issues before finally concluding with the anti-Movement anthology *Mavericks*, which I co-edited with Howard Sergeant. John Heath-Stubbs was very much featured in the magazine. In No. 1, his poem 'Meditation on a Name' appeared; in No. 3, 'The Hundred and Thirty-Seventh Psalm Paraphrased'; in No. 7, 'Mors Poetarum' – all poems in which John Heath-Stubbs exhibited his wit, scholarship and technical virtuosity. In No. 2, he himself reviewed Auden; in No. 5, an anthology *Images of Tomorrow* which he had edited was noticed, as was his own *A Charm Against the Toothache* in No. 7. He would have appeared in *Mavericks* also, but in order to match the relative youthfulness of The Movement anthology *New Lines*, Howard Sergeant and I set the birth deadline of our contributors at 1920. John Heath-Stubbs was born in 1918, as readers of this magazine are all aware.

One reason I agreed to co-edit *Mavericks*, apart from a quarrel about linguistic style, was because I disliked the insular attitude of some of the *New Lines* contributors, their parochialism, their consciously contrived philistinism, their posture of being tough, cynical and sardonic. They rarely chanced themes that transcended barriers of custom and nationality. Much could be said in favour of linguistic tact and decorum but those who championed Movement verse did not appear to value 'feeling' in poetry or any ambitious excitements beyond discipline. They saw poetry as a modest art. Donald Davie, a poet with a genuine winter talent, in asking himself the question, 'how can I dare to feel?' wrote:

> Alas, alas, who's injured by my love?
> And recent history answers: Half Japan!
> Not love but hate? Well both are versions of
> The 'feeling' that you dare me to. Be dumb!
> Appear conceived only to make it scan!
> How dare we now be anything but numb?

A neutral tone was welcomed in the 1950s. Besides, many of the contributors to *New Lines* were truly gifted, not least Philip Larkin who, in his poetry, far from negated the plangent tones of feeling. Conquest's anthology proved to be a great critical success and the fashion of Movement-like verse thrived for the rest of the decade.

I recall a conversation I had with John Heath-Stubbs in Soho during the later Fifties. (Was it at the Mandrake Club in Meard Street?) We were discussing the popularity of *New Lines* and how so many of the plain, uninspiring and unaspiring poems that appeared in journals such as the *New Statesman* and *Spectator* were influenced and hampered by the Movement's critical strictures. John Heath-Stubbs commented somewhat ruefully, 'It'll be a long time before the brand of poetry we write will become fashionable.' I'm still waiting, John.

From: *Aquarius* – Tribute to John Heath-Stubbs on his 80th birthday, 1998

2. Autobiographical Fiction

From: *Ash on a Young Man's Sleeve*

Lol was three years older than I. Seventeen years from his shadow he stood, tall and well built, with a lolling massive head full of air, instead of brains, and with no neck at all worth talking about. If Modigliani had painted him, he would have just looked about normal. As Keith had said – if Lol was blessed with a neck he would have been a giant almost. Lol's father who'd recently come out of jail had become rich suddenly, so now Lol, dressed in big-shouldered suits and gaudy extravagant ties, lounged round street corners talking to newspaper boys. I was lying down on the grass near the quarry, chewing a blade of grass when I heard his voice.

'Hello,' he called. Lol sat down beside me, pulled a stem of grass from the earth and started chewing at it like me.

'Whassermarra with your brother Leo?' asked Lol. 'Saw 'im in town with a white thing round his leg.'

'Broke it,' I said. 'Mam's pleased because that's stopped him going to Spain.'

'What's wrong with Spain?' demanded Lol.

'Don't you know, Lol? – there's a war going on.'

He looked at me incredulously. We sat there awhile looking over the rooftops at the distant Bristol Channel shimmering in the sun that shone out of a bald blue sky. Below us the dark primitive quarry with its rusted stone jutting in and out savagely. Stone abandoned, cold, cruel, ancient...

'Why ar't you at school?' he asked me finally in his Canton accent.

'Don't feel like it,' I replied.

'Wish I was you,' he said miserably.

'Why?'

'Dunno. Wish I was anybody but me.'

Lol pulled his creased trousers up from his suede shoes, revealing gay yellow socks.

'What do you do all day?' I asked him.

'Goes to the pitchers venyer every afternoon,' he said. 'Likes gangsters best.' He made a fist of his right hand, then slowly extended his index finger like a gun. 'Bang, bang, bang!' he said.

'What else do you do?'

He frowned, trying to think. 'In the mornin', these weathers, I likes goin' for a walk early. Picks mushrooms.'

'On your own, Lol?'

'Oh yes, in the mornin', very early. Sometimes I takes a bus to Rhwbina – I gets up especially early – and I takes a threepenny bus ride. They gives you a blue ticket for threepence. I collects 'em. Tickets. I got lots. And I goes walking in the 'ills. It's dirty, misty I mean, early mornin' and you know, sort of true. Know what I mean? Fresh air, when you breathes. Very good for you, fresh air, Dad says.'

Lol began to breathe violently in and out, in and out, expanding his chest, making a noise like an engine with brakes on, until his face was red.

'Good for you,' he explained. 'Fresh air.'

'You pick mushrooms, Lol?'

'Yes. It's easy. You find 'em, then you pick 'em.'

'And you're on your own?'

'Natcherly. It's nice, mun. Fresh air. Mist. Bloody birds singing.' I laughed and he smiled at me benevolently.

'What you going to do when you grow up?' I asked him.

'I'm 'aving elecuit lessons.'

'What lessons?'

'You knows, for speaking proper,' he said.

'You mean elocution lessons,' I said.

'Yes, 'em,' he nodded vaguely.

'What for?' I asked.

He took a blade of grass out of his mouth once more and looked at me with bright eyes.

'Goin' to be a film star,' he said proudly and he threw back his head, closing his eyes, pointing his finger at me. 'Bang, bang, bang!' he bellowed.

'What do you want to be a film star for?' I asked him.

'Go away,' he said. 'You're 'aving me. Leave me be.'

'No, serious, Lol. Why do you want to be a film star?'

'Garn,' he answered.

'I'm interested. Honest.'

Lol looked at me suspiciously. His brow puckered, and his big head lolled forward on his chest.

'They gets their pitchers in the papers.'

'And...?' I asked.

'Shut your gob,' he ordered. 'You're 'aving me.'

'No, I'm not, really, Lol.'

'You knows Lydia Pike,' he shouted. He stood up and looked around at the house across the street. Fiercely, he said, 'If you touches 'er, I'll do you in, proper.' He pointed a finger at me. 'Bang, bang, bang!' he screamed. 'Bang, bang, bang!'

'Don't be silly, Lol. Sit down.'

'Shurrup,' he yelled. 'You're 'aving me.' And he walked away leaving me there, on the sparse grass, near the old disused quarry, under a sun that was too dazzling to look at.

The next evening after tea I walked out of the house, and there he was again, evidently waiting for me. There was a steamroller down the road and you could smell the new tar. Shadows of houses were slung across the street because the sun was low in the sky.

'Steamroller,' said Lol, nodding his head.

'Yes,' I said.

'I been waiting over an hour for you,' he remarked.

'Why?'

He didn't answer and we walked towards the Park. I wondered what was inside the new briefcase he carried.

'What do you want, Lol?' I asked.

He combed his greasy hair and straightened his sky-blue and dandelion-yellow tie.

'I just wants to walk with you.'

In the Park, we watched the tennis-players for a while, and afterwards stared at the waterfall, watching the foam bubble like shaving soap.

'Let's go into the summer-'ouse, bachan.'

'What for?'

'I want to tell you something.'

'Can't you tell me here?'

'Too many people about.'

'They're not listening, Lol.'

'I want to *show* you something.'

'What?'

'Come to the summer-'ouse.'

We passed the magnolia tree. Its wax blossoms had already begun to fall. The shadows stretched themselves across the grass. They were long. Because of Lol I felt uneasy. You couldn't be sure of Lol. Only last year I remembered, the day Dirty-face and his dog suddenly came round the corner, the other side of the street. I was with Lol then. The dog growled, recognising us. Dirty-face was shouting, 'Come back, boy, come back, boy!' and there was a shriek of brakes before the motor-car gathered speed again to disappear down Albany Road. The dog lay in the gutter and Dirty-face looked down upon it, stupefied. We ran across the road, Lol and I. 'The car didn't stop,' I said. The dog was stretched out in a pool of its own urine and something was funny about its back. Its hairy belly heaved in and out as it breathed. And the brown eyes gazed at Dirty-face sadly, with a sort of 'You are responsible' look. The smell of burning rubber from the auto-mobile's brakes still hung finely in the air. 'Could you go and get a vet?' Dirty-face asked me, nearly crying. Just then the dog barked. It barked and whined rather as it would in the night when a stranger approached.

'There, boy,' said Dirty-face. 'It's all right, boy.' Dirty-face had bent down to stroke the dog's head. Suddenly, the dog cocked up its ears, listening to something.

'What can it hear?' I asked.

'Go and get the vet!' shouted Dirty-face.

But by then the eyes of the dog stared on brownly at nothing and its belly was still.

'He's dead,' whispered Dirty-face.

'It's not,' said Lol.

'Poor chap,' I said.

'It's not dead,' shouted Lol. 'It's not, it's not.' Dirty-face burst into tears. 'It's not dead,' screamed Lol. All the muscles of his face seemed to tremble at the same time and he brought down his fist again and again on the dog's belly and face.

'Stop it, Lol,' I shouted.

But he still flayed the dog, screaming now something incomprehensible. A man intervened finally and they took Lol to a doctor who gave him an injection.

I had been frightened by Lol then. And, yesterday, when he had stood over me as I lay on the grass near the quarry, he had been odd, strange. You couldn't be sure of Lol.

Wilfred said once that Lol was harmless. Backward, of course, but harmless, and I was not to pull his leg, like the other kids did. I was to be kind to him, Wilf had said. Yet last year as he was striking the corpse of the dog, he was dangerous surely? And yesterday, he had been a bit crazy; the way he shouted about Lydia Pike. Harmless... hell. What did he want to go to the summer-house for? What did he want to show me?

'Show me here, Lol,' I said.

He gripped my arm tight.

'Come,' he said urgently. 'I gotter speak to you private.'

Near the summer-house I looked back, and the blossom lay under the magnolia tree like bits of useless paper. I was glad that there were a couple of lovers in the summer-house. The man looked at us meaningfully. 'Get to hell out of here,' his eyes said and the girl looked down at the floor.

'Let's go, Lol,' I said.

'We stays 'ere,' said Lol.

The man coughed, waiting for us to leave. There was a musty, dusty, stuffy odour in the summer-house.

'We stays by 'ere,' repeated Lol loudly.

The seamed walls, lettered with signatures and initials of lovers of past years, looked down upon us askance.

'Let's go and get some sun, Arthur,' said the girl and, though I prayed they would not, the couple walked out. The man turned round before he left, scowling at us.

We were alone. The voices and the sound of tennis-players seemed far away.

'Whassermarra with you?' said Lol. 'What you shake for?'

'It's cold in here' I said. 'The sun never gets in.'

'I'm 'ot,' said Lol, and he took his coat off. 'Did you see how that girl's dress was all creased and mauled?' He smiled.

'What do you want to tell me, Lol?' I asked.

Lol blushed.

'I want –'

His sentence was interrupted because the man who had been with the girl reappeared in the doorway. He walked over to the corner of the summer-house, where he had been when we first came in, and picked up a pair of gloves which the girl must have left behind.

'You kids got nothing better to do than sit in a summer-house?' protested the man.

'Shurrup!' said Lol.

The man started towards us, but Lol stood up; so he changed his mind. He said something obscene and Lol pointed his finger at him shouting, 'bang, bang, bang!' The man looked at him amazed and walked out.

'Some people got some cheek,' I said.

'I should 'ave bashed 'im,' said Lol. 'Like in the pitchers.'

'Well, Lol?' I asked casually.

Lol pulled out a writing-pad from his dispatch-case. 'I wants...' he said. 'Listen,' he went on, 'I want... I want you... to write a letter for me.'

'Sure, Lol,' I said, relieved. 'Who to?'

'If you 'ave me, I'll get you,' he warned.

'Who to?' I repeated. 'I mean whom to?'

'What?' asked Lol.

'Who to?'

He looked at me, sizing me up.

'To Lydia Pike,' he explained.

I didn't dare laugh, though I did almost in surprise.

'What about?' I asked, and then, 'is that what you wanted to tell me?'

'You knows. About me. About me having talking lessons and my becoming a film star. About me being strong an' being able to bash anybody what asks for it. I'm no good at writing,' he added, 'though my Uncle Fred is a clerk. Your cousin, Clive, told me you're goin' to be a writer and I can't spell proper. That's my trouble – spelling.'

'I haven't got a pen,' I said.

He pulled out a fountain-pen from his inside pocket.

'Begin,' he commanded.

Lol stood over me, forcing me to write.

'*Dear Miss Lydia,*' I wrote, '*Excuse my presumption in writing to you ...*'

'What's that word?'

'Presumption?'

'What's 'at mean?'

'It means impudence, cheek, boldness.'

'What's cheeky about it? Lots of folk write to folk. Fred 'ad a letter last week. Leave out the cheek word.'

'*Dear Miss Lydia,*' I began again, '*Excuse me writing to you but I want to tell you about myself and...*'

'What do you want to write "excuse me" for?' said Lol. 'I haven't belched or farted.'

'*Dear Miss Lydia, I'm writing to you because I want to tell you about myself. I'm taking elocution lessons and I'm going to be a film star...*'

'With pitchers in the papers.'

'*...with my picture in the journals.*'

'Good,' said Lol.

'What else can I write?'

'You write it. I'd do it if I 'ad your education – if I could spell proper.'

'Do you want me to say you like her?'

'Don't be soppy,' said Lol. 'Tell 'er I think she's neat.'

'*...I should like to make your acquaintance and I think you're most attractive.*'

'That's nice. I like big words. That's what I want. Now say about me being able to bash anybody. Ask 'er if she'd like anybody particular bashed.'

'I think I'd leave that out, at the moment, Lol.'

'Well...'

'I'll put your address on it and sign your name.'

'I can sign my own name.'

'Fine, Lol.'

'And what'll you put for a PS?'

'A PS?'

'Natcherly.'

'You don't have to write a PS.'

'Now don't do that to me. Don't 'ave me. Do what's right by me. You wouldn't want to 'ave me bash you.'

'But Lol. You don't have to add a PS, honest.'

Lol looked at me uncertainly, searching my face to see if I was taking him in.

'OK,' he said. And then he signed the letter, folded it up and put it in an envelope which he had extracted from his briefcase.

'You're my pal,' he said tenderly, when I wrote Lydia Pike's name and address on the envelope.

We went out into the sun again. The end of the sun. The magnolia tree in the dusk. Lots of insects about. The players going home and the sound of the waterfall. Near the shops stood the red pillar-box.

'Got some money for a stamp?' I said.

'A stamp? What for?'

'You have to put a stamp on it, Lol, otherwise they have to pay the other end. Pay double.'

'I'm not goin' to post it,' said Lol.

'Not going to?'

'No. I was only jokin'. Christ, catch me writing stuff like this to a girl!'

I looked at him surprised. 'Do what you will, Lol,' I said, and started off home.

'Think I'd write letters to girls,' he called after me. I could hear him laughing. Gosh, to think Lol had kidded *me*! Yet at the corner of the road, I looked back and he was still standing by the pillar-box, with the letter in his hand.

'What you looking at?' shouted Lol. 'Beat it.'

From: *Ash on a Young Man's sleeve*

'What's the matter?' asked Keith.

'Who me? Nothing. Why?'

'I thought you were in a trance.'

'Just thinking.'

'What about?'

'Oh, er... trying to work out whether Ends justified the Means.'

'Yesterday you said Marx was all wrong,' said Keith.

'Where's Miss Cobb?' I asked.

'Talking to my father,' said Keith, combing his long hair.

We walked into the gravel sunlight towards Lydia Pike's house. When we were half-way up the hill, he pulled a packet of cigarettes from his pocket.

'Have a drag,' he said.

'Let's wait,' I said doubtfully.

He looked at me, his eyes blue as a poison bottle.

'Scared?' he asked.

'It'll be dark soon,' I persuaded him.

Keith ignored me and lit up expertly, cupping his hands to keep the match from going out in the light breeze.

'Remember what we were talking about yesterday?' he said, blowing out a cloud of grey-blue smoke.

'What?' I said. 'Dialectical Materialism and the Spanish War?'

'No... afterwards... what you were saying about the Oedipus

Complex.'

'Yes.'

His cheeks sucked in, pulling at the cigarette, making the fag-end glow brick-red.

'Tell me,' he said. 'Can you still have an Oedipus Complex if you haven't got a mother?'

'Dunno,' I fenced, 'I haven't read all Freud yet...'

Keith suddenly hid the cigarette behind his back and I looked up the hill to see Mr Blackburn, our English Master, come around the corner from Melrose Avenue.

'Crikey! Old Blacky,' grunted Keith.

Mr Blackburn took long steps, using his umbrella like a walking-stick.

'Good evening, boys,' he said, stopping.

'Good evening, sir.'

The smoke came out from behind Keith's back, just faintly.

'You should wear your caps,' complained Mr Blackburn. 'You're not ashamed of your own school, are you?'

'No, sir.'

'Have you done your week-end essays?' he asked.

'Yes, sir,' we said.

'Last week your essays were uncommonly alike,' said Mr Blackburn. 'You were asked to write on "Tea" and you insisted on depicting the horrors of exploitation. Both of you.'

'A coincidence,' said Keith, raising his eyebrows.

'Remarkable,' I stuttered.

'Some paragraphs were *identical*,' said Mr Blackburn.

'Telepathy,' muttered Keith.

'I beg your pardon?'

'How odd,' said Keith.

'Most odd,' agreed Mr Blackburn.

'We think alike, sir,' I volunteered.

Keith was getting worried. If the conversation continued the cigarette would burn his fingers.

'Is there something burning?' asked Old Blacky.

'It's my hair-oil,' mumbled Keith. 'It has an oriental smell.'

'I don't want you to think alike this week,' went on Mr Blackburn, not listening. 'It's English literature I'm interested in – not political diatribes, or anarchist propaganda. Good evening.'

'Good evening, sir.'

Keith carefully transferred his cigarette anteriorly as Mr Blackburn strode down the hill.

'Bloody Tory,' said Keith.

'He reads the *Daily Telegraph*,' I said.

Near the quarry, Lydia Pike was waiting for us, honey-haired, grey misted eyes, what a figure, Lydia Pike (I bet she doesn't wear a brassiere). We looked down, the three of us, into the dark hole of the disused quarry. The grey stone was rusted with mustard colour; at the bottom, rainwater had collected. I imagined a thousand men, stripped to the waist, toiling – striking picks into the stone sides of the quarry to the rhythm of Capitalist whips.

'Nancy can't come out tonight,' said Lydia.

'Oh, what a pity,' Keith said casually in his best accent.

'She's got a headache,' explained Lydia.

'Not bad, I hope,' Keith inquired, pronouncing every syllable carefully. 'No.'

'A pity,' said Keith.

He lit another cigarette. Then said, 'Either of you care to partake of the brown weed?' He spoke with breeding, slowly, changing his voice. 'Either of you... care... to... partake... of the brown... weed?'

'No, thanks,' said Lydia.

I took a cigarette and blushed when the match went out. It took three matches to light the damned thing. My face bloomed like a geranium.

'I like men to smoke,' said Lydia, 'it's so manly.'

We walked towards the fields; it was dusk now and the skies had changed to translucent green and purple. We strolled through a gate, puffing cigarettes madly, Lydia between us. On an allotment, a man wearing bicycle clips looked up at us amused. Towards Cyncoed you could see the wooded hills. Below us, the lights of the City and the Bristol Channel. The grass lay wet with dew and in the farther field there was a ground mist. Behind us, the allotment man, now chopping wood, disturbed the loneliness of the fields.

'I think I'll turn back here,' said Keith suddenly.

'Why?' asked Lydia. 'It's quite early yet.'

'No, I've to be home early,' Keith said, inspired. 'Dad's got sciatica – and he's not to worry about me...'

'Psychosomatic?' I said.

'Yes,' said Keith sadly, 'psychosomatic.'

'What is?' asked Lydia.

'His sciatica,' I explained.

'You know what psychosomatic means, surely?' said Keith.

'Of course she does,' I said.

Lydia smiled... I didn't like it that Keith thought Lydia stupid. Keith threw his cigarette-end on the grass and stepped on it professionally.

'Do you have to go, Keith?' I said.

'But definitely.'

'Shall we walk back with you?' asked Lydia.

'Heavens, no!' I protested. 'Keith's not afraid of the dark, are you?'

'No,' said Keith mournfully.

'I'm sorry you have to leave us,' I said.

'We could walk back with him,' suggested Lydia.

'No... oh... please... please... don't spoil... your walk... because of me...'

'Not at all, Keith,' Lydia sympathised.

'Well... you'll probably get back quicker if you're on your own,' I said.

'Yes... probably.'

'What a shame your father has sciatica,' said Lydia.

'Well, good-bye, Keith,' I said finally.

'Good-bye,' he frowned, shaking hands with Lydia. 'Give my condolences to Nancy.' And then to me, 'If you can't be good, be careful.' ... I laughed awkwardly. We watched Keith strolling down the path, past the allotment. The man who had been chopping wood came out on to the path, pushing his bicycle, and Keith opened the gate for him.

'Shouldn't we walk him back?' asked Lydia.

'No,' I said, 'he likes walking home alone.'

Keith turned round and waved. Then he shouted, 'Shall I leave some fags with you?'

'Don't bother,' I called back.

He waved again, sadly, and disappeared into the road, leaving Lydia and me high up in a spring-chilled field, close to a moon that hardly shone because it was not yet dark.

We continued through the fairy-tale fields up to our ankles in grey mist and I gave my school scarf to Lydia to keep away the cold. She looked lovely in my green and gold scarf. I hummed the school song to myself:

'Green and Gold, Green and Gold,
Strong be our hearts and bold.
To remain unsullied our Great Name
Adding to Ancient Glory, Modern Fame.
Green and Gold, Green and...'

I nearly stepped on some cow-dung, humming. At the top we gazed down at Cardiff, at the lights dotting the shadows below, window lights, lamp-posts, flashes of electricity from the trams. Away towards the direction of Newport a train rushed through the dark, a chain of lights, like a glimmering thought, across the blank mind of the countryside. Somewhere down there amongst the lights, Mother would be in the kitchen preparing the evening meal. Leo would be in his room writing a speech for some Labour Party meeting, rehearsing it perhaps before the mirror. Dad would be in the armchair under lamplight reading the *South Wales Echo*, the spectacles slipping down his nose, and his mouth silently forming the words as he read.

'I think Keith is very nice,' Lydia said.

'Yes, he's a good chap,' I condescended.

'And attractive too.'

I looked at her – was she joking? 'Do you think so?' I asked doubtfully. I tried to see Keith through the eyes of Lydia. A scruffy, scraggy youth with red-brown hair falling over a high forehead without fuss – the freckled wide flat face, the snub nose, and eyes blue as a poison bottle...

'Oh, I don't mean physically,' said Lydia.

'No?'

'But he attracts me mentally.'

'That so?'

I was taken aback. Imagine *anybody* being attracted to Keith *mentally*. Perhaps Lydia was a little backward after all! But Lydia slipped her hand into mine.

'Of course *you* attract me mentally *and* physically,' she reassured me.

'I don't know why,' I said, 'there's nothing to me.' I looked at her beautiful face. 'Nothing at all really.'

'Oh, but there is,' protested Lydia.

'Besides, I'm no good for women,' I pointed out. 'I'm so selfish, so egocentric, inconsiderate. And I'm moody, shockingly moody. I think of suicide quite a lot, you know. I'd be hopeless to live with. Can't do anything in the house. Only concerned about myself. Yes, I'm an evil influence on women.'

'You shouldn't speak of yourself that way,' said Lydia passionately. 'You're a good person.'

'Oh no,' I protested. 'I'm rotten really. I know myself. Rotten through and through.'

The fields traced our signatures in moonlight and shadows. Under the clear stars we looked at each other with wonder, anew.

'You're beautiful in this light,' I said.

Lydia looked down at her feet.

'I'm going to kiss you,' I said.

She feebly tried to stop me. After she said: 'You're not like other boys. You kiss differently. You don't make me feel sick when you kiss me.' I wondered how other boys kissed her and *which* boys.

'How do you mean?' I questioned her.

'You keep your lips closed when you kiss,' she whispered. What did she mean? Of course I kept my lips closed. Was there another way of kissing?

I tried to embrace her again but she pushed me away saying: 'A girl mustn't be cheap with her kisses.'

We turned back down the path and later I stepped on the cowdung which earlier I had avoided.

My Father's Red Indian

Look at a good map of South Wales and you'll see Ogmore-by-Sea plainly marked. It is half-way between Swansea and Cardiff, on the coast, of course, facing the small hills of Somerset that I can now observe hazily, fifteen miles away, across the grey, twitching, Saturday evening sea of the Bristol Channel. Not quite a village, not quite a resort, it is a place where sheep outnumber seagulls, where seagulls outnumber dogs, where dogs outnumber its human denizens.

My father loved Ogmore. He regularly drove the car down the A48 so that he could fish where the river, trying to rid itself of all the Welsh rain from the inland mountains, pours itself ceaselessly into the sea. 'I'll catch a salmon bass today,' my father would say optimistically in those far, long-ago days before the war when I was a small boy flying low over that Ogmore beach with my arms outstretched, or kicking a pebble into the rocks and shouting 'Goal!' or just playing with my yo-yo and whispering, 'Knock, knock, who's there?' while the sea-wind replied threateningly, 'Me, the bogeyman, me, Adolf Hitler, and I'll make you and little Audrey cry and cry and cry.'

I love Ogmore as much as my father did. That's why, since I've been in South Wales a week now, staying with my mother at her Cathedral Road flat in Cardiff, I drove out here on my own today. I like the open acres of sheep-cropped turf that spread upwards from the rocks to the bluish ribbon road where the post office is and the petrol pump and the small Sea Lawns Hotel. I like the green ferns, the gorse in yolk-yellow flower that smells of Barmouth biscuits, and the old grey stone walls flecked with mustard lichen. I like the tons and tons of sweet air, and the extra air between the fleeing clouds and the blue. I like the dramatic, slow, chemically coloured sunsets – unpaintable, unbeatable – and those lights of Porthcawl across the bay that in an hour or so will suddenly appear, so many shivering distant dots as darkness deepens. I like even those scattered bungalows over there that scale the slopes of Ogmore-by-Sea, hideous as they are with their tidy lawns and hydrangea bushes and their neat, little, surrounding red-brick walls. Bungalows called Sea Breeze or Cap Dai or Balmoral or Cartref.

Just after tea I overheard a lady, a stranger to me, who lived in one of the bungalows, say in the post office, 'Jack Evans, 'e ought to be put away, I'm tellin' you, stark ravin', stark ravin', duw'.

Jack Evans, I thought, I wonder if it's the same Jack Evans. He would be an old man now.

A common enough name in Wales. I did not like to question this lady who wore a green scarf tied about her head and who said nothing more about Jack Evans. 'Ta-ta,' she called as she closed the door that made a bell briefly, sadly, tinkle.

'*South Wales Echo*, please,' I said, and carrying the newspaper walked down towards the sea, towards a dog barking.

After the war, when I was a student, my father continued regularly to visit Ogmore-by-Sea. But the river had been become polluted, the Bristol Channel more of a sewer, and he caught no more salmon bass, no more of those little flat dabs either, that my mother liked so much. Even the skate, with their horrible human lips, had vanished. Nothing lived in that sea except an occasional conger eel and the urine-coloured seaweed. Still my father stood there with his rod, all day, uselessly, until sunset when his silent silhouette listened to the crashing, deranged rhythms of the sea.

'Stark ravin', stark ravin',' the woman had said in the post office. And didn't my mother think Dad stark ravin' as he stood in his footprints throwing a line of hooks and raw pink ragworms into the barren waves?

'Might as well fish in the dirty bathwater upstairs,' my mother grumbled.

'But I'm not the only one,' father growled one day defensively. 'Since two weeks now another fella comes to fish near me. We'll catch something one of these days.'

'Who's this other crazy fisherman?' my mother asked.

'Name of Jack Evans,' my father replied. Then he hesitated and with his left thumb and index finger pulled at his lower lip. He was obviously going to announce something important. But he mumbled something. I didn't hear what he said that made my mother laugh.

She laughed, stopped, laughed again, and choking cheerfully gasped, 'That's a good one, ha ha.'

My father, uneasy because of her response, ignored me when I poked, 'What did you say, Dad?'

My mother, chuckling, tried to wipe tears from her eyes. 'Your father says, ha ha ha, that this Jack Evans is ha ha ha ha ha ha, oh dear, oh dear.'

'What?' I asked, irritated.

'Ha ha ha,' my mother continued, 'a *Red Indian*, ha ha ha.'

'He is too,' shouted my father, angry now. 'For heaven's sake, stop laughing. His mother was an American Indian, his father Welsh. What's funny about that?'

My father picked up a newspaper but didn't put on his glasses. He just stared at the paper and said, 'He's a Welsh Red Indian. When his mother died, Jack was sixteen, so his father brought him back to Bridgend which is where the Evans family comes from.'

'We're Welsh Jews,' I said to my mother. 'So why should we laugh at Welsh Indians?'

'You and your old fishing stories,' my mother said dismissively and disappeared into the kitchen.

My father put down the newspaper. 'He's a very interesting man is Jack Evans,' my father said, pensively, quietly.

Next time my father went fishing by the river mouth at Ogmore maybe I would go with him and meet Jack Evans, interesting Welsh Red Indian. My father drove the twenty-odd miles to Ogmore most weekends but somehow I never found time to go with him. There was a film to see, a party to go to, or I just wasted time playing poker in the students' union. So I did not meet Jack Evans. My father, though, became more and more expert in the culture and history of the American Indian.

'Oh, aye,' said my father. 'We do 'ave some very hinteresting conversations, me and Jack.'

'No fish, though,' I said.

'Had a definite bite yesterday,' said my father.

My father was not a religious man, not a philosophical man either, but standing there, by the side of the sea with Jack Evans, both men silent for the most part I should think, they must have thought thoughts, dreamed dreams that all men do who confront the man-absent seascape for hours and hours. My father never spoke a word of praise about the altering light in the water and the changing skies but he did occasionally stammer out some of his newfound Jack Evans knowledge, and when he did so my mother gazed at him with unaccustomed, suspicious eyes as if he were unwell, or as if he had brought home, uncharacteristically, a bunch of flowers.

'D'ye know,' he told us, 'the American Indians are a bit like Jews?
They 'ave no priest between man and his Creator, see.'

'No mediator, no intercessor?' I asked.

'Exactly,' my father continued. 'And like Jews, would you believe it,
they don't kneel to pray. They stand up erect, aye.'

'So what?' my mother said, disturbed.

'They don't try and convert people either – like Jews, see. And they
have a sort of barmitzvah, a sort of confirmation, when they're
thirteen.'

'I don't like Jack Evans,' my mother suddenly declared as if she had
decided he was a savage. 'What does he want?'

But I was curious to learn more about the Red Indian confirmation
ceremony and so I asked my father to tell us more about it. It seemed,
according to Jack Evans anyway, that after a purifying vapour bath
the thirteen-year-old Red Indian would climb the highest point in the
vicinity. Wishing to stand before God in all humility the youth would
strip and stand naked and motionless and silent on tip of hill, or top
of mountain, exposed to the wind and the sun. For two days and one
night, for two sunrises and two sunsets, the naked boy would stand
erect watching all the stars coming out and all the stars disappearing.

'Good night,' said my mother. 'What an ordeal for a young boy.'

We sat in the room, none of us speaking for a while. Then mother
said, 'I bet that Jack Evans could do with a vapour bath. Bet he smells
and could do with some Lifebuoy soap under his armpits.'

My father looked up, pained. 'I'd like to meet Jack Evans,' I said
quietly. 'I'll come to Ogmore with you next weekend, Dad.'

'All right,' my father said. 'I've told 'im you write poetry. He was
very interested to hear that. Soft in the head I told him you were. But
I 'spec' he'll be glad to meet you.'

'Fishing by there in Ogmore, both of them,' my mother said.
'Blockheads.'

The next weekend I sat in the back of my father's Morris Minor
next to his fishing tackle, next to the worm bait in an old tobacco tin.
My mother, at the last moment, decided to come too. 'Just for the
ride,' she explained. Like me, though, I'm sure she was curious to
meet my father's own Red Indian. On the other hand, my mother
always took delight in travelling in a car. Always she sat next to the
driver's seat, the window on her side open a little, however chill a wind
screeched in to freeze the other back-seat, protesting passengers.

'Just an inch,' she would plead. And content to be driven, to rest from her house chores, ten miles outside the town she'd sit there regal, giving my father directions or humming happily the gone music-hall songs that have faded into nostalgia.

As we came down Crack Hill to leave the A48 for Ogmore her hum became louder and soon words, wrong words, replaced the hum. 'I know she loves me, because she says so, because she says so, she is the Lily of Caerphilly, she is the Lily – Watch the sheep,' she suddenly shouted. The hedges and green fields raced back-wards and there, ahead of us in the bending road, forty yellow eyes stared at us. Afterwards, when father accelerated again, my mother asked in a voice too loud, 'He doesn't wear feathers an' things, does he?'

'For heaven's sake,' my father said. 'Don't be tactless. Don't ask him damn soft things like that.'

'Good night,' my mother replied. 'I won't speak to the man at all.'

She pulled out some Mintoes from her handbag, gave me one and unwrapped another to push it into my father's mouth as he stared steadily ahead at the road. Through the window now the landscape had changed. Down there in the valley, beyond turf and farms, the river snaked its way this side of the high sand dunes and then, abruptly, as we climbed an incline the open sea fanned out, the dazzle on the sea, the creamy edge of it all visible below us as it curved elliptically on the beach from the promontory of Porthcawl all the way round Happy Valley towards Ogmore and the mouth of the river. Such a deception that sea. So beautiful to look upon but so empty of fish. Even the seagulls of Ogmore looked thin, famished, not like those who feasted on these shores before the war.

'Can't see anyone fishing down there,' I said to my father. 'Tide's coming in,' he replied. 'Jack'll be by presently.'

Jack Evans seemed in no hurry. My father fished alone and my mother and I waited until we became tired of waiting. We went for a turfy walk and when we returned we found my father on his own still, casting his line into the incoming sea. We decided to go for tea in the Sea Lawns Hotel and we left my father the flask and sandwiches. When we came back again, still Jack Evans was absent. There was just the derelict wind and, out there, a distant coal tramp steamer edging its way on the silver dazzle towards Cardiff.

'Brr,' my mother said. 'It's an arctic wind. We'll wait in the car. Don't be long.'

We did not meet Jack Evans that day and the next weekend was raining monotonously. Besides, I wanted to see Henry Ford in a film called *Strange Incident*.

'Duw, you want to see a cowboy film,' my father mocked, 'when you could come with me an' meet a real live Red Indian.'

'It's raining, Dad,' I said.

'He'll be down there this week, sure as eggs,' my father said.

So father drove that Saturday to Ogmore alone and that night when he returned he gave me a note. "Ere,' he said. 'Jack Evans 'as written this out for you. He said sorry to 'ave missed you last week. But you might like this Red Indian poem of his. Read it out loud to your mother. It's short, go on.'

I opened up the piece of paper. I have never seen such big handwriting – bigger than a child's. You up there, I read to myself and then I read it out loud for my mother sat there inquisitively. 'It's about a falling star,' I said.

> You up there
> you who sewed to the black garment
> of endless night
> all those shining button-stars
> how your big fingers
> must have been cold.
>
> For the buttons do not hold
> some are loose
> some fall off.
> Look how one drops now
> down and in towards us
> and out of sight.

My mother nodded. 'Very nice,' she said. My father seemed triumphant. 'Even I understand that, son – it's about a shooting star – now why can't you write clear stuff like that instead of those modern poems you produce?'

'That's how Red Indians think,' my mother interrupted him. 'They don't understand about shooting stars. I mean they don't know the scientific explanation. They think God's fingers were just numb with cold. Fancy. Good night.'

I stared down at the handwriting. Nobody genuinely wrote like that, I thought. And then it occurred to me: Jack Evans didn't exist. My father had made him up. Why not? Some people wrote novels, others plays, or worked at poems like me. So why shouldn't my father have invented a character? And yet? How would my father have got hold of that poem or all those facts about Red Indian religion? My father was no scholar. Somebody with erudition had talked to him... so why not Jack Evans? All the same I looked at my father suspiciously.

'I'll come with you to Ogmore again one of these days,' I said.

I did too. About once a month I accompanied my father on his fishing trips. But I never met Jack Evans.

'Funny,' said my father, 'how he never makes it when you or your mother come.'

'He's got Red Indian second sight,' I muttered.

I remember it was 21 June, the longest day of the year, when I ambled into Cardiff Central Library and saw in the spacious reference room my own father studiously reading a book – something he never did at home. At once I guessed the book was about American Indian culture. Now I was certain he had invented Jack Evans, that his recently acquired knowledge about American Indian history and religion and poetry had been culled from books – not from any real, gossiping individual. My father sat, the other side of the room, at a long black table, bent over a book, unaware that his son was watching him. And I felt guilty standing there, finding out his secret. I felt furtive and quickly left the reference room lest he should look up.

My own father... crazy! Fooling us like that. As I ran down the steps of the library, disturbed, I do not know why I wanted to cry. My own father whom I loved, who was a bit eccentric, yes – but I'd thought not this crazy – living in a fantasy world, having a fantasy companion fishing with him in the sea that contained no fish. Hell, I thought, good grief! I decided not to say anything to my mother.

That night after a silent supper my father brought a piece of paper out of his pocket. 'I went to the library today,' he announced. 'I wanted to find a Red Indian poem for Jack. They were very helpful. The girl in the library let me 'ave a look at a book called *Literature of the American Indian*. Very hinteresting. I found this in it. It's an Eskimo poem, really. I'm not sure whether it's the same thing as a Red Indian one.'

He handed me the piece of paper and I felt relieved. I wanted to laugh. So my father hadn't made up Jack Evans. Now I felt ashamed that I had ever thought he had. I stared at my father's handwriting that was simple but small, mercifully small.

'Read it out, son,' said my mother.

'It's called "The Song of the Bad Boy",' I said.

My father stared at me bright-eyed, his mouth a little open. My mother smoothed back her hair. They were waiting so I read it out loud, 'The Song of the Bad Boy'.

'I am going to run away from home, *hayah*
In a great big boat, *hayah*
To hunt for a sweet little girl, *hayah*
I shall get her some beads, *hayah*
The kind that look like boiled ones, *hayah*
Then after a while, *hayah*
I shall come back home, *hayah*
I shall call all my relations together, *hayah*
And I shall give them all a thrashing, *hayah*
I shall marry two girls at once, *hayah*
One of the sweet little darlings, *hayah*
I shall dress in spotted seal-skins, *hayah*
And the other dear little pet, *hayah*
Shall wear skins of the hooded seal only, *hayah*.'

My mother laughed when I finished and said, 'The little demon.' And my father said, 'What does *hayah* mean?' I didn't know. Did it mean anything? Did it mean Hooray?

'You can ask Jack Evans!' said my mother.

He never did though. Jack Evans never turned up in Ogmore again. Regularly my father went fishing, regularly he stood near the river's mouth on his own. First he assumed that Jack Evans was ill. He did not know exactly where he lived. In Bridgend, probably. In some ways, my father admitted, Jack Evans was a mystery man. 'An' I can't look him up in any damned phone book,' Dad said. 'There are so many Evanses about.'

Gradually, catching nothing except seaweed week after week, and having no companion, my father became discouraged. Only in the best blue weather would he drive the car to Ogmore and even then he would rarely go fishing. His chest already had begun to play him up. He would sit in the car and cough and cough, gasping for breath, while my mother muttered anxiously, 'Good night, I do wish you'd give up smoking.'

The next year he did give up smoking. He gave up everything. The one Sunday we did go to Ogmore he did not even take his fishing tackle with him. He sat for hours silently, then almost shouted, 'They spoilt it, they ruined it. Oh the fools, the fools!' And he stared morosely at the polluted sea.

The years have not made me forget the timbre of his voice, nor the righteousness of his anger. I strolled over the turfy hillocks above the rocks and stared at the wronged sea. I remembered my mother, now an old widow in her Cardiff flat, still saying, 'Good night', and I continued walking towards the sea and the sunset. I wondered if there would be any fishermen this Saturday evening down by the mouth of the river. Because of the woman with the green scarf in the post office I half expected Jack Evans to be fishing there – an ancient grey-haired man not quite right in the head, standing where my father stood, wearing Wellingtons like my father did, as the smallest waves collapsed near his feet. 'Stark ravin', stark ravin'.'

I quickened my pace as the strong sea-wind moistened my eyes. There was not going to be much of a sunset. A few seagulls floated like paper towards the flat rocks on my left. Soon I would be beyond the small sand dunes on my right and the grey wall and the last bungalows. Then the river mouth would be visible. Indeed, three minutes later I saw the river below me and, in the distance, one solitary man holding a bending rod. I wanted to run. I scrambled over the rocks, shuffled over pebbles until my feet became silent on sand. As I approached the fisherman, I saw that he was, alas, quite young and I felt stupid as I walked towards him, still carrying my *South Wales Echo*.

He had seen me and I veered away a little but the stranger called, 'Got the football results?'

I glanced momentarily at the newspaper in my hand. 'No,' I said. 'I got this paper earlier. Too early.'

The fisherman nodded and I asked, hesitating, 'Any fish in these seas?'

Perhaps the wind carried my words the wrong way for he replied, 'Costs 'ell of a lot these days, mun. The price of bait, duw, shocking.'

'Do you ever catch fish here?' I asked again, louder.

'They caught a cod down by there near the flat rocks last week,' he replied. 'I'm 'oping for a salmon bass meself.'

He probably lived in Ogmore-by-Sea. Perhaps he would know

about the Jack Evans 'who ought to be put away'.

'Jack Evans?' he replied. 'No.'

I nodded and was about to turn back when he surprised me with, 'You don't mean Mac Evans by any chance?'

I wanted to laugh. I was looking for a Welsh Red Indian not a Welsh Scotsman!

'No, no,' said my new-found fisherman friend. 'Max Evans, mun. We just call him Mac for short.'

'Is Mac... Max Evans a bit... er... crazy?'

His hands tightened on his rod so that his knuckles whitened and he laughed. Suddenly he stopped laughing. 'By Christ,' he said. And solemn, he paused again as if to tell me of some disaster. 'You should see Mac on a motorbike,' he continued.

I grinned, half turned and raised my hand. He smiled back. I walked away up the crunching pebbles, over the rocks, onto the turf. Way at the top, on the road, the lamp-posts jerked on and Ogmore-by-Sea immediately became darker. Lights came on, too, in the post office and the Sea Lawns Hotel, and as I walked up the slope the moon in the sky became more and more bright.

From: *There was a Young Man from Cardiff*
(London 1991)

The Deceived

I was astonished when I opened my mail. For one letter proved to be from my Uncle Eddie and, accompanying the letter, was a cheque for a hundred pounds. 'The cheque,' he wrote, 'is for Services To Be Rendered by you. Please contact me at the above address.' The notepaper heading was Metatron Hall.

I knew about Metatron Hall. I had learnt about it in the newspapers, how it had become a healing centre because of The Marvellous Girl, Sandra Gibbs. I had read, with some scepticism, how this local young woman had been blind and then how, during a thunderstorm, a miracle had happened. Afterwards, not only could she see, but she had apparently acquired certain psychic gifts. She had appeared on stage for a year before giving up the theatre, and such inconsequential pursuits, to become the saintly, serious, Medicaster-in-Residence at Metatron Hall.

'How did your uncle get involved with that lot?' asked my wife, Joan.

'I don't know,' I said. 'I haven't seen him for twenty years.'

When my mother was alive she called Uncle Eddie, 'a real twister, the black sheep of the family'. I stared at the cheque for one hundred pounds. Uncle had always been disarmingly generous, always quick to put his hand in his pocket – other people's too, according to my mother. Over the years, he had quarrelled with all his numerous brothers, sisters, and in-laws. Those still alive spoke with venom about how he had double-crossed them, persuaded them with that glib tongue of his, to invest in one crazy business scheme or another. Even my Uncle Max would have nothing to do with him. 'You have to count your teeth anyhow after you've seen Eddie,' he growled.

The women in the family particularly disapproved of Eddie. For he had abandoned Aunt Hetty, his two daughters and their apple pie home for a succession of gullible women, all wealthy enough to keep him. 'Gone off with another of his chorus girls,' my mother used to exclaim with breathless, condemning fascination. 'What a rotter!' But now he was in his seventies so surely women could no longer think of him as Gorgeous Eddie, even if he called them 'My flower'.

A few evenings later – I happened to be watching the Prime Minister being interviewed on television – I had a follow-up telephone call from Uncle Eddie. Reluctantly, I agreed to go and see him at Metatron Hall. As soon as I'd replaced the receiver I regretted saying 'Yes'. Anyway, there was no point in brooding over it. I returned to the living room and the television screen. There were those who believed that in two week's time Margaret Thatcher would be elected Prime Minister for a third term of office. Entrepreneurs like Uncle Eddie, I thought, thrive in Thatcher's Britain.

The Vale of Glamorgan is studded, not only with the ruins of Norman castles but also with concealed, centuries-old, ivy-hugged mansions that only become visible when you meticulously explore the narrowest, high-hedged, minor roads and turn down some unlikely by-way. That Sunday afternoon in May, after passing several megaphoned cars out electioneering, I drove towards emptiness, down butterfly-haunted country lanes a dozen miles or so from Ogmore before I came to the signpost I was looking for. As soon as I turned into the long drive of Metatron Hall I heard the great clanging bell of the private chapel that adjoined the mansion.

I parked the car just as the sun luminously silvered the edge of a cloud before lighting up the whole landscape, not least the spectacular rhododendron bushes in blood-red flower and the dozen faces of the weary and the sick who were filing into the small chapel. 'They're hoping for a miracle,' I thought as I joined them beneath a flock of noisy rooks wheeling over the chapel.

The chapel itself, inside, was intimate and plain – except for one garish window which reminded me of the coloured glass that decorates so many front doors of older semi-detached, surburban houses. The ceiling had been washed an unconfident blue to match the frayed and fading blue carpet on the floor. A woman at my elbow whispered to me, 'The day of our death is the most beautiful day of our life.' Before I could refute that outrageous statement the service began. I became aware of the sun drizzling through the stained window onto a brassy-gold candelabra and a gold statuette of an angel. The angel Metatron, the heavenly scribe perhaps? There and there blue, the colour of healing; and there and there gold, the colour of money.

After a short service led by an absurdly round-faced clergyman, The Marvellous Girl appeared – she could not have been any other.

She was dressed modestly in black, pale of countenance, wearing no make-up, and she laid her hands on those who inched forward. A young father hugged a child in his arms, the child probably not yet three years of age. The little hand was bent on the wrist oddly. It kept on twitching. The Marvellous Girl, Sandra Gibbs, solemnly placed her own two hands firmly on the head of the spastic child and prayed – as did the others in the pews. Then, from outside, I heard some harsh cries. They were the terrible dark sounds of the dozen rooks that must have resumed flying about the roof of the chapel.

Afterwards, behind the pews, at the rear of the chapel, I observed the young father with the child still cradled in his arms. Surreptitiously, he bent down and kissed his little son's head. I saw the naked face of a father, a naked face of a grown man close to tears. He was unaware anyone had observed him. For some reason I felt angry with myself and urgently left the church. I walked on to the mansion.

A young woman with streaky blonde hair led me into a dilapidated, high, oak-panelled room whose long, dust-flecked windows overlooked an extended, tidy lawn on which I could see a man and a woman talking together.

'Your uncle won't be long,' the woman said. 'I'll tell him you're here.'

She closed the door behind her, leaving me alone with the Sunday newspapers on a desk. My small journey from the front door, through the long hall with its peeling wallpaper to this shabby, once elegant room, had given me a glimpse of how tatty and rundown Metatron Hall had become. All the more paradoxical then was the studied tidiness of the mowed lawn outside.

I moved nearer to the window. The two people on the lawn faced each other. They were both exceedingly tall, both very straight-backed. The man in a cream-coloured suit, though athletic looking, was quite old, and the woman probably not much younger. They seemed to be talking earnestly, standing a few feet away from each other, he on my right, she on my left. They were about a hundred yards away from the window so I could not see their faces with great clarity. After a minute, the man moved so that he had his back to me and the woman immediately changed her stance, too, so that now she faced me directly. They stood near a white-painted garden bench but still continued their rapt conversation standing up. Again the man slewed round and the woman followed as in a slow ritual so that the tall, old man was now on my left, the tall woman on the right. 'Sit down,' I thought. 'Why don't you both sit down?'

I turned away, picked up one of the newspapers on the desk and settled in an armchair that was in desperate need of upholstering. Almost at once the door opened and Uncle Eddie came into the room. 'Dan?' he asked. 'Duw, you've changed. I'd never have recognised you in a 'undred year.' He looked pretty sprightly himself, his plastered-down hair with a conspicuous parting was now, unfairly, darker than mine, despite his age.

'I saw you on TV only a year ago. They sure must have made you up,' he said, making me feel the age in my mouth.

'You're looking fine, Uncle,' I said lamely, thinking whatever happened to his glib, buttery tongue?

'TV flatters some people,' Uncle Eddie said, puzzled. 'Anyway, I'm glad you've come.'

He evidently realised he had been less than tactful for he tried to make amends by telling me how he had heard only good things about me, how I was this and how I was that, not like the rest of the family. 'What a shower they are,' he said. Then he took out of the desk drawer a box of Black Magic chocolates. 'See,' he continued, 'I remembered how much you liked these.'

'It was my mother who was keen on them,' I said.

This stopped him smiling. 'Oh, I quite like them too,' I added quickly.

He opened the box and studied the key to the different centres of the chocolates. 'Now, what do you like best?' he asked. 'Turkish Delight? Marzipan? To be honest, I'm fond of the cherry one myself, but if you'd like it you have it...' I selected a chocolate at random. 'What is it?' he asked as I bit on it.

'Caramel, I think,' I said. He hunted through the box to select the cherry chocolate. When I looked towards the window I saw that the tall couple had left the lawn.

'I popped into the chapel,' I said. 'I witnessed Sandra Gibbs at work.'

'They don't pay a penny,' Uncle boasted. 'Not one penny. We open up the chapel to the public on Sundays. You were impressed by Sandra, I hope? She has the spiritual blessing, you know, of this Bishop and that – the sanction of the church.'

'I'm a Welsh Jewish secular fundamentalist,' I said.

'I bet you're dubious about The Marvellous Girl,' said my uncle, 'but you haven't witnessed what I have. Sandra's crazy, says little, but when she does speak in that deep, husky voice of hers I've seen a woman fall to the ground, pronto. I've seen a farmer, a very matter-of-fact bloke, having a convulsion so that he had to be held down. She can have an extraordinary effect upon people. She's so mentally fragile, so wistful, so sincere, so possessed by the holy spirit. Some who've visited Metatron Hall have already testified to miracle cures. The place could become a beacon of light for the sick everywhere – like Lourdes. A beacon. And we could make a packet.'

'We?' I asked.

'I mean May Gibbs, Sandra and me. And perhaps, one day, a Medical Director. Why not? The National Health Service isn't much cop these days, is it? All those waiting in queues for ops, they need a place like Metatron Hall, right? If the other marvellous lady is elected again, places like Metatron Hall will do better and better. Mark my words. Listen, Dan, Metatron Hall at present is in an 'ell of a mess. No facilities. No central heating. All fourteen bedrooms in need of repair and decoration. And only two lavs in the whole place. Well, mun, if you're going to charge guests who stay here for The Marvellous Girl's healing touch, you have to offer them luxury, right? Well, we have this idea of building a luxury hotel-nursing-home annexe in the grounds. Out there, beyond that lawn, there's plenty of room for building. But, to be honest, the bank won't lend us more. However, Harri Jenkins is interested in extending his hotel business.'

'Harri Jenkins?'

'Of the Sunset Hotel near Ogmore.'

'I don't know him. I've never been to the Sunset Hotel. That's a bit inland, isn't it?'

'He knows you – of you, I mean. Because of our surname he asked if we were related. He knows you're a doctor. He's very impressed by doctors. He's likely to call on you since you live only a couple of miles away from the hotel. To be honest, that's why I wrote to you. I said that... er... who knows, one day you might consider becoming Medical Director at the Hall. I know it's not your cuppa tea, but I thought no harm in me saying it.'

'It's not my cuppa tea,' I said.

My uncle picked up the box of Black Magic chocolates, then put it down again on the desk. 'I know your mother never thought me to be the bee's knees – because of Hetty. Two sides to everything, right? I'd be much obliged if you'd be very careful if Harri Jenkins asks you anything about me.'

'OK,' I said. 'But I don't need to be bribed.'

I took the cheque he had sent me out of my pocket and tore it up. He laughed. Perhaps he was laughing at me being so dramatically self-righteous. Or would the cheque have bounced anyway?

'Yes, Sandra is sort of remarkable,' Uncle Eddie said. 'Last winter she had a premonition. She had a vivid dream of a car ferry capsizing and sinking outside a French port.'

'The *Herald of Free Enterprise* sank outside a *Belgian* port,' I said. 'Well, it was damned near, wasn't it?' exclaimed Uncle vehemently.

Outside, on the lawn, the tall couple appeared again, this time accompanied by a woman in a blue dress. 'Dan,' said Uncle Eddie quietly, 'it's important to me that this business deal goes through. My last chance maybe. I mean I've buggered up so many things in my life. I'm depending on you being discreet.' He looked towards the window and his face visibly softened. 'There's May Gibbs,' he said, 'in the blue dress.' He came closer to me, too close. 'You know, Hetty was a great whore in the kitchen and a great cook in bed. With May it's the other way round. She's a goer. She keeps me young. She's twenty-five years younger than me but, to be honest, it's good between us. Listen, Dan, I'm telling you that for the first time in my life I care more about another person than myself, know what I mean?'

Vulnerably, he looked out of the window. All three on the lawn were walking towards us. The woman in a blue dress, in her fifties, had a pleasing face, a delicate bone structure, and when young must have been entirely beautiful. Now she waved as she stood at the tall, dusty window, and called, 'C'mon and join us, Eddie. Get some sun.'

'Coming, my pigeon,' he called back.

As we left the panelled room he told me, 'That Llantwit couple with May, they're religious and rich as Croesus but I bet they won't invest in Metatron Hall. They're not so susceptible to May's charms as Harri Jenkins is.'

'And your Marvellous Girl,' I asked. 'I take it she's sincerely religious too?'

Uncle halted. 'She's not a charlatan if that's what you think. She's mad, yes, sort of insane, but not a charlatan.'

After Mrs Thatcher won her third term of office the election posters were taken down. In their stead notices had been put up for miles around – from Ewenny to Merthyr Mawr, from Colwinston to Southerndown. At Ogmore-by-Sea they blazoned forth from the windows of Hardee's, the post office and the village shop: AT THE SUNSET LOUNGE, 21 June 8 p.m. Midsummer Night. One performance only. THE MARVELLOUS GIRL; SANDRA GIBBS IN PERSON. In aid of the Blind Children's Fund.

Harri Jenkins had never contacted me but I had made some enquiries about the Sunset Hotel. Brian Clark, who used to come over once a month to do some gardening at Green Hollows and who lived a stone's throw from the hotel, was far from reassuring. The Sunset can't compete with the Craig or Sea Lawns. They're in sight of the sea. I think Harri's up to his neck in debt. As for that show being in aid of blind children, I wouldn't like to bet on that,' Brian said. The more I heard about Harri Jenkins, the more he sounded like my Uncle Eddie!

On Sunday, 21 June, Joan had no wish to watch 'a magic show'. She suggested that if Sandra Gibbs really had psychic powers she could solve the financial difficulties of Metatron Hall by visiting a casino and forecasting which numbers would turn up next. 'Besides,' she remarked, 'I think it would be better if you had nothing to do with either your dubious uncle or the dubious Mr Jenkins.'

She was quite right of course, but I was curious. So I set out to walk the two miles to the Sunset Hotel on my own. On my way I had to pass through the tiny village of Gwylfa. Only very occasionally did a car or a van travel down the narrow winding lane, its hedges filled with so many wild, delicate flowers the names of which I didn't know, this one and that one delinquently incognito. Just before I reached the village I saw a sheep close to the hedge, apparently asleep. When I reached it I realised the creature was dead. It had been hit by a car. I hesitated. There was nothing I could do. I walked on.

The large lounge of the Sunset Hotel, with all its indoor greenery, was crowded that Sunday evening. Soon after I had sat down on a chair in the back row I espied my uncle sitting on the side at the front. I had arrived just in time because the lights were lowered almost immediately. Harri Jenkins came on to the specially raised platform on which had been arranged a couple of chairs, a table covered by a black velvet cloth and, in the background, a blackboard.

'Privilege,' said Harri Jenkins, a middle-aged man with glassy, sparkling eyes and distinctly rosy cheeks that made him resemble a ventriloquist's dummy. 'Privilege,' repeated Mr Jenkins louder so that the humming conversation of the audience began to subside to an expectant hush. He waited dramatically for complete silence before he undid his double-breasted, too tight, purple blazer and continued, 'Privilege for me to introduce the *famous* celebrity, The Marvellous Girl, and her mother, May Gibbs. You've all read about The Marvellous Girl so she hardly needs me, um, to introduce her, oh dear no. Lately I've got to know her and her mother who should be called marvellous too, got to know them both personally. Well, um, many of you here know me, know how good I am at sussing out qualities in men and women. An hotel proprietor does have to be a bit psychic and –'

'Get on with it, Harri,' shouted out Lol, one of the local shepherds, who evidently had had several jars in the bar beforehand.

Harri Jenkins's hands had been raised in the air like a conductor's. He let them drop. 'As I was saying, mun, we have two marvellous women on stage at the lounge tonight. Makes me feel like a glutton,' he added smiling, showing all his teeth. 'As for The Marvellous Girl herself – just to be near her is to feel a great bronze bell silently ringing.'

'Aw, put a sock in it,' Lol suddenly shouted, amusing some in the audience but embarrassing most.

'Lol?' asked Harri Jenkins, peering into the shadows of the lounge. 'What's the matter with you?'

'I'm pissed,' called back Lol, standing up, swaying a little.

There was a general hum of sighings and tuttings and someone shouted out, 'That man must leave the lounge. He must leave.'

'Go,' said Mr Jenkins, pointing like the Angel who directed Adam and Eve from Paradise. 'If you don't go I'll see you never get another drink at the Sunset ever.'

He stood there with his hand pointing towards the door for a full minute while Lol, obediently, mumbling to himself, made his way past knees to the gangway. At the door, he paused to face the intrepid, pointing Harri Jenkins. 'You're a fart,' he said, then stumbled backwards through the door and disappeared.

Inappropriately, as if he had just heard great good news, Harri Jenkins smiled again at the audience. This absurd, semi-comic prole-

121

gomenon was hardly appropriate for the 'mystery show' that was about to follow but the Master of Ceremonies, Harri Jenkins, valiantly continued, 'The stage appearance of The Marvellous Girl is a one-off. She has basically given up stage appearances. Instead she works selflessly at that healing centre, that wonderful healing centre, Metatron Hall in the Vale of Glamorgan. Um. It's the cause of the Blind that brings her here tonight. And my own personal interest in Metatron Hall. Ladies and Gentlemen, please welcome The Marvellous Girl and her marvellous mother.'

The audience applauded and, at once, Mrs Gibbs came on to the stage carrying a lit black candle which she placed on the black velvet cloth, followed by The Marvellous Girl who was wearing bow tie, tuxedo and shiny top hat. Her face had been powdered an unnatural white to emphasise her large, staring eyes. She stood behind one of the crimson chairs while her mother pronounced, 'When the angels descend to this world to fulfil a mission they wear the garments of this world and they take on the appearance of the people of this world. Otherwise they would not be tolerated here on this earth and we, in turn, could not endure them.'

Was Mrs Gibbs suggesting that her daughter was divine? I recalled my uncle's remarks about Sandra Gibbs that she was 'sort of insane'. Perhaps the mother was too?

The show began. It seemed that the slim, haunted-looking girl in disturbing top hat and in evening-dress suit owned psychokinetic and telepathic gifts. She, at first, did not speak, utter one single word, yet this somehow did not diminish her almost palpable charisma. The mother vocalised everything – quite a joky auctioneer's patter she had too – as Sandra Gibbs, in a kind of cataleptic trance, stared at the flickering lit candle with terrible concentration and made solid objects apparently dematerialise and rematerialise.

After about half an hour of this The Marvellous Girl was blindfolded and a few members of the audience were invited to clamber onto the stage. Each, in turn, was asked to write the name of some real, concrete object on the blackboard. One of my neighbours wrote down 'Tusker Rock', the young woman with streaky blonde hair that I had seen at Metatron Hall chalked up 'Niagara Falls', and Mrs Maddocks, our local wit, started to write the name of the village in Gwynedd fifty-eight letters long. She had got as far as 'Llanfairpwll' when May Gibbs stopped her saying that the village's name,

Llanfairpwllgwyngyllgogerychwyrndrobwllllantysiliogogogoch, would be too easy for The Marvellous Girl. 'So give her something more difficult,' urged May Gibbs. After much laughter Mrs Maddocks wrote down, 'Lol the shepherd' and again everybody laughed.

Sandra Gibbs stood very still, blindfolded, in front of the stage while her mother took a billiard cue and pointed to the words 'Tusker Rock'. 'Concentrate your minds,' commanded May Gibbs addressing the silent audience. 'Bring into your minds a vision of what is written here. Think, think of it, picture it.' She cleared her throat and mumbled something I couldn't hear, then added, 'Ye-es, let it float into your minds. It's coming, it's coming, that's right, into your minds and now it will be seen by The Marvellous Girl.'

The audience waited. The girl with the white powdered face opened her mouth as if to speak but uttered no word. The Sunset Lounge was quite silent. Then, in an unexpectedly deep voice, The Marvellous Girl said, 'Tusker Rock'. And everybody applauded. The same routine was followed before Sandra Gibbs pronounced 'Niagara Falls' and then, with even greater hesitation and more patter from her mother, 'Lol, the shepherd'. Again everybody applauded. Was this exhibition of telepathy somehow faked? Others followed in similar fashion. Did Mrs Gibbs' patter conceal a code? I suspected so. What did somewhat unnerve me was The Marvellous Girl's remarkable, eerie voice. Deep as a man's. And her clothes were like a man's. Was her evident charisma expressed in the mythic apprehension that man and woman once were one person, a god and goddess dwelling in one body?

'Now, another phenomenon,' May Gibbs solemnly announced after the show had lengthened to almost two hours. She placed a large glass vase on the black velvet cloth next to the one lit candle. 'The Marvellous Girl will now, by a further concentration of psychic energy, shatter this vase into a hundred pieces. She will not, I promise you, touch it.'

Seemingly more white-faced than ever, her eyes hardly blinking and conspicuous beneath her top hat, Sandra Gibbs stepped forward to stand a foot or two from the table. 'Silence, please, utter silence,' called May Gibbs who then raised her right foot on its heel before letting the sole slap down, up and down repeatedly on the floor to evince a regular pattern of noise.

'Slower,' The Marvellous Girl surprisingly objected. 'Slower. The same rate as my heartbeat.'

The foot tapped slower, tap tap tap, about seventy beats a minute, I reckoned. Meanwhile The Marvellous Girl, Sandra Gibbs, passed her hands back and forward horizontally, arms outstretched, above the vase. Suddenly, May Gibbs stopped tapping the floor, the candle flame, which had been increasingly flickering, inexplicably went out and there was a great crash behind me. One of the pictures on the wall had, for no evident reason, smashed down onto the floor. Everybody looked away from the stage over their shoulders and the woman next to me mumbled, 'They say when a picture frame falls down on its own there'll be a death in the family.'

The vase on the velvet cloth remained whole, unshattered. May Gibbs looked dismayed. 'Oh my God,' uttered the Marvellous Girl in her dark voice, 'I'm sorry, I'm sorry. I visited the Void. That was a malefic influence. I'm sorry.'

May Gibbs quickly took the vase away. She told a joke about how things can go wrong that made everybody laugh while Sandra Gibbs sat down again, unsmiling, somnambulistically, on one of the crimson chairs, hands on her knees, palms turned upwards.

'Yes, that picture is of Foxhunting and The Marvellous Girl is an anti-vivisectionist and a vegetarian,' May Gibbs declared.

The audience did not notice, at first, the return of Lol the shepherd. He had abandoned the lounge somewhat tipsy earlier, he was now indubitably quite drunk. As May Gibbs spoke he drifted up the aisle with the obvious intention of climbing up onto the stage. 'You bastards,' he shouted out abruptly. 'You're all bastards.'

Mrs Gibbs looked at her daughter wildly. And as Lol advanced on the stage, Harri Jenkins came forward to impede his progress. 'Leave him alone,' Sandra Gibbs said quietly. 'It will be all right.' Lol had raised his right arm and his right hand had become a fist. He moved threateningly towards Harri Jenkins but Sandra Gibbs stepped forward. 'This way, my dear child,' she commanded in her husky male voice. Lol hesitated. The audience were rapt, quiet. 'This way, my dear one.' Lol changed his direction. 'Come.'

He dropped his fist and, docile, moved towards her. 'Life is so hard for you, I understand,' she intoned quietly. Lol nodded assent. 'What do they know out there,' she said, 'in their comfortable seats, the hardships you have to endure every day. The insults, the injuries, the loneliness. Kneel my child and pray. Afterwards you will feel refreshed, grateful and happier.' Lol sank to his knees, seemingly hypnotised, and uttered, 'Our Father, which art in Heaven, hallowed be Thy Name, Thy Kingdom come...'

While he prayed The Marvellous Girl placed her hand on his head. At the conclusion of the prayer she said, 'Rise now, dear child, and go home in peace.' Lol rose and without stumbling, apparently quite sober, left the lounge. As soon as he had vanished the audience all clapped and Harri Jenkins came forward to conclude the 'show'. His vote of thanks was a masterpiece of hyperbole which would not have shamed the medieval Welsh poets. 'We've seen here tonight, ladies and gentlemen, great inexplicable splendour. We've had torrents of surprises and, um, entertainment. Absolute torrents. The Marvellous Girl has a talent that could put an oak tree into flames. Like the preachers of old she could light the lamp to direct us away from the chasm beyond Hell's gate. As for her mother, an eagle amongst women, we must thank her too. We, of this parish, are truly privileged to have them visit us tonight.'

He diligently continued to extol the virtues of May and Sandra Gibbs before reminding the audience that the evening's takings would be going to the Blind Children's Fund. 'But one should not forget,' he concluded, 'the inspiring, valorous work going on at Metatron Hall. Healing skill they have, money is what they need. So the boxes are going around for notes only, ladies and gentlemen. Remember those who visit Metatron Hall are those the doctors have despaired of. Count your blessings and give in order that these two noble ladies, pure as nuns, may carry on their merciful work. Cheques will be accepted. I deeply thank you.'

I waited until the lounge had cleared before approaching Uncle Eddie who had not moved from his chair. Sandra Gibbs and her mother had disappeared but a few near the door had buttonholed Harri Jenkins. Uncle Eddie stared at me uncomprehendingly when I greeted him. I was curious about the picture frame, how it, deranged, had crashed down unaccountably, surprising – or so it appeared – even those on stage. Had that genuinely been unplanned? I wondered, too, whether the journalist who had originally dubbed Sandra Gibbs 'The Marvellous Girl' had done so ironically, to evoke comparisons with the teenage Thomas Chatterton, that gifted eighteenth-century poet and forger whose deceptions had, for a time, bamboozled the literary world and antiquaries alike, and who had been labelled by William Wordsworth as 'The Marvellous Boy'. But it did not seem the appropriate moment to air my scepticism. Instead I said, 'It went well, Uncle. She certainly has the true hypnotic powers.'

He stood up and said morosely, 'Let's get some air.'

I followed him to the door where Harri Jenkins said to him, 'We'll be leaving in about twenty minutes, Eddie.' But my uncle brushed past him angrily. I remembered how Brian Clark had suggested Harri Jenkins was up to his neck in debt and could hardly invest in Metatron Hall. Perhaps my uncle had become aware of this?

Outside the hotel, the sun was setting so that the trees, drawn in charcoal, barred the width of a streaky coloured sky. Midges, restless specks of energy, had begun their sundown Sisyphus work and, in the distance, doors were slamming shut in the hotel car park. My uncle seemed loath to speak.

'What's the matter?' I asked him.

'The pig, Harri Jenkins, that's what's the matter.'

The cars leaving the car park had their headlights switched on. In the failing light I saw how much older my uncle now looked.

'I don't know what to do, I don't know what to do, I don't know what to do,' Eddie murmured distressingly.

'Maybe someone else will invest in Metatron Hall,' I said.

'That's not the trouble,' Uncle said dismissively as if I were utterly stupid. 'May's persuaded that couple from near Llantwit to put cash in. No, it's Harri Jenkins. Harri Jenkins and May, they're having an affair. He's moving into Metatron Hall.'

'They know you know,' I said, at a loss what to say.

'I've had it,' my uncle said. 'They won't let me stay there much longer. May's the only woman I've ever really cared for.'

He stepped towards the hotel, defeated, then stopped to say helplessly, 'I don't know what to do. I don't know where to go to. All Sandra does is pray, pray, pray. She's doing that now – asking God's forgiveness for giving a show. And May, she's infatuated by that crook Jenkins. Hypnotised by him.'

He stood there without moving. I thought he was going to cry. Instead he added, 'I could kill him.' The deceiver had been deceived. He looked past me, as if into the future. 'What are we here for, Dan?' he asked quietly, 'What the hell are we here for?' before turning to disappear into the Sunset Lounge. His shoulders were round. His back was the back of an old man.

By the time I had walked to the village of Gwylfa it was quite dark. A few desolate sodium lamp-posts lit up a short bend of the road within the village boundaries. Then it was dark again. I expected to see the carcass of the sheep. It had gone. Someone had taken it away. It was as if it had never existed except in my imagination.

From: *There was a Young Man from Cardiff*
(London 1991)

3. Journals

From: *Notes Mainly at the Clinic* 1981-2

On Suggestion

On one hand the power of denial, on the other the power of suggestion. A number of my patients need to give up smoking because they have been exposed to blue asbestos – there is a synergistic effect with the inhalation of tobacco smoke and blue asbestos fibres. I mentioned this to one of my colleagues, Dr Margaret MacDonald, who has begun to practise acupuncture with what seems to be total enthusiasm. I thought perhaps acupuncture might help those who had difficulty in kicking the habit, through the power of suggestion.

'That is not how acupuncture works,' Margaret insisted.

The continued existence of acupuncture in a 'modern' state like China has sanctioned doctors like Margaret MacDonald, as well as quacks, to practise this form of treatment in the West. In the last decade or so newspapers and popular periodicals have given acupuncture much free publicity; there have been medical journalists who have tried to give acupuncture a scientific gloss. In Britain, and no doubt elsewhere, there exist acupuncture clinics where men in clinical white coats, resembling the glamorous doctor heroes of television medical romances – though frequently they are not, in fact, qualified doctors – stick needles into hopeful patients. Most of the patients leave the clinic (the decor of one I visited resembled a cross between a lush private nursing home and a Chinese restaurant) with the symptoms they had when they entered. All leave with less money in their wallets or handbags.

It is significant that one acupuncture doctor interviewed in the *Sunday Times* declared that he preferred to treat 'chronic ailments which have defeated Western medicine: for instance, migraines and other types of headaches; duodenal and stomach ulcers; indigestive disorders; lumbago, fibrositis, sciatica, neuralgia; acne and other skin troubles; asthma, hay fever; high blood pressure; depressions and anxiety states' – all symptoms or ailments known to be related to stress or other psychological disturbance. The doctor would probably obtain the same results, providing he believed in the efficacy of it all, by sticking the needles into himself while his patients watched him. However, the acupuncturist could well respond, 'Do orthodox physicians prescribing placebos, tonics and vitamins obtain better results with those patients suffering the same intractable conditions?'

Of course, the power of suggestion can be packaged in a capsule or concentrated at the point of a needle. Or, for that matter, in any object which has for the patient certain potent associations. Some years ago I was asked to give a gas and oxygen anaesthetic for a minor operation – a removal of an infected toenail. My colleague had nearly finished scrubbing up so I placed the mask over my patient's mouth and nose ready to administer the gas and oxygen anaesthetic. 'It will be over soon,' I had reassured the patient – and so it would have been but, at the last moment, the theatre door opened. An intruder's mouth opened and closed noiselessly in oral gesture. Then shufflings, whisperings, eyes meaningful behind masks. I gathered my colleague needed to answer, immediately, outside, an urgent telephone call. He temporarily quit the theatre and so I removed the mask from the patient's face. I was about to explain everything as best I could to the inconvenienced patient, to apologise to him for the delay, but he lay there with eyes closed, his head as still as a statue's. He had had no anaesthetic whatsoever. He had breathed in only ordinary air through the mask yet he had swooned. For a half-minute the mask had been over his face and he presumably thought he was breathing in the gas. Accordingly he had fallen into a profound sleep – as profound as Adam's – and I suspect that in that trance he could have had not only his toenail removed but a rib as well. My patient was roused only by strenuous shouting and shaking!

So much for the reports concerning operations undertaken in China with patients 'anaesthetised' by acupuncture needles.

Chest Clinic and Albert Poem

Early next year, 1 February 1982, I am to be made redundant. As part of a quarter-of-a-million-pound saving there has to be 'contraction and rationalisation'. So, as they say in the football world, I am for an early bath.

It will be strange to vacate this consulting room. I have been lucky, until now, in my medical career. I originally took up chest work because of a sweet accident. When I was conscripted into the RAF for National Service and was sent, with a number of other young doctors, to Moreton-in-Marsh for one month's induction (square-bashing) in May 1951, I resented being separated from Joan Mercer (my future wife) who lived (with me) in Belsize Square, London. So when, one evening in the mess bar, I heard that the RAF Mass Radiography Section was based in Cleveland Street, *in London*, I became very interested, suddenly, in mass radiography. After all, Cleveland Street was near Goodge Street station, a short tube ride on the Northern Line. Moreover it was halfway between the BBC and my publisher, Hutchinson!

Towards the end of our induction period a form was circulated to us all in which we were invited to put down our geographical and professional preferences regarding future postings. Though it was rumoured that little attention was paid to our responses, on the form I firmly entered 'HOME COUNTIES' and 'VERY KEEN ON MASS RADIOGRAPHY'. The idea of mass radiography had never crossed my mind until that bar conversation but I figured that while my colleagues would ask for 'GENERAL PRACTICE' or 'SURGERY' or 'DERMATOLOGY' or some other speciality they had some engagement with because of this or that house job, not one of them, no one at all, would elect for 'MASS RADIOGRAPHY'. Probably, in the whole history of the RAF medical services, no neophyte ever had.

I was posted to HQ Mass Radiography, Cleveland Street, in London for a further month's training. Then, to my horror, I was to join the mobile X-ray unit in Northern Ireland! However, soon after, I was returned to HQ to become an assistant to the squadron leader in charge of all radiography units. The squadron leader had a PC, i.e. a permanent commission. I liked him; he was an easygoing fellow who frequently absented himself from his office without explanation. Too easygoing, the RAF thought, for a year later, because of certain incidents about which I am still not clear, he was court-martialled and I found myself promoted to Squadron Leader in charge of five doctors, five units, the central chest clinic, etc. So began my chest experience.

And when I left the RAF I was offered the job here, a job limited to office hours and of a diagnostic nature only, a repetitious job, one frequently boring, but one that has given me time to write and to pursue a more general academic interest in medicine. Besides, as a doctor practising within the strict confines of my own small speciality, I have been quite good! I do not want an early bath.

My patient, G., was ostentatiously polite. I had the feeling that he would hurry to open a door for me; but now it was time for him to quit, to open the door for himself. Instead he hesitated, then said, 'I wonder if I might ask you a personal question, Dr Abse?'

'Of course.'

'Have you a son called Albert?'

'No,' I said. 'My son's called Jesse David.'

He then mysteriously withdrew a piece of paper from a pocket of his suit.

'This poem of yours is very very meaningful to me and my wife, Dr Abse,' he said.

Surprised, I glanced at the paper, at an early poem of mine, one that I had written when a medical student. It was called 'Albert' – I still liked it well enough though I would hardly expect that particular poem to be very special for anyone:

> Albert loved dogs mostly though this was absurd
> for they always slouched away when he touched their fur,
> but once, perching on his shoulder, alighted a bird,
>
> a bird alive as fire and magical as that day
> when clear-eyed Héloïse met Peter Abelard.
> Though cats followed him the bird never flew away.
>
> And dogs pursued the cats which hunted the bird.
> Albert loved dogs deeply but was jealously hurt
> that they pursued him merely because of the bird,
> the bird alive as fire and magical as that day.
> So one morning he rose and murdered the bird.
> But then the cats vanished and the dogs went away.
>
> Albert hated dogs after – though this was absurd.

I handed the paper back to G. 'It's the only poem I've ever written derived from a dream,' I said. 'I dreamed years ago of someone with a bird on his shoulder followed by cats, followed by dogs...'

G. nodded. He rose from his chair. 'You see,' he said at last, 'I have a son called Albert. He's six now. A year ago he murdered our canary.'

Plath

Over Christmas I have been rereading the *Collected Poems* of Sylvia Plath which have recently been published. The notion that poets must suffer in order to write well, be deranged as Sylvia Plath was, has a long tradition. There are those who continue to see in the Philoctetes legend of the wound and the bow the predicament of the poet who, while owning special gifts (the magic bow), is alienated from his fellow men by his suffering psyche (the stinking wound). The lives and writings of a number of modern American poets, in particular, have been illustrative of the Philoctetes predicament. It has been pointed out how even that apparently impersonal major poem of the twentieth century, 'The Waste Land', was written while T.S. Eliot recovered in Switzerland from a nervous breakdown. In a lecture at Harvard University many years after the poem was published, T.S. Eliot, afflicted with modesty, admitted to a half-truth:

> Various critics have done me the honour to interpret the poem ['The Waste Land'] in terms of criticism of the contemporary world, have considered it, indeed, as an important bit of social criticism. To me it was only the relief of a personal and wholly insignificant grouse against life; it is just a piece of rhythmical grumbling.

Of course 'The Waste Land' is much more than that. In any event, some more recent prominent American poets – Robert Lowell, Anne Sexton, Sylvia Plath – have been altogether less reticent than T.S. Eliot about their personal mental suffering. On occasions, they have boasted of their breakdowns and suicide attempts as warriors might of their war wounds; and these very boastings, it must be said, helped to crank the machinery of a fame-making mythology.

This same machinery continued to be active in Sylvia Plath's case after her death, after her 'successful' suicide in 1963.

Yet, leaving all the sentimentality and all the theatrical hooha aside, it is translucently evident that her talent was extraordinary, that her work, though limited by neurotic elements in her nature, was vibrant and arresting partly because of those same elements.

Al Alvarez was probably right when he maintained, 'The real poems began in 1960 after the birth of her daughter Frieda. It is as though the child were a proof of her identity, as though it liberated her into her real self. I think this guess is borne out by the fact that

135

her most creative period followed the birth of her son two years later.' There are intimations in Sylvia Plath's work that her sense of her own identity was far from secure. Perhaps she felt most herself when she was at work on a poem. In that early, fine poem 'Black Rook in Rainy Weather', she talks of the 'rare random descent' of the inspirational angel who allows her to 'patch together a content of sorts', to gain – and this is the point I'm trying to make here – 'a brief respite from fear / of total neutrality'.

There is no doubt that she felt herself, on one level, to be possessed by the malevolent ghost of her once beloved father. 'I am,' she wrote in 'The Bee Meeting', 'the magician's girl who does not flinch.' She conceived herself to be a passive victim manipulated by a magician's power or a Hiroshima victim or a kind of Jew who survived a concentration camp. As a 'victim' she made her own inward devastation a mirror of recent history.

Many of her late poems have an oneiric quality. It is not surprising that they should be so, given the time of night when they were written. 'These new poems of mine have one thing in common,' she wrote. 'They were all written at about four in the morning – that still blue, almost eternal hour before cockcrow, before the baby's cry.' They were also written apparently when she felt herself to be, once more, a victim – lonely, separated from her husband and, because of her mental make-up, clearly desperate. She was a prey to overwhelming separation anxieties. She had been separated from her father when she was a small girl – by dying he had abandoned her, an act she had not felt as being inadvertent.

In *The Savage God* A. Alvarez wrote:

> As the months went by her poetry became progressively more extreme... the last weeks each trivial event became the occasion for poetry: a cut finger, a fever, a bruise.

But to go a little deeper, it is obvious that these 'trivial' events had enormous significance for her. They represented her deepest feelings and her most central resentment. She wrote a poem called 'Contusion'. She felt bruised spiritually. She wrote a poem about a cut finger called 'Cut' – and that's how she felt herself to be, her whole being, cut. Cut and bruised and wounded.

Besides, the cutting of her thumb ('the top quite gone', she wrote, 'except for a sort of hinge of skin') no doubt nourished her feelings of separation. The separation of a bit of her own body was resonant with her long-held, submerged separation anxiety. Of course, all this may be a wild guess and there will be some who will think it not proper to hazard guesses of this kind. Nevertheless, the nature of her late poems is such that one is tempted to look at her poetry as medical evidence of a state of mind. For her desperation is so clearly touching and so painful even when encapsulated in genuinely wrought poems which do more than express a private terror.

From: *Intermittent Journals*, Seren, Bridgend, 1994

From: *Journals from the Ant-Heap* 1984-86

Parable and Football, May 1984

I went for a morning walk on the beach at Ogmore-by-Sea. The post-Easter blue skies still persisted and sunlight threw down its mercury-backed mirror dazzle on the sea. The beach was empty. I looked towards the barely-outlined coast of Somerset across the Bristol Channel and walked on, half-listening to the erratic rhythm of the sea.

Then, ahead of me, I saw a man, alone, sitting on the pebbles, his trousers tucked into his socks. Nearby lay a white stick. The man looked out, seemingly towards Somerset but, of course, he was blind. And I, walking on sand, and hence silently, suddenly felt myself to be a voyeur, watching him watch nothing.

I noticed how he was feeling the pebbles around him one by one. He picked them up, weighed them, felt, perhaps, the sun's faint warmth in them before replacing them, each one deliberately. He looked my way and seemed to smile so that I wondered, what parable is this? From behind a rock a woman now appeared, obviously his companion, and I strolled on listening once more to the sea and to the sorrowing of some seagulls.

That Saturday afternoon I went, for the last time this season, into Cardiff to watch The Bluebirds play at Ninian Park. Quitting the ground, I moved as quickly as possible back to my car. There was no crowd trouble on this occasion and I did not feel menaced as I have done earlier this year – because of running feet, because of a sudden stampede of rival supporters, because of raw shouts, over-alert policemen and police dogs barking.

These days, even approaching Saturday-afternoon football grounds has its suggestions of hazard. Not such a long time ago I used to enjoy the preliminaries to a football game. It began from the moment you locked the door of your car and some small boy would extend his hand saying, 'Mind it for sixpence, sir.' Afterwards you would join a stream of people, a benign stream that, in turn, would join another to form a river of supporters all flowing in the one imperative direction towards the mouth of the tall Stands.

Waiting there, and somehow contributing to the small excitements, would be the vendors wearing their white laboratory coats, selling rosettes, shiny programmes, ghastly onion-smothered sausages. And, in the ground itself, the dramatic crowds would be good-natured. Never would you hear, as I did at the Millwall ground recently, even before the game began, a whole mass of razor-headed young men shouting in unison, 'Kick their fuckin' 'eads in, kick their fuckin' 'eads in.' And brandishing their right fists rhythmically to this threatening cry, with routine malevolence.

Perhaps it is better that these lynch parties gather at football matches rather than elsewhere. To be sure these ranting, lead-irritable, broken-homed, frustrated, violent youths are a symptom of our unhealthy and increasingly uncaring society. But can football managerial staff attempt to undertake some palliative measures?

I was told by a Rumanian how they solved a crowd problem in Bucharest. Apparently the citizens of Bucharest are not given to queueing up. They have no discipline, the East Germans say. So, in their splendid football stands they would not sit in the seats numbered on the tickets that they had bought. Simply, they acted on the principle of first come, best seat. Then the faceless ones decided that at important games when the Stands were full a car would be given away to one particular occupant of a certain numbered seat. A kind of raffle. However if that occupant did not have the ticket with the right seat number the car was kept in the kitty, as it were, until the next big game. Soon the citizens of Bucharest became as obedient as East Germans.

Meanwhile, lethal crowds or not, I still enjoy watching Cardiff City, the Bluebirds, play. I'm involved. I almost sing to myself. 'Roll along

Cardiff City, roll along, to the top of the League where you belong...'
Some years back a friend lent me his season ticket to watch Spurs
play. At White Hart Lane I had the pleasure of encountering Hans
Keller or Professor Ayer. Refined company. Alas, that kind of
bonus did not make up for not watching my home team. Despite
the classy company, despite the classier football, I could not feel
pure enthusiasm. I even felt the referee was fair!

Aphorisms

I put on an old sports jacket I had not worn for years. In one of its
pockets I found an envelope on the back of which I had written: 'I'm
never at home in a garden; I'm always a visitor.' I quite like that, but
did I make it up myself or did I copy it from some book I had read?
I don't remember.

I am a sucker for aphoristic sayings. I love wisdom stories, parables,
proverbs. Many seem to stick in my head. When I was a student I
stayed in a boarding house which had a card on the wall. It read: 'If you
have two pennies to spend, spend one penny on bread that you may
live; spend the other on a flower that you may have a reason for living.'
This was purported to be an Old Chinese saying and is, I realise now,
rather twee. But I liked it at the time and it has stayed with me.

Then there's the old Zen saying I came across and which I'm still
not ashamed to know and quote: 'To a man who knows nothing,
mountains are mountains, waters are waters and trees are trees. But
when he has studied and knows a little, mountains are no longer
mountains, waters no longer waters and trees no longer trees. But
when he has thoroughly understood, mountains are once again
mountains, waters are waters and trees are trees.'

Some 'wise' sayings stay with me from the days when I was a
medical student. For instance, there's Pliny's complaint that the
Greek physician was the 'only person who could kill another with
sovereign impunity' or the dictum of a certain twentieth century
London consultant that 'the anus is the sentinel of social security.'

Parables? Here's one I learned from Martin Buber of the Baal-
Shem that particularly appeals to me: 'Once some musicians stood
and played, and a great group moved in dance in accordance with
the voice of the music. Then a deaf man came there who knew

nothing of music and dancing and thought in his heart, "How foolish these men are: some beat with their fingers on all kinds of implements and others turn themselves this way and that".'

I wish somebody would edit an Oxford Book of Parables and Wisdom Sayings. I would be the first to buy a copy. I hope such an editor would sensibly include in it wry Yiddish jokes for some, in fact, are very close to being proverbs. Take, for example, that modern definition of a psychiatrist: 'A Jewish doctor who hates the sight of blood.' Or better still that older one: 'If the rich could hire other people to die for them the poor would make a wonderful living.' I wonder what shadowy, bearded figure dressed in ridiculous black, walking somewhere in Latvia or Lithuania, Poland or Russia, suddenly pulled out his pencil and, inspired and feelingly, wrote that down on the back of an envelope.

Coincidence, August 1984

I do not know why, just before I sat down at this desk, Paddy Muir came to mind. I have little in common with him. I have not seen him these many years, not since he and his wife emigrated to Canada. Yet suddenly, for no apparent reason, a minute or so before the telephone sounded, I thought of him. I walked into the hall, picked up the receiver and heard his voice. I felt curiously cold at the back of my neck. It's time, I thought, time to consult oracles, pay attention to inklings and omens. Simply, though, he was in London, and he decided well, why not, he would just telephone me, old mate, to see how I was getting on. Still writing poems are you? 'I've just had a haircut,' I said.

Coincidences. They occur all the time, increasingly, I fancy, as the years pass by, as the pages are blown over. Things happen that we knew would happen before the door opened. The feeling of having been here before. And 'déjà vu' we say, as if the mystery named is the mystery solved. And 'synchronicity' we say, as if that word itself were a diagnosis and an explanation of all coincidences.

Was it Jung who first used the word 'synchronicity' to indicate a meaningful coincidence? But what was meaningful about P. Muir telephoning me 35 minutes ago? And why am I thinking now of another coincidence, one more odd, which concerns a Saturday morning journey across London in 1948 when I was a medical student?

That morning in June, I had set out from my digs in 38 Aberdare Gardens, NW6, carrying a bag and a cricket bat, for Finchley Road underground station. I was on my way to play cricket for Westminster Hospital whose sports ground was located in those of a mental institution in South London. So I had to travel to Charing Cross, change to the Northern Line, continue to South Clapham before taking a final short bus ride.

When I entered the train at Finchley Road I was not thinking of my journey or of cricket but of a telephone conversation I had had the previous day with Louis MacNeice whom, at that time, I had not met. I sat down and, soon after, overheard an animated conversation going on about poetry-drama. I looked up in surprise and with some alarm for one of the two men in conversation opposite me looked like Louis MacNeice – or rather, looked like a photograph I had seen of Louis MacNeice in a book.

At Charing Cross Station the man resembling Louis MacNeice got up and quit the carriage at the same time as I did, and on the platform I dared to stammer, 'Excuse me, are you Louis MacNeice?'

'No,' the man said, unsmilingly.

Embarrassed, I moved away as fast as I could and, in adolescent confusion, lost my way. Eventually I discovered the correct platform for trains on the Northern Line travelling south. As I approached, the doors of a waiting train began to close and I spurted forward, managing to extend my cricket bat just in time to prevent the doors shutting completely. All the doors of the train had to open again so, victoriously, if somewhat self-conscious, I strutted into the carriage.

He was sitting opposite me. He was staring at me and at my cricket bat with transparent distaste. I did not look again at Louis MacNeice's doppelganger but gazed at the back of my hand entranced almost all the way to South Clapham where, to my horror, he stood up preparing to exit.

I allowed him to get ahead of me. He shot forward purposefully; I loitered. He walked up the ascending escalator; I rested on its rail with chronic inertia. I pretended not to notice how, when he reached the top, he looked over his shoulder rather wildly.

It must have been all of three minutes before I found him at the bus queue. I had almost decided to walk but the damned bus came trundling in. Because he went downstairs I took my bat and bag upstairs.

Five minutes later when I descended, he was ready to alight also. It was incredible. We had journeyed from Finchley Road Tube Station to this same bus-stop in South Clapham. On the pavement, as the bus moved away, he swivelled towards me, pulled out his wallet, extracted delicately from it a visiting card which he offered me as proof that he was not Louis MacNeice.

'I'm not following you,' I protested vehemently. 'I'm going to play cricket in there.'

I pointed my cricket bat towards the main gates of the hospital. He followed the direction of my bat and read the big sign which indicated that these were the gates of a Mental Asylum.

Mouth open, he walked away with undignified haste.

Ask the Bloody Horse and Rilke, May 1985

I've sent my new book of poems to Anthony Whittome at Hutchinson today. It contains work over five years. I've called the book *Ask the Bloody Horse* because I don't know and still don't know, where I'm going. I should have liked to put, as an epigraph, a quotation by Martin Buber: 'All journeys have secret destinations of which the traveller is unaware.' Alas, Charles Causley has done exactly that in one of his volumes. Instead I have prefaced the book with:

> While Freud was tracing the river to its source
> he met Itzig unsteadily riding.
> 'Where are you going?' he asked that wild-eyed rider.
> 'Don't ask me,' said Itzig, 'ask the bloody horse.'

Simply I've adapted the old joke about the novice horseman Itzig. Apparently it was Freud's favourite joke, presumably because he perceived the horse to be an emblem of the unconscious and recognised the truth of Itzig's response. Hence I introduced Freud into the quatrain. The best jokes, I think, often turn out to be humorous parables. Anyway, what is writ, is writ – Would it were worthier!

Fraser Steele has invited me to contribute to the Poet on Poet Radio series he is producing. I was tempted to recycle the lecture I gave at the Poetry Society – *The Dread of Sylvia Plath*. On second thoughts, I decided to be less lazy. I have let Fraser know that I would like to write a piece on D.H. Lawrence. I've chosen Lawrence because I think that, generally, he is still under-estimated as a poet.

Years ago, when I was a medical student, I happened on his poems for the first time and responded at once to 'The Ship of Death' and 'Bavarian Gentians'. I did not know then, being untutored, that these poems were among his last, were by a man dying of pulmonary tuberculosis. Re-reading these poems, aware of the fact, I find I am even more deeply touched now than I was then.

What a double-streaked man Lawrence was. His poems reveal it over and over again – at one moment he's gentle and patient, at another he is shrill, irascible. He was ambivalent about so many things, not least sex. That's why I like that early poem of his, one that critics do not much remark upon, and which begins, 'She said as well to me: Why are you ashamed?...' That poem not only shows, dramatically and precisely, Lawrence's ambiguous sexual preoccupations but articulates, characteristically enough, his vivid awareness of the mystery and, indeed, divinity of life – human and non-human life. When Keith Sagar writes, 'His vision becomes increasingly sacramental,' it is not entirely true. It is there from the beginning in the earliest poems, blurred, myopic, as in such bad poems as 'Mystic Blue' – the secretive, living dark (its blueness) was there then but abstract, not wonderfully concrete as the dying Lawrence was later to order it in 'Bavarian Gentians'.

I was about to leave the Tate Gallery when Mark Gertler's painting 'Merry-Go-Round' made me hesitate. It intrigued me: the background of night, the tense, open-mouthed figures in the artificial light whose enjoyment, if it were such, was akin to that of spectators at a horror film. Gertler painted it in 1916 and no doubt was making some allegorical statement about the First World War.

On the way home I kept thinking of Gertler's painting, its ambiguity, the terror in it, and then I recalled Rilke's poem about a Merry-Go-Round at night. How typical, I thought, of Rilke to focus on such an image, interested as he was in the mediation of the invisible to the visible. ('The Angel of the Duino Elegies,' he wrote, 'is the being who vouches for the recognition of a higher degree of reality in the invisible, terrible to us because we... still cling to the visible.') Yes, the Merry-Go-Round at night was a given metaphor for Rilke: fairground spectators have the optical illusion of night's invisible creatures becoming tangible, as the roundabout turns them from darkness into light.

It was years since I had read Rilke's poem. When I arrived home I picked out Rilke's poems from the bookshelf. I read J.B. Leishman's translation of 'Das Karussell' (I have no German, alas) and was astonished to discover I had misremembered the poem, that the Merry-Go-Round Rilke portrayed was not even one revolving at night! Somehow I must have merged Gertler's vision with my own weak remembrance of Rilke's poem. Doodling, I sat down to write the translation I thought I had remembered:

> The roof turns, the brassy merry-go-round crashes
>   out music. Gaudy horses gallop tail to snout,
>   inhabit the phantasmagoria of light
>   substantial as smoke. Then each one vanishes.
>
> Some pull carriages. Some children, frightened, hold tight
>   the reins as they arrive and disappear
>   chased by a scarlet lion that seems to sneer
>   not snarl. And here's a unicorn painted white.
>
> Look! From another world this strange, lit retinue.
>   A boy on a steer, whooping, loud as dynamite –
>   a sheriff, no doubt, though dressed in sailor-blue.
>   And here comes the unicorn painted white.
>
> Faster! The children spellbound, the animals prance,
>   and this is happiness, this no-man's land
>   where nothing's forbidden. And hardly a glance
>   at parents who smile, who *think* they understand
>
> as the scarlet lion leaps into the night
>   and here comes the unicorn painted white.

Graves, Larkin and Ogmore, November – December 1985

Now comes news of other casualties: Robert Graves, Philip Larkin, Geoffrey Grigson.

I met Robert Graves but once and in *A Strong Dose of Myself* (Hutchinson, 1983) I wrote an account of the meeting which I doubt Mr Graves would have enjoyed. But I liked, and continue to like his poetry. He composed poems in the central English lyric tradion and he used a conservative diction and a logical syntax without display, though not without the power to surprise. His was an essentially romantic sensibility, with belief in phantoms and miracle; in the terrifying and terrific supernatural; in his interest in myth as a surviving, operative power even in our so-called rational societies; and in his enduring preoccupation with the creative and destructive element that waxes and wanes in the man-woman relationship.

Indeed, almost one-third of Robert Graves's poems refer to this relationship. In 1963 he opined: 'My theme was always the practical impossibility, transcended only by miracle, of absolute love continuing between man and woman.' He seemed to believe in the mythographic story of woman as the lover and the destroyer of man. As Ronald Gaskill has put it – 'the story of man drawn inescapably to woman by her beauty, immolated in the act of love and finally supplanted by her son.'

Unlike D.H. Lawrence, Graves did not dwell on the physicality of man-woman love. With Graves one seldom senses a man and woman most and least themselves, coupling beneath the sheets. Rather we encounter the emotions of lovers or ex-lovers, and usually they are fully-clothed and courtly always, and civilised always, even in dismissal and disappointment. (Not surprisingly Graves called D.H. Lawrence a 'wretch', a man who is sick, muddle-headed and sex-mad). When we do discover Robert Graves's lovers in bed as in the poem 'Never Such Love' they are groping for words rather than for each other:

Turned together and, as is customary,
For words of rapture groping they
'Never such love,' swore 'ever before was.'
Contrast with all loves that had failed or staled
Registered their own as love indeed.

I hardly knew Larkin either. We met only at the Poetry Book Society committee meetings. As a chairman he was always courteous, always considerate, relieving argumentative tensions with humorous one-liners. He did not seem shy, though I'm sure he was.

In committee, he had a problem with his deafness. In earlier years he suffered, I understand, from a dire stammer. There was no trace of that handicap at the PBS meetings. Apparently that crippling stammer had dramatically cleared up when his father died. He was suddenly free to say what he wished. Yet later he suffered another kind of block. He could not write poetry.

> They fuck you up, your mum and dad.
> They may not mean to, but they do.

From all accounts Philip's father, the Coventry City Treasurer, had been a most dominating, authoritative figure, mercilessly tidy and solemn. According to Noel Hughes who had been at school with Philip Larkin, he, Sidney Larkin, went on visits to pre-war Germany and was struck by 'qualities of decisiveness and vigour in German public administration that compelled his admiration'.

Sooner or later someone will write a biography of Philip Larkin. My guess is that the biographer will not have to be a crude Jake Balokowsky to discover that Sidney Larkin was an unambiguous, fervent Nazi sympathiser.

How much did Philip model himself on his father? I do not mean politically, although Philip Larkin's own knee-jerk, right-wing views I find deplorable enough.

However much I admire Philip Larkin's poetry it was his social attitudes that made me feel distanced from him. It was predictable that when the PBS had to shift from the Arts Council's sheltering roof to either the care of the National Book League or to the Poetry Society, Philip supported the NBL because of its larger economic sources and despite its 'non-record' concerning poetry.

'I'm for the Big Battalions,' Philip argued, not being ironic, as of course Voltaire had been when he wrote, 'On dit que Dieu est toujours pour les gros bataillons.' The Big Battalions are what I've never been for. It's not for nothing that Cardiff City FC are now right at the bottom of Division Three!

It is good to be back in Ogmore. Because of the American trip we have not been here since October 6th. This time of the year one can take an oxygen walk to Southerndown without seeing anyone – for company there's only the sheep, the crows and the gulls, and perhaps an occasional self-absorbed, solitary dog. This morning we took the sand route at first, for the tide was right; then we climbed up and over the rocks to the high, breath-holding cliffs. We observed a sheep utterly motionless. It seemed to be reading a red danger sign on which was written DANGEROUS CLIFFS. To mis-quote Shelley: there is only one better walk in the world than from Ogmore to Southerndown and that is the walk from Southerndown to Ogmore. The return journey is especially good to take at dusk when one can watch the slow Western mobile sunsets below the aeroplane vapour-trails.

In the 1930s, when we lived in Cardiff, our car, a Riley, seemed to know only one route. It would go instinctively to Ogmore-by-Sea. My father only had to sit in the driving seat, turn on the ignition, and off it would go along the A48, up Tumble Down Dick, through Cowbridge, up and down Crack Hill, all of the twenty-three miles to the sea, the sea at Ogmore. Every half sunny Sunday, every holiday, the car knew we wanted to play cricket on the sands of Hardee's Bay while its boss, my father, fished near the mouth of the river for dabs, salmon bass, and ghosts.

Not only my immediate family homed back to Ogmore. Uncles and aunts, fat and thin, cousins short and tall, from Cardiff, Swansea, Ammanford, singing in their closed saloons, 'Stormy Weather' and 'She was a Good Girl until I took her to a Dance' returned to meet and quarrel and take a dip in the unstable Ogmore estuary.

My sister, Huldah, once confided that she had lost her virginity in one of the secret caves of Ogmore while my Uncle Max, unaware, played the violin on the rocks nearby, and cousins and their friends munched gritty tomato sandwiches and stared at the incoming, loosely-chained sea.

Not everybody in the Abse family is stuck on Ogmore. I have an American nephew, Nathan. When he was ten he came to stay with us at Ogmore. His voice was inordinately deep and husky and Virginian. He arrived after nightfall, gave the slate-black emptiness of Ogmore the once over, heard the sheep munching in the dark, then gazing towards the funfair's shimmering lights across the bay of distant Porthcawl, said, 'Hey, man, let's take off for civilisation.'

I wish we could stay here longer. I'm fed up with driving up and down the M4, from and to London. But I don't see any solution to that. In the new year we shall still be making the same tedious journeys. No matter, now, as I breathe out the air of London and breathe in the air of Ogmore I know it's all worth it. I walk beside the cutlery-glinting sea, consoled by the sound of the waves' irregularities, by the pitch and tone of them, the 'sssh' of shingle, the way the sea slaps on rocks or shuffles sinking into the sand that sizzles as the tide recedes. And there, quite near really, the steamers pass, slow and hushed, around the breath-holding cliffs on their seamless way to the ports of Barry, Cardiff, Newport and, in dream, further, mysteriously, into 1986.

From: *Journals From The Ant-Heap*, Hutchinson, London, 1986

From: *New Journals* 1987-93

Eliot and Anti-Semitism, 1988

In the back pages of the Sunday newspapers and weekly journals there has been much discussion of T.S. Eliot's anti-Semitism. This follows the publication of a book by Christopher Ricks called *T.S. Eliot and Prejudice*.

Leonard Woolf (a Jew) once remarked that T.S. Eliot was 'only slightly anti-Semitic'. I am reminded of how Sir Adolph Abrahams on his ward rounds at Westminster Hospital used to forbid medical students to utter the words 'slight' and 'slightly'. I recall how once, after examining a woman, I had told Sir Adolph that the patient has a slight swelling in her abdomen. 'Slight,' he said imperiously. 'Slight! Either a woman is pregnant or not pregnant. She cannot be slightly pregnant, boy.'

In the early Fifties, at the inaugural poetry-reading of the Institute of Contemporary Arts in London, I happened to be sitting a yard away from T.S. Eliot. The chairman, Herbert Read, called upon Emanuel Litvinoff to read. Litvinoff touched his spectacles, then announced 'To T.S. Eliot' and the audience settled back complacently, expecting to hear a text in homage to Eliot. Instead, Litvinoff declaimed a frontally passionate poem about T.S. Eliot's anti-Semitism:

> I am not one accepted in your parish.
> Bleistein is my relative and I share
> the protozoic slime of Shylock, a page
> in Sturmer, and, underneath the cities,
> a billet somewhat lower than the rats.
> Blood in the sewers. Pieces of our flesh
> Float with the ordure on the Vistula.
> You had a sermon but it was not this...

The poem continued in the same passionate, biting tone and when Litvinoff sat down a wailing arose as if from a battlefield. Some hurled abuse at Litvinoff while, enraged, Stephen Spender rose, tall, to defend Eliot stridently against the charge of anti-Semitism. Anarchist Herbert Read banged a coercive hammer on the table to impose order! Meanwhile, Eliot leaned forward, his head on his hands, muttering over and over, 'It's a good poem, it's a good poem.'

Eliot, in the early Thirties, had been a sick man and it was during this period that he expressed his racial prejudices more blatantly. His eighteen years of impossible marriage to a neurotic woman who, in her later derangement, became a paid-up member of the British Union of Fascists, caused him so much distress that he compared himself to Prometheus whose liver was perpetually gnawed by the vulture. Escaping from the torment of his domestic life, he lectured in the U.S.A. and at the University of Virginia delivered a diatribe against the America that was 'worm-eaten by liberalism' and 'invaded by foreign races'. He specifically deprecated the presence of free-thinking Jews.

But after the war – in 1954 – T.S. Eliot commented on anti-Semitism in the Soviet Union: 'I have long held that any country which denies the rights of its own nationals – and most especially the Jews – will sooner or later have to pay the full price for so doing; and even the "uninvolved" people whom it governs will have to expiate the crime of having allowed such a government to lead them.'

By 1954, of course, History had turned over certain monstrous bloody pages which carried names such as Auschwitz, Belsen, Dachau, and Eliot had read them. That is why, I believe, Eliot contrite, hearing Litvinoff's accusatory poem, leant forward, head in hands, muttering the assent of 'It's a good poem.'

Larkin, February 1993

In the November-December 1985 entry of these *Journals* I speculated amongst other cheerless matters that, 'Sooner or later, someone will write a biography of Philip Larkin. My guess is that the biographer will not have to be a crude Jake Balokowsky to discover that Sidney Larkin (Larkin's father) was an unambiguous, fervent Nazi sympathiser.' Soon after the publication of the first edition of these journals in 1986 I received an imperious, how-dare-you, 'upstairs' letter from Larkin's future biographer, Andrew Motion.

But just over a year ago, at a pre-election Neil Kinnock rally, Andrew Motion approached me and apologised for his earlier letter. 'You were damn near right,' he said quietly. It was generous of him to tell me so. We were at a political rally. Politicians never apologise. Poets do.

I have now read further into Andrew Motion's biography, *Philip Larkin, A Writer's Life.* He does not flinch from recounting how Larkin's father 'had been an ardent follower of the Nazis and attended several Nuremberg rallies during the 1930s; he even had a statue of Hitler on the mantelpiece (at home) which, at a touch of a button, leapt into a Nazi salute.' Sidney Larkin decorated his office in Coventry's City Hall with Nazi regalia until war broke out. Then the Town Clerk ordered him to remove it. Nor does Motion hesitate to dwell on Philip Larkin's own repugnant racialism and right-wing, Blimpish prejudices.

Admirer though I was and still am of Philip Larkin's memorable poetry – his poems have given me much perdurable pleasure – they are so sharp-eyed, appropriate with arresting detail and do not eschew sentiment, feeling – I am reminded of my 1950s quarrel with him, or rather with the Movement thesis. Howard Sergeant and I at that time edited *Mavericks*, an anthology intended to rival Robert Conquest's forthcoming Movement anthology, *New Lines* (1957). On the surface, our publicised arguments were about poetic style, about different linguistic strategies in the making of poems, about romantic or anti-romantic allegiances; but underpinning these postures opposing socio-political attitudes occasionally peeped through.

I disliked their insular gestures, their parochialism. One of the Movement's most influential propagandists, J.D. Scott, the literary editor of the *Spectator*, was revealing when he reviewed William Golding's *Lord of the Flies* in the *Sunday Times*: 'This is a strikingly un-English novel. In abandoning the parochiality which so often irritates foreign students of the contemporary English novel, and in seeking universal experience, Mr Golding may have walked with kings but he has lost the common touch which is particularly appreciated by English readers... perhaps it will be his fate to become one of those English writers more deeply appreciated abroad than at home.'

Similarly, in a Fabian tract, Socialism and the Intellectuals, Larkin's friend and fellow Movement writer, Kingsley Amis, sounded off: 'Romanticism in a political context I would define as an irrational capacity to become influenced by interests and causes that are not one's own, that are outside self.' The only social consequences, Amis felt, with which we should be concerned were those that might have a direct, immediate impact on an English way of life. It would not be caricaturing Amis's attitude (which Larkin shared) to summarise it thus: foreigners don't matter and we should only be moved to moral indignation when a particular injustice or pressure threatens English vested interests.

Once, when asked how he enjoyed holidaying in Portugal, Kingsley Amis replied without irony, 'It's a bore. It's just that the place is located abroad and the people are foreigners.' Larkin, with Amis, relished a consciously contrived philistinism. One or two other Movement poets, though not so crassly nationalistic, exhibited right-wing, proto-Thatcherite views. 'The Movement is anti-wet,' announced Conquest before 'wet' had become a political curse.

So prior to reading Andrew Motion's book I had inklings of Philip Larkin's views and prejudices. I did not know, though, about his stinginess, his almost comical 'Jack Benny' focus on money. Motion's references to it made me recall a telephone conversation I had with Philip Larkin in 1973. That winter I happened to be Writer-in-Residence at Princeton University. Though abroad, I co-judged with Larkin the current Poetry Book Society choices and recommendations. Every now and again a batch of poetry books would be sent by the Arts Council to our temporary trans-Atlantic home in Pine Street, Princeton, New Jersey. But there was a gap in the post. When I received a letter from Philip Larkin in which he outlined his preferences for the quarter I realised that some books must have gone astray. Several of those he cared for had not arrived. Because of an Arts Council deadline a swift response from me was required. So I telephoned Philip Larkin to explain what had happened. It was not as customary in 1973, nor as cheap, to make telephone calls to or from the U.S.A. as it is nowadays. Thus, when he heard my voice, Philip Larkin seemed puzzled.

'Where... where are you speaking from?' he asked.

'From Princeton.'

'Princeton?'

'Yes, Princeton.'

'But that's where I've been writing to,' Larkin said.

'Well, I'm still there.'

'At the University?'

'Yes.'

'You're phoning from the U.S.A.?'

'Yes.'

'The U.S.A.!'

'I want to talk to you about the books.'

'Are you phoning from the University?'

'I'm phoning from home actually but listen, the books never...'

'Are you paying for this call then?'

'Yes, I am. I haven't received the books from the Arts Council so I can't comment on...'

'Can you reclaim the money, do you think?'

'How do you mean?'

'From the Arts Council.'

'I don't think so. Look, in your letter...'

'I've never had a phone call from the U.S.A. before!'

'About the choice and the recommendation...'

'It must be costing you a packet.'

There is a story I like about Jack Benny. A masked highwayman, gun in hand, says to Jack Benny, 'Your money or your life.' Benny pauses, 'Let me think.'

Music and the Family, December 1993

Over breakfast I read letters. The first Xmas card has arrived already. One letter proves to be from Gavin McCarthy of B.B.C. Wales. He invites me to participate in a radio programme which involves an interview interspersed with six or seven pieces of music that hold a significant place in my life. Soon, upstairs in the bathroom, I find myself sub-vocally thinking nostalgic tunes – so much so that I cut my lip shaving. I bleed. Damn.

Oh the ineffable potency of old melodies! Like a faded photograph or a whiff of a strong scent they remind us of gone days, gone nights. Even as they pleasure us they induce feelings of small regret and greater loss. Soren Kierkegaard once confessed, 'In Stralsund I almost went mad hearing a young girl playing the pianoforte, among other things Weber's last waltz over and over again. The last time I was in Berlin it was the first piece I heard in the Tiergarten, played by a blind man on the harp. It seems as though everything was intended to remind me of the past'. Yes indeed. Those old remembered tunes can make a man bleed!

It is some twenty years now since I chose eight Desert Island Discs for Roy Plomley. Half a dozen of them were classical pieces; but these I shall not repetitively choose for Radio Wales. One classical composition that has entranced me over the last two years, ever since my daughter, Keren, gave it to me on a cassette, is Mozart's Divertimento K563. We play it sometimes in the car, journeying from London to Ogmore-by-Sea. It is a spiritual unguent, one conducive to calming driver and passengers in the tensions of the M4. It is, as Rilke would put it, 'The breathing of statues'. I think it is a musical medicine. Iamblichus, writing in the fourth century A.D., in his *Life of Pythagoras*, relates how a raving, lovesick youth, insane with jealousy and about to burn down his rival's house, heard a flute player sound a Phrygian melody and was as a result, restored in time to quietude and sanity.

I am glad Mr McCarthy has asked me to contribute to his 'Music of My Life' programme. I have an excuse not only to listen to musical medicine but to wallow wonderfully in obstinate nostalgia. I can indulge myself with musical calories. I can put on old records and pretend I am slaving away, working like billy-o, preparing myself in a melodic sweat for a radio programme.

I sit at this desk half in a trance. I am transferred more than half a century back to a house in Cardiff, to a room with too much furniture in it. My eldest brother, Wilfred, is playing his favourite 'Georgia' on the gramophone as growled out by Nat Gonella and I remember each nuance of the trumpet solo. I go back even further to hear Leo singing that politically-sound bitter lyric, 'Once I built a railroad... they called me Al', and my sister, more romantically, crooning, half to the mirror and with such a drastic look on her face, 'Some Day He'll Come Along' or 'Mad About the Boy'.

When my parents focussed on popular music it would be that, of course, which was fashionable for an even earlier generation. Those jaunty tunes of the Music Hall! And could anybody, in the whole wide world, whistle so skillfully as my father 'Daisy, Daisy, Give me your answer do', and 'The Lily of Laguna'? My parents took me sometimes to the ornamented – all crimson and brass – New Theatre for a Saturday night Variety Show. Two Ton Tessie, Vic Oliver or The Mills Brothers topped the Bill. And suddenly, now, as I write, The Mills Brothers are heavy-breathing in my ear: 'Where's that Tiger? Where's that Tiger?' I wait for silence but all I hear is my father laughing inexplicably at someone dressed up, surely for Budget Day, someone called Max Miller. Was it he who sang with innocent vulgarity: 'I never knew what a little girl could do... She did her dancing in the East, she did her dancing in the West, but she did the dancing where the dancing was best'?

Those occasional Saturday nights my father would buy a rustling box of Black Magic chocolates for my mother and, of course, they would let me dip into it. Marzipan, Turkish Delight, Coffee Cream, Nougat, Cherry Liqueur, I cannot bite now into the dark hearts of such chocolate without experiencing a Proustian evocation of a time and a place and a circumstance. So it is with the lovely malice of music that can take a man back and further back down the indigo roads.

From: *Intermittent Journals*, Seren, Bridgend, 1994

4. The Theatre

Failure

The stage is a scaffold on which the playwright is executed.

Chekhov (Letters)

I

On my thirteenth birthday one of my mother's best friends – the one who laughed more often and louder than any person in Wales and whom I had to call Aunt May not Laughing Gas – gave me a thick, heavy, blue-bound volume of plays by G.B. Shaw. Since it contained 1220 pages (I own the book still and its leaves have not spotted or turned brown) it was considerably more substantial than the William and P.G. Wodehouse books that had, until then, been intermittently engaging me. Suspiciously, I opened this thick-as-a-bible volume at its preface, which oddly turned out to be 'A Warning from the Author'. I was accustomed to such brief admonitions as could be found in GWR carriages, which had 'Penalty for Pulling Communication Cord £5'; but G.B. Shaw's authoritarian warning ambled on for a page and a half to conclude:

> When you once get accustomed to my habit of mind, which I was born with and cannot help, you will not find me such bad company. But please do not think you can take in the work of my long lifetime at one reading. You must make it your practice to read all my works at least twice over every year for ten years or so. That is why this edition is so substantially bound for you.

I had no intention of reading the edition once. To tell the truth, I had never heard of G.B. Shaw who seemed somewhat conceited from his introductory remarks and, besides, his 'Warning' was not all that well written. Mr Graber, my English master at school, had told us that to begin a sentence with *But* and to use such words as *get* showed a weakness of style.

However, before I was thirteen and a half, measles visited me and since I was bored during my convalescence, I opened again the pages of my unwanted present. Not many people, I suspect, come to read Bernard Shaw because of a virus. First I turned to *Widowers' Houses*, then to *The Philanderer*, then to *Mrs Warren's Profession*. I became addicted. Over a period of months, though now healthy, I read all Shaw's plays. I liked them enough to investigate the work of other dramatists. Indeed for a time, berserk, I read only plays.

I had been once to the theatre. That had been three years earlier when the big boys from Marlborough Road Primary School were conscripted to see a matinee performance of *The Merchant of Venice* with Donald Wolfit as Shylock. All of us had been impressed by how far Mr Wolfit could spit. Philip Griffiths decided if we could spit like that it would be worth sitting at the back of a Western Welsh bus and having a go at the driver's neck. It would be worth paying the inevitable £5 fine, bloody worth it. 'My gob's as good as Donald Wolfit's your honour... I couldn't resist it your honour.' 'Quiet, boy. £5 fine or jail.'

I had told both my elder brothers – Wilfred and Leo – of Wolfit's prowess in projecting sputum convexly after the departing Antonio. Wilfred, not listening, said reflexly, 'Well done,' but Leo was fired by my information. Suddenly he was Shylock. 'Fair sir,' he was saying, his seventeen-year-old eyes rolling as he hunchbacked himself, 'you spit on me on Wednesday last; you spurned me such a day; another time you called me dog; and for these courtesies I'll lend you thus much moneys.' Leo stared like a madman, arranged a nasty noise in his throat, ignored Wilfred's 'Now watch it,' and deposited a heavy round of spit onto the grate of the coal fire where it momentarily sizzled like sausages. Leo was already quite an actor, for all orators are surely actors?

By the time I was thirteen and a half my brother had become entirely professional, as befitted a future Member of Parliament. Leo, twenty years of age, would stand on a soapbox in Llandaff Fields – the local Hyde Park Corner – and denounce with righteous passion the unemployment in the Welsh valleys, the paradox of slums and cripples in a world of colours. He always sounded wonderfully spontaneous but I knew that like an actor he would carefully rehearse his fresh-languaged speeches. He would lock the door of his bedroom and then his voice would rise and fall remarkably. 'It is given to man,' I could hear him roar. He was very good.

Along with Wilfred he became my temporary hero. 'When you shut yourself in like that, Leo,' I asked him with sincere interest, 'do you practise your speeches before a mirror?' I didn't get a reply. It was like asking a poet whether he used a rhyming dictionary.

'What do you think of Bernard Shaw?' I cross-examined my knowledgeable brothers.

'*Saint Joan*'s good,' Wilfred said.

'Shaw? A castrated monkey,' Leo said dismissively.

I remembered my brothers' considered judgements of Shaw. Two years later Leo told me about Eugene O'Neill. There was an O'Neill play at the Prince of Wales Theatre called *Desire under the Elms*. 'Now that's got more guts, is much more visceral than Bernard Shaw,' Leo proclaimed. I had never heard the word *visceral* before. I liked the word. I repeated it to myself.

I went with my friend, Sidney Isaacs, to see the O'Neill play. On the way, in the lurching tramcar, I confidently informed Sidney that *Desire under the Elms* would be better than any play of G.B. Shaw's.

'I thought you admired Bernard Shaw,' said my friend.

'Not so much as I used to. Shaw's plays don't wear well, you know, except perhaps for *Saint Joan*.'

'Have you seen *Saint Joan*?'

I ignored that. 'The trouble is,' I continued, 'Shaw has got no balls.... He's a eunuch. But O'Neill, now, he's really gutsy... er... visceral.'

From the corner of my eye I could see that Sidney, who had become strangely quiet, was staring at me with a new, inadvertent admiration. Perhaps he felt that I should be one of those fancy, bitch theatre critics who pronounce in the Sunday papers after they have sat, free-ticketed, proud and pampered, in a gangway seat, row G.

We enjoyed *Desire under the Elms* from the gods, so much so that we began occasionally to frequent the Prince of Wales Theatre instead of the Olympia Cinema, the Park Hall, the Empire. We saw *Young Woodley*, *Little Women* and beheld Donald Wolfit again, this time as King Lear:

> Come, let's away to prison;
> We two alone will sing like birds i' the cage:
> When thou dost ask me blessing, I'll kneel down
> And ask of thee forgiveness; and we'll live,
> And pray and sing and tell old tales, and laugh
> At gilded butterflies, and hear poor rogues
> Talk of court news; and we'll talk with them too,
> Who loses, and who wins; who's in, who's out;
> And take upon's the mystery of things,
> As if we were God's spies, and we'll wear out
> In a wall'd prison, packs and sets of great ones
> That ebb and flow by the moon.

Ill-produced *King Lear* may have been, ill-acted for the most part too, but the language of England soared and I soared with it. I sat in the high gods of the Prince of Wales Theatre and I heard the active words of Shakespeare as I had never heard them before and I was exhilarated in a way I could hardly explain or define. Somehow, young as I was, silly as I was, I felt most wonderfully altered and refined. More than that; when, later, I licked the back of my own hand and brought it to my nostrils, like old King Lear himself, I could smell the smell of mortality.

II

When I was a medical student in London I had a book of poems accepted, which encouraged me to try and earn some money – for my patient landlady's sake as much as my own – by occasional freelance writing. Later, because of an inept poetry-drama I had written called *Fire in Heaven* I was invited to become a sporadic critic for a fortnightly theatre magazine. I boasted of this part-time appointment when I returned home to Cardiff for Christmas. 'Stop wasting your time,' my father advised me, 'and get on with studying medicine.'

The magazine was not important enough to be offered first-night free tickets by theatre managements and I was not important enough to cover the main plays in the West End. This the editor did himself. So on second-night performances of plays, frequently new plays, and frequently staged it seemed to me in the vicinity of Notting Hill Gate (I was forever taking a 31 bus) I took my seat in row G among a sparse audience – how sparse depended on how many friends the actors had, the size of the cast and whether or not the author was alive and well and living in Notting Hill Gate. No matter; before the house lights came down and the curtain went up, there I sat with my swanky chest stuck out, an invisible sceptre in my left hand and my two eyes narrowed, ready to write my best worst.

Since that stint as second-string, second-night theatre critic, I have never envied those columnists, however important, who year in, year out have to provide hebdomadal copy. What a job for an adult! Even when the production is of a justly admired classic – a Greek play, a Shakespeare, a Chekhov – some self-infatuated director, probably called Peter since most directors are so named, will decide the script needs pepping up a bit. To ensure Peter's production will make its mark, *Lysistrata* is given an all-male cast, dwarfs only are allowed to appear in *Julius Caesar* and *The Cherry Orchard* is set in industrial Newark, New Jersey. Hazlitt, referring to the egomania of so-called creative people, tells us in *Table Talk* of a friend of his who discovered a very fine Canaletto in a state of curious disfigurement, the upper part of the sky having been smeared over and fantastically variegated with English clouds. On inquiring to whom it belonged and whether something had not been done to it, Hazlitt's friend was informed 'that a gentleman, a great artist in the neighbourhood, had retouched some parts of it.' That great artist of the neighbourhood, I suggest, could well have been christened Peter.

Mary McCarthy once cast a cold eye on current drama for the American magazine *Partisan Review*. Readers of that magazine, being serious people, did not really want to visit the New York theatre. She, by giving all plays truthful, some would say acidulous notices, confirmed their prejudices. After reading her in *Partisan Review* they were able to mutter comfortably, 'I guessed that play wouldn't be worth seeing.' She did those Partisan Review readers a wonderful service. By giving them no fashionable reason to attend this or that play Mary McCarthy saved them an immense amount of trouble, time, and money. She was a public benefactor.

The theatre magazine that I wrote for, alas, had quite a different readership: men and women keen to see plays week after week, month after month, year after year. They did not want to be put off by negative copy. I did not do too well. I was too sincere. The editor did not suggest I should be more temperate but when I managed to remain awake through the whole of a play called *The Same Sky* by Yvonne Mitchell at the Lyric Theatre, Hammersmith, I softened my critique. At that moment I understood the furtive circumstances, the occasional guilt-tinged feeling of every journalist in the world who has to supply overlooked copy.

Some imagine writers to be encouraged by other writers' impoverished creations. Bad poems, they believe, allow an aspiring poet to think, 'I can do better than that'; bad plays, similarly, tempt a potential dramatist to try his hand at the game. This notion is wrong. Rather it is those rare poems that thrill, those rare plays that enchant which prove to be seminal. Academic critics, some of them anyway, seem somewhat puzzled that any living writer has enough arrogance not to be crushed by tradition, by the unsurpassable works of those artists who have preceded him. But of course writing has nothing to do with arrogance or humility. Simply, there are needs to be gratified and besides 'there is no competition'.

I soon gave up pretending to be a theatre critic and over the next decade enjoyed certain plays I visited as a paying customer, among them Ibsen's *The Wild Duck*, Pirandello's *As You Desire Me*, Eugene O'Neill's *The Iceman Cometh* and Tennessee Williams's *The Glass Menagerie*. Those plays stage-struck me sufficiently to think that one day I might try again to write a play. Should not a poet, I secretly asked myself, be able to contribute something uncommon to the theatre?

Not poetry-drama – I did not deeply admire the then fashionable plays of T.S. Eliot, Christopher Fry, Ronald Duncan. There was such a thing, though, as *poetic* drama. It was not just a question of diction. *The Tempest* was more of a poetic drama than *Macbeth*; Pirandello's plays closer to poetry than those of Eliot. Nor was it a question of raising the language at appropriate moments: there were too many plays where the language suddenly became moonlit and the audience treated to a patch of artificial poetry. 'Poetic drama must be written by dramatic poets,' wrote Alan S. Downer. 'If the truism is chiastic, truth yet lies in the figure.' Poetic drama, not poetry-drama – that was the crucial point. And was poetic realist drama, I wondered, possible – or was it a contradiction in terms?

In 1958, I adapted a poem of mine for radio, dramatised it – a poem called 'The Meeting'. It was broadcast on the Welsh Home Service. My father listened to it and groaned. Perhaps he was right. It would be better to write a play proper with more distinctive characters – a stage play. I would try and write it as Poetic drama.

'It'll fail,' my father said. 'That's not what people want. You'd do better to write for TV. Terrible rubbish they put on. Even you might have a chance there.'

I finished my play and called it *House of Cowards*. By then poetry-drama was discredited in the British theatre, T.S. Eliot and Christopher Fry no longer fashionable. Nobody would notice the difference between the designation *poetry-drama* and *poetic drama* so I did not give it any tag at all. In the summer of 1960, my play – my first real play as far as I was concerned – would be produced at the Questors Theatre in Ealing and directed by John McGrath.

I asked my father if he would care to come to London and see it.
'You say the Questors Theatre is amateur?' he asked.

'Duw, an *amateur* theatre,' my father said sadly. 'That won't bring
the butter home, son.'

Though performed at the Questors, *House of Cowards* won the
Charles Henry Foyle Award for 1960. 'The Foyle Award,' I explained
to my father, trying to impress him, 'is for the best play produced
outside the West End. It's the first time an amateur theatre has been
given that award.'

'Amateur dramatics, that doesn't count,' my father said,
unimpressed.

'£100 goes with the award too,' I added.

'You'd do better in the football pools,' Dad said with scorn.

It was a game, of course, that my father and I were playing. He
invited me to report to him my self-directed gossip and then he, in
turn, liked to tease me. I knew that and he knew that. In any case, I
was encouraged by winning the Foyle award and I got myself a
theatre agent, Peggy Ramsay, who had, and has, the just reputation
of being one of the best in Britain. In her office she said to me
imperially, 'Dr Abse, you come in here today a duck. One day you'll
leave this office a swan.'

From: *A strong dose of myself*, Hutchinson, London, 1983

5. Interviews

Conversations with Dannie Abse

The first interview took place at the end of May, 1982, over the long bank holiday. The weather was warm with sustained sunshine, and Dr. Dannie Abse and I talked at length sitting in his garden behind his home in Golders Green. The irises had reached their peak and were fading, but the roses were in their first full bloom when we held our discussions, not unaware that this particular weekend was marked by other dimensions than literary ones. For the Pope's visit to England had just begun, and in the Falkland Islands, the British assault to retake Port Stanley was underway. The seriousness of these historical matters notwithstanding, we began our leisurely discussion.

J.C. You've shown me the letter that Hutchinson's wrote to you, September 5th, 1946, saying that they accepted *After Every Green Thing*, your first book of poems, for publication. You were a medical student at the time. You must have been delighted.

D.A. Yes, but Hutchinson's took over two years before they actually published *After Every Green Thing* – the title, by the way, comes from the Book of Job... the ass that goes after every green thing.

J.C. Those early poems were very romantic, indeed lush. They show a vitality of imagery, much that's memorable, yet mostly they're immature. I assume you agree for you've only included one of them, 'The Uninvited' in your *Collected Poems*.

D.A. Yes, they *are* immature. I was immature. I caught like an infection, the neo-romantic fashionable mode of the time.

J.C. How would you characterise the qualities of these neo-romantic poets? Were they much influenced by Dylan Thomas?

D.A. Grigson, who was antagonistic to Dylan Thomas's poetry, thundered that 'the romance we are drifting back to is a romance without reason, it is altogether self-indulgent and liquescent.' Those poets contributing to neo-romantic periodicals such as *Poetry Quarterly* held Dylan Thomas in high regard and were much less gifted than he. Their diction was florid, rhetorical, and their subject matter often wilfully obscure – due to an excessively private vision. This was the case sometimes, too, with Dylan Thomas.

J.C. Yet some of these young *Poetry Quarterly* poets like Alex

Comfort and Denise Levertov had real talent. I believe you were a friend of Alex Comfort's?

D.A. Alex Comfort had shown me – he was a little older than me – nothing but kindness. And Denise Levertov who was my exact contemporary was a friend.

J.C. Did you and Levertov discuss poetry together?

D.A. As a matter of fact there is one poem in *After Every Green Thing* that was – perhaps I can admit to it now – addressed to Denise Levertov. It begins 'Lady of black hair I see you dead in a red dress.' That lady of black hair was Denise Levertov.

J.C. That poem isn't in your *Collected Poems*. So would you read it out loud.

D.A. It's not very...

J.C. Never mind.

D.A.

'Lady of black hair I see you dead in a red dress,
I bend over to kiss your face of ivory in moonlight,
I touch your ache of branches weighted with fruit.

I touch your fruit. What terrible cry is this?
You open the gangrene of birds in your breasts,
in pain of roses you open your mouth to speak.

And think, all these years you have been dead,
wonderfully silent in a red dress,
beautifully white and dead in moonlight.

I am in no way accustomed to a corpse speaking.
I cannot enter and walk through the mists,
and depart as both boy and girl, alive as a voice,
with my eyes in terror of two worlds.

I cannot follow the music out of the room,
leaving those I love, standing there, gesticulating,
and return, return as before, sane and accepted.

For I should not speak again being of two sexes,
being knowledgeable with the terror of two worlds.
I know no man who has lived in a female grave.

And think, all these years you have been dead,
wonderfully silent in a red dress,
beautifully white and dead in moonlight.

I am in no way accustomed to a corpse speaking.'

J.C. That's a very odd, a very erotic poem.

D.A. Not long before I wrote it I learnt from my elder brother, Leo, who's 6½ years older than me, that between his birth and mine my mother had had a miscarriage, a stillbirth, a girl. I was 22 or 23 when I learnt this surprising news and had recently met Denise Levertov with whom I felt much in common. For instance, Denise's mother was a very Welsh, Welsh lady and her father a Russian Jew who'd become a Church of England Divine. So this background of hers, Welsh and Jewish, made me feel kinship with her. Besides we were both writing poetry in that neo-romantic tradition; also our political views were not too dissimilar. And she had been a nurse and I was a medical student.

J.C. I didn't know she'd been a nurse.

D.A. She tended to think in the same way as I did – saw the same face in a cloud, the same pattern in a carpet. I suddenly began to have the extraordinary feeling that Denise Levertov was an embodiment of the dead-at-birth sister that I never knew.

J.C. 'I am in no way accustomed to a corpse speaking.'

D.A. When I published the poem in *Poetry Quarterly* I received a few letters from homosexual readers who, misunderstanding the poem, thought I was declaring that I was homosexual or bisexual. It so happens I've not had a homosexual experience in my life – nevertheless, I recognise, as Freud tells us, that we all have within us a masculine and a feminine component and in that poem I was unconsciously projecting this; though consciously, in a private way, I was only referring to my dead sister and Denise Levertov – I might add that my feelings spoilt my relationship with Denise. I was a promiscuous young man, but I had a feeling that Denise, attractive as she was, was not for me, that to make overtures to her would...

J.C. Would have been incestuous?

D.A. That's right.

J.C. That's very interesting because if you had not mentioned this personal aspect, there'd be no way of knowing...

D.A. Yes, it's too private. One should eschew such private references in poetry.

J.C. But there are several things that are not merely private which came through to me as you read the poem, among them the combined feminine and masculine principles. As I said, it's a very erotic poem.

D.A. Necrophilic?

J.C. The poem succeeds in that it recognises the masculine and feminine aspects of ourselves. It recognises that duality, I'm reminded of Tiresias, and the use of him made by Eliot and Durrell. By the way, you never had in the back of your head the image of the Sleeping Beauty when you wrote that poem?

D.A. No, not at all. Of course, for all I know Sleeping Beauty had a mother who before she was born had a miscarriage!

J.C. O.K. Whereas I think 'Lady of black hair' succeeds, I know many of the others fail. For instance, I've read a lot of war poems, but your early war poem, 'Tonight slippers of darkness fall', is about the worst one I've ever read.

D.A. O.K.

J.C. The best quality in this first book is its lyrical intensity – and a more controlled lyricism is evident in your later work. Your poem 'Epithalamion' comes to mind, though that, also, is quite an early poem. It was published in your second book *Walking Under Water* which contains poems written between 1948 and 1951. You were still a medical student.

D.A. I qualified in 1950.

J.C. *Walking Under Water* shows little *stylistic* development. There are more successes in it than the previous volume but many poems are flawed and most are still neo-romantic in tone. There are exceptions. A poem like 'Letter to Alex Comfort' about the nature of scientific inspiration and its misapplication of scientific knowledge to war technology is cast in a less intense way, is more relaxed in diction.

D.A. Yes, that poem is more conversationally pitched. It's a drier, wittier poem than the more hortatory poems I was then, in 1948, tending to write. 'Letter to Alex Comfort' in some ways predates the Movement poetry of the fifties – all those Movement poems you can find in the 1956 *New Lines* anthology edited by Robert Conquest which included the then 'new' poets, Larkin, Donald Davie, etc. Their poems, also, tried for a more chaste diction, a more neutral tone.

J.C. Conquest, I seem to remember, claimed their poems had a more intellectual backbone than the neo-romantic poetry of the Forties, and owned a 'notable aridity.'

D.A. 'Letter to Alex Comfort' has in it such lines as 'Ehrlich certainly was one who broke down the mental doors' and 'Koch also, painfully and with true German thoroughness / eliminated the impossible.' I mean there was a naming of names. Seven years later, the Movement poets were writing lines like 'That was not what Berkeley meant.'

J.C. By?

D.A. By Donald Davie. Thom Gunn began one of his poems, 'Shelley was drowned near here.' D.J. Enright began one, 'Was Freud entirely right?' Then worst of all there's Conquest's

> Perhaps Karlsefni saw it to starboard
> On the voyage to Hop from Siraumfjord.

J.C. Ha ha ha.

D.A. Such naming of names became for a while a Movement tic. But I hope that in 'Letter to Alex Comfort', the naming of names was not simply name-dropping. Nor, though conversationally pitched, was the diction of that poem too arid.

J.C. In succeeding years your diction has varied from the more relaxed language of 'Letter to Alex Comfort' to the lyrical intensity of 'Epithalamion.' I've always found that poem to be especially appealing which accounts, I suppose, for its being frequently anthologised. I assume it came out of actual experience. Do you recall that marvellous passage right at the end of Molly Bloom's soliloquy in *Ulysses* where she's reminiscing about her courtship with Bloom and says 'they might as well try to stop the sun from rising tomorrow the sun shine for you he said the day we were lying among the rhododendrons on Howth head in the grey tweed suit and his straw hat the day I got him to propose to me yes first I gave him the bit of seedcake out of my mouth and it was leapyear like now yes 16 years ago my God after that long kiss I near lost my breath yes he said I was a flower of the mountain yes so we are flowers all a womans body yes...' But to get back to your barleyfield.

D.A. I don't recall ever making love to a girl in a barley field! You know some months after I wrote that poem I happened on a paper in a psychoanalytical journal called 'Barley, Wedding Rings and Styes in the Eye.'

J.C. Styes in the Eye?

D.A. I mentioned earlier about my mother being pregnant, a stillbirth. Another thing I learnt about my mother's pregnancies – was that, on each occasion, my father developed a stye in the eye. It was a family joke. So when I came across that psychoanalytical paper I read it with interest. It pointed out that a primitive method of treating styes in the eye was by rubbing them with a golden wedding ring – and that to this day golden eye-ointment is used to treat styes though that ointment is a weak antiseptic and there are many better ones.

J.C. Barley too is golden.

D.A. It's a fertility symbol. So 'my white girl in a barley field' is apt – though in placing her in that topography I did so without awareness of such a thing.

J.C. It was unconscious.

D.A. Yes. Incidentally, after I read that paper, while a medical student, I must have been a nuisance in the Ophthalmology Department. For whenever I encountered a man with a stye in his eye, I asked him if his wife or mistress had missed a period!

J.C. May I turn now to the poems 1951-1956 which you collected in *Tenants of the House*, a volume which shows a significant advance on the two previous volumes? *Tenants of the House* has shaken off the neo-romantic mannerisms, it's a highly individual volume, as Edwin Muir indicated when he reviewed it; and I'm not surprised it's the first book of yours, poems I mean, to be published in the U.S.A.

D.A. Many of the poems in *Tenants* used an allegorical or a symbolic framework. I got into the habit of working that way, off and on, for about a decade so such poems are to be found also in my next book *Poems, Golders Green* published in 1962.

J.C. Yes, I think *Poems, Golders Green* is a transitional book linking your later work to your earlier. But what do you mean by allegorical?

D.A. On one level I was saying one particular thing, on another something more general.

J.C. You were writing about mountaineering in 'The Mountaineers' but really referring to the creative process rather as Frost did in his poem 'Apple-Picking'.

D.A. I wrote about mountaineers, yes, but as you rightly say I was thinking about the creative process. I wrote about a particular football game in Cardiff but was referring to the evil and good propensities in man, how they were in conflict with each other. I sang a song about five men warring over a deserted island – territory something like the Falkland Islands – but I was really making a noise about the danger of a nuclear holocaust. Such poems were simple parables, allegories. Other poems in that same volume were symbolically ordered.

J.C. By which you mean? The difference between allegorically ordered and symbolically ordered?

D.A. The difference is between a sign and a symbol. 'X' can be a sign or a symbol. It can be an emblem and stand for one particular thing or 'X' can stand for many things and remain finally an enigma. Poems like 'The Trial', for instance, cannot be totally paraphrased, as can say 'The Mountaineers', or 'Emperors of the Island'.

J.C. Still 'The Trial' comes through in a concrete way. It's an existentialist ballad.

D.A. Yes, in the 50s I was interested in existentialist literature, in Sartre, in Camus, and how they dramatised philosophical questions.

J.C. Do you maintain that interest in existentialism? You continue to touch on the theme of absurdity – the absurdity of existence in the 20th century.

D.A. Indeed. In 'Lunch and Afterwards' the protagonist in that recent poem, on learning from a pathologist how after death, the first organ to disappear is the brain and how the last organ to endure is the uterus, finds that he needs to *act*. So he, standing next to a telephone, thinks of a number, then doubles it. It's an act, even though it is one of total absurdity.

J.C. I think there's a lot of despair in that recent poem and I recall how, when I first read *Tenants of the House* years ago I was aware of how much despair about the human condition haunted the poems – and that despair seems to be a part of the whole existentialist *gestalt*.

D.A. I wouldn't admit to unrelenting despair in *Tenants of the House*. You'll find lines in such poems as 'Poem of Celebration' as:

Any man may gather the images of despair.
I'll say 'I will' and 'I can'
and, like an accident, breathe in space and air.

In the next volume, *Poems, Golders Green*, there are lines from 'The
Grand View' which read:

There are moments when a man must praise
the astonishment of being alive,
when small mirrors of reality blaze
into miracles...

I've known the mood of jubilation and the mood of despair. Who
hasn't? My poems reflect that. True, as the years turn over the pages,
my poems become more sombre. My consciousness of recent
history: the nuclear crimes in Nagasaki, Hiroshima; the crimes of
Auschwitz, Dachau; the geography of Vietnapalm; the awful opening
mouths of the lethal crowd; this awareness does not diminish with the
years. On the contrary.

J.C. You are talking about general and public aggressiveness. But
'The Trial' postulates an individual helplessness, an existential
despair. He who is on trial for throwing off his masks will be found
guilty, will be hung. He may be hung high, he may be hung low, but
he'll be hung.

D.A. That's so.

J.C. I think 'The Second Coming' suggests a similar despair. I find
this poem enormously interesting in several respects. You seem to
suggest that people expecting a messiah are deluding themselves.
The saviour emerges from the earth like an old vegetation god to get
his head lopped off by the technology of our civilisation. This killing
machinery precludes the possibility of a spiritual rebirth.

D.A. Yes.

J.C. Are you aware also of the affinities it has with a couple of Dylan
Thomas's poems? The one about the birth of the baby who, emerging, utters 'If my head hurt a hair's foot.' Also that other Thomas
poem which begins 'Light breaks where no sun shines.' In 'The
Second Coming' you have the line, 'Still his body in darkness, light-
ward pushing.'

D.A. I'm happy to acknowledge influences where I see them, and

Dylan Thomas was an early influence, but the line of mine you quote owes much more to my experience, experience of delivering babies, rather than reading Dylan Thomas.

J.C. It is finally, in some ways, a political poem. I'm struck, as a matter of fact, by how many of the poems in *Tenants of the House* are political. There's a consciousness of the obligation to resist the official destructive forces of the twentieth century. Daniel in the lion's den must reject these value systems, must remain a maverick and resist being murdered.

D.A. I would have liked to have written more political or rather more public poems. There are a few in *Tenants of the House* and those there are do proclaim my continuing emotional imperative of 'oppose, oppose orthodoxies.' 'Outside is a lonely place.'

J.C. Yes, from 'New Babylons':

> Let spellbound lions know
> an angel in the den
> lest they bite to please
> the vast majorities.
>
> Outside is a lonely place.

D.A. When I wrote those lines I more frequently leaned on mythological references. Since *A Small Desperation* I think I've written much more directly.

J.C. I recall that in writing about *A Small Desperation* Jeremy Robson observed that you explore those areas of experience which defy articulation. That observation's true, I think, not only for *A Small Desperation* but for many poems written since then. For instance, in that dialogue poem 'Hunt the Thimble' you allude to mysteries we all perceive but cannot explain. It seems in such poems you're trying to probe the reality beyond our general, commonplace reality. You seem to be moving toward defining the undefinable.

D.A. Not long ago, after a poetry-reading a very small lady approached me. 'You didn't swear like the poet we had here last,' she said. I wasn't sure whether she was complaining or commending me for my chaste diction. 'You don't use swear words,' she insisted, 'in your poems.' I came to the conclusion she was more disappointed than pleased. I became curious to know which poet had evidently impressed her on the previous reading at that literary society. 'Nuttall,' she told me. 'A man called Nuttall.'

J.C. Nuttall?

D.A. 'What swear words did Mr. Nuttall use?' I asked as innocently as possible. She hesitated. 'Ah,' she said finally, 'that would be telling.' Then she turned away presumably to some barracks for better verbal refreshment.

J.C. Swear words very rarely come into your poetry as a matter of fact, or for that matter in other Anglo-Welsh poets.

D.A. We are a respectable people. I remember how, in 1956, Vernon Watkins invited my wife and me to his house on the Pennard cliffs, the Gower side of Swansea. He's been editing the correspondence between Dylan Thomas and himself for Faber and Faber. Vernon was mightily angry because an editor had censored Dylan Thomas's letters. 'He deleted,' Vernon said excitedly, 'a certain word whenever it arose and it arose frequently, for Dylan, do you see, freely used this word both in speech and in his letters.' I became aware of how aware Vernon was of my wife's presence. He resolutely stared away from her as he continued, 'It's a word that is somewhat stronger than bloody. Indeed Dylan used this word quite innocently. These days many people speak it, not merely those who are ill-bred. Readers are accustomed nowadays to read this word. Why it's hard to read a modern novel without encountering it. How dare they alter the character of Dylan's letters by censoring this word?' Vernon became more and more angry. For another two minutes he raged against his publisher – and righteous his protestations. Yet not once did Vernon, being a correct and courteous man...

J.C. And Welsh...

D.A. ...utter, in front of my wife, that word which is so much worse than bloody.

J.C. Nor have you, for that matter. We seem to have gone off on a tangent. I'd like to return to your poetry – the fact that you're a doctor, the fact that you're a Jew, how these facts have affected your poems. All this we haven't discussed. Nor have we touched on your plays. Maybe we can continue this interview, at a later date, after you've come back from Wales and I've come back from Ireland?

D.A. Sure. Let's call it a day, now.

★★★

J.C. A number of Jewish writers in America – to name just two, Karl Shapiro and Bernard Malamud – have made explicit statements about the Jew being the symbol of the central victimised and alienated figure of our time.

D.A. As this century continues more atrocities occur and recur in different parts of the world. Man has been a wolf to man irrespective of whether he's a Jew, a Christian or a Moslem. So that central symbol of the Jew is likely to become diluted. On the other hand, the crime against the Jews in war-torn Europe, the immensity of that crime cannot diminish, even in a small measure, in the minds of those who have truly apprehended it. For them, whatever other crimes against nations occur, nothing is annulled. That sickening apprehension has changed their minds forever, deepened their distrust in man.

J.C. Changed *your* mind forever, deepened *your* distrust?

D.A. Yes.

J.C. I asked you about the Jew being a symbol of the victimised figure of our time and you've answered me; but I also asked you about the Jew as being the alienated figure of our time. What about the title of your most recent book of poems?

D.A. *Way Out in the Centre?*

J.C. Yes.

D.A. Does that title suggest to you a geographical spiritual position?

J.C. It suggests to me that in a complicated way you think of yourself as being an Outsider.

D.A. It's a dualistic position. The title, after all, is a paradox. As you know I was born and brought up in Cardiff, a border town. Though Cardiff's the capital of Wales, it's not very Welsh. One aspect of it faces West to Welsh Wales. One East to confident England. There are some who are scornful of such a mongrel city but out of the tensions of a double tradition a city may just as well be enriched as impoverished. So it is with its inhabitants. In my case, moreover, I'm a Jew – and to add to the complication one who's hardly part of the Jewish community.

J.C. You say that even though, in recent years, you've admitted that in

writing your poems you've raided Midrashic texts, legends of the bible.
D.A. Right. In recent poems of mine you'll find images I've stolen, images and aphoristic sayings from the Talmud. But one can be fired by Talmudic or Chasidic stories, even occasionally adapting them, and still feel isolated from the Jewish community at large.

J.C. You feel yourself to be a maverick.

D.A. If you like. All my life I've had an enduring feeling of being way out in the centre. When I left Cardiff I went, eventually, to Westminster Hospital to study medicine. And most of the students there, in my day, were ex-public school boys, and not a few had afterwards gone to Oxford or Cambridge. I went to a working-class Catholic school in Splott, Cardiff where I was taught by Christian Brothers.

J.C. A middle-class Welsh Jewish boy in a working-class Irish Catholic school.

D.A. Exactly. It was no way a classy establishment. Boys from there *never* went to Oxford or Cambridge. Only a small minority progressed to University. I hasten to add that I was happy enough at that school, mainly because I was interested in playing games, in cricket and rugby. But for the first lesson of the day, the religious lesson, I with a few Protestant lads was banished to another, empty classroom. I was way out in the centre there and at medical school. So it was, too, in the R.A.F. later. I was an officer but I was conscious, in the Mess, of not sharing my fellow officers' social and political views about occasions, ceremonies, and issues. I daresay that dualistic or paradoxical situation in which I've always found myself is common to most poets who live in a Philistine society. All the same, some poets may be made aware of being a maverick more than others.

J.C. Some of your feelings about being *Way Out in the Centre* inform your poems. And perhaps it leads you to be critical of those who thrive uncomplicatedly in the centre. For instance, in your poem, 'Tales of Shatz' you seem to be mildly critical of the modern-type English Jew who's more and more assimilated – the 'Baruch Levy who changed his name to Barry Lee / who moved to Esher, Surrey, / who sent his four sons – Matthew, Mark, Luke and John – to boarding school...' What you're doing here is what the prophets did in drawing attention to how Jews had moved away from their spiritual values.

D.A. That's much too grand. All I was trying to do in 'Tales of Shatz' was to catch the wry flavour you find in certain Yiddish stories. I don't know Yiddish but I admire in translation, such writers as Sholom Aleichem – their wryness, their humour, their humanity. That tone, that's what I was fumbling for in 'Tales of Shatz' and like Sholom Aleichem I hope I was affectionately satirical.

J.C. Your origins, as we know, apart from being Jewish are also Welsh. Your mother spoke Welsh, I believe.

D.A. Yes, when she was a young girl in Ystalyfera. As a matter of fact my grandmother, Annabella Shepherd spoke Welsh also. True, it was a broken Welsh, a peculiar Welsh, and the inhabitants of Ystalyfera – a village in the Swansea valley – wondered if she were a Patagonian. You see, in the 19th century, there'd been a Welsh settlement in Patagonia and no doubt when these Patagonians returned to Wales their Welsh was somewhat different to those who'd stayed behind. They used to say to my grandmother, because of her execrable Welsh – 'Tell the truth, Annabella fach, you're not Jewish, you're Patagonian!'

J.C. Though I know you don't speak Welsh yourself, given your background, aren't you attracted to the *Matter* of Britain in the way you're attracted to the *Matter* of the Eastern European *shtetls*?

D.A. The early Welsh tradition was often focussed on the fabulous. The *Mabinogion*, for instance. I'm not excited by highly romantic Arthurian tales as I am by that component of the Jewish tradition that presents fallible characters recognisably, absurdly, human. I'm more interested in fools talking to their dogs than knights killing dragons. Sometimes, of course, it's Welsh fools talking to Welsh dogs that intrigue me.

J.C. How should a poem declare itself to be Welsh?

D.A. Best of all by being written in Welsh – though there is such a thing as an Anglo-Welsh tradition.

J.C. I've noticed how many Anglo-Welsh poets, especially in recent years, plant an occasional Welsh word in their poems.

D.A. I don't scatter my poems with token Welsh. That would be a condescension. Almost one hundred years ago Emrys ap Iwan spoke satirically of those Welshmen who found it poetic to conclude each speech in English in barely tolerable Welsh, 'Long live the Welsh language.'

J.C. But you do have a strong sense of place.

D.A. Perhaps. For Ogmore-by-Sea where I think I was conceived, for Cardiff where I was born, for London which educated me, and for another place that has no name and you'll find on no map.

J.C. How do you mean?

D.A. It's something lost. It's not innocence, it's a form of knowledge that is lost. It's more than 'hiraeth' which is an untranslatable Welsh word that has something to do with a longing for home, the yearnings of an exile for something lost. No, perhaps a Chassidic story best dramatises what I mean. May I quote it? It's a kind of parable.

J.C. Another parable?

D.A. I'm afraid so. 'When the Baal Shem had a difficult task before him, he would go to a certain place in the woods, light a fire and meditate in prayer – and what he had set out to perform was done. When a generation later the 'Maggid' of Meseritz was faced with the same task he would go to the same place in the woods and say: We can no longer light the fire, but we can still speak the prayers – and what he wanted done became reality. Again a generation later Rabbi Moshe Leib of Sassov had to perform his task. And he too went into the woods and said: We can no longer light a fire, nor do we know the secret meditations belonging to the prayer, but we do know the place in the woods to which it all belongs – and that must be sufficient; and sufficient it was. But when another generation had passed and Rabbi Israel of Rishin was called upon to perform the task, he sat down on his golden chair in his castle and said: We cannot light the fire, we cannot speak the prayers, we do not know the place, but we can tell the story of how it was done.'

J.C. I like that. But it does strike a rather pessimistic note.

D.A. I wouldn't say that. It's a recognition of a loss but...

J.C. It has the same pessimism as 'Dover Beach.'

D.A. True 'Dover Beach' is a recognition that ignorant armies clash by night but it's also a prescription. For individuals on a personal level to be true to each other. And the parable, the Chassidic parable, prescribes that we must tell the story, must bear witness. The imperative for poets to bear witness is an old one. No doubt, one could find it in several cultures. The sixth-century bard, Aneurin, told us that of more than three hundred wearing gold torques at Catraeth only two returned from battle – one, Cibno, and the other, the bard himself, 'soaked in blood for my song's sake.'

J.C. Let me raise another question about *Way Out in the Centre*. I read a review recently which I'd like to quote from. Philip Owens wrote, 'It appears that the main problem these poems tackle is a substantial one – the question of how truth or reality is most accurately to be apprehended – and underlying it is a tension between two methods of approach (which we might define as the empirical and the imaginative) which, one presumes, emerges from the interplay of Abse's vocations as doctor and poet.' How do you feel about that?

D.A. Was that from *The Anglo-Welsh Review*?

J.C. Yes.

D.A. Many of my recent poems do seem to be about appearances, about what seems to be real, and how we may be deceived. There are those, I think, you're one, who wish to compartmentalise my occupations of doctor and poet. Oh there he's a doctor, here he's a poet. I don't think I'm that divided. Of course I have conflicts, tensions and I do contradict myself. In that, I'm like everybody else, and such oppositions within oneself do help to breed poems. Besides, though I start with the visible, I don't know where I'm going to end.

J.C. There are a number of poems in *Way Out* that are about different kinds of deception.

D.A. Right. There's a poem about vagrants but, imaginatively, are those down-and-outs what they seem? There's a poem about a door of a so-called haunted house banging and banging in the wind – how does one perceive that? There's a poem on how, looking out of a window four hoofmarks in the snow can be seen but suddenly these dark marks rise up like crows and fly away. At least three of them do.

J.C. What's particularly interesting is one dark mark remains behind!

D.A. That apprehension may only be a consequence of the optic nerve of the soul not yet having been severed!

J.C. To conclude, if I were to ask you to read a poem from *Way Out in the Centre* without thinking about the choice, which one would you turn to?

D.A. There's a poem of Amir Gilboa, the Israeli poet, I've adapted. About how we observe blood but we're told, officially, it's paint. With all the euphemisms and propaganda coming from the Middle East, at the moment, perhaps I could read his 'Lesson in Reality'?

They held up a stone.
  I said, 'Stone.'
Smiling they said, 'Stone.'

They showed me a tree.
  I said, 'Tree.'
Smiling they said, 'Tree.'

They shed a man's blood.
  I said, 'Blood.'
Smiling they said, 'Paint.'

They shed a man's blood.
  I said, 'Blood.'
Smiling they said, 'Paint.'

J.C. Thank you. Thank you very much.

From: J. Cohen: *The Poetry of Dannie Abse* (London: Robson Books,
1983)

Section B: Writings on Dannie Abse

Preface

Section 6 includes only a very small number of the hundreds of reviews of Abse's poetry books which have appeared over the last sixty years. Four are devoted to key single volumes which appeared roughly fifteen years apart, from *Poems, Golders Green* (1962) to the latest single collection *Running Late* (2006). The others cover his three *Collecteds* and the 1994 *Selected*. Given Abse's roots it is not surprising that many of the more extended and considered reviews have appeared in 'Poetry Wales' magazine. The two pieces by Tony Curtis reflect his long advocacy of Abse's work; he is the author of the only single volume critical book on Dannie Abse's writings.

The essays in section 7 have been written over a period of forty years and reflect different critical approaches. All but two have been published elsewhere; those two, by John Pikoulis, rather psycho-analytical in approach, and Laura Wainwright, with its twenty-first century perspective, were especially commissioned for this volume. Three of the essays appeared in Joseph Cohen's extremely valuable *The Poetry of Dannie Abse; Critical Essays and Reminiscences* (1983) now unfortunately out of print (See also part of one of his 'Conversations with Dannie Abse', taken from this book, in section 5.). Of these, Alan Brownjohn's historical piece is an evocative account of the literary scene during Abse's early career. John Tripp's very personal, stimulating article was originally published in 'Poetry Wales' and has never been reprinted. James A. Davies has written about Abse's work in a number of places; included here is his essential introduction to the author's dramatic writing and his fascinating, contextualising article on Abse's relationship to Modernism. The extract from Jasmine Donahaye's article has been included for its insights into Abse's Jewish context. All the reviews and essays are testimony to the importance of Abse's work, and to his unusual position as both maverick and popular poet.

6. Reviews

John Smith
Poems, Golders Green

Four of the poems from this collection appeared in the Spring number of this magazine and readers will therefore have some idea of the kind of poetry they will find in Dannie Abse's fourth book of poems which is, justly, a Poetry Book Society Choice. Among the many careful and fastidious voices of contemporary poets Dannie Abse's sounds with a distinct and distinctive timbre, human, compassionate and real. Like so many poets who began to publish in the forties his early work was often too cluttered up with mythology, was too allegorical, often too clogged with romantic adjectives. Gradually this language has been pared down, but not emasculated, and his preoccupations have become more closely concerned with the predicaments, the lonelinesses, longings, hopes and fears of the human animal. I can think of no other poet of the moment who catches so exactly the tone of suburban man's anxieties, love and unrest – Auden perhaps in some early poems but his tone is more clinical, his preoccupations are with the upper rather than the middle class. There is none of the impersonal smoothness of fashionable poetry in these poems. They are the poems of and for the man who sees the morning stubble of beard on his face, who suffers the common cold, is worried by the trifles that wear away our lives, but by being human both suffers and is calmed by intimations of the divine. They lay before us the worried agnosticism of twentieth-century man.

As the title perhaps almost belligerently announces, these are the poems of a Jew and I think the Jewishness is sometimes rather overdone; occasionally, too, I find him being tricked into writing from a good idea that is not finally the right one for transmuting into that indefinable object, a true poem. There are also lines like

> till some genius on a gramophone
> holes defences, breaks all fences.

which I find curiously lacking in verbal taste. But to compensate for these there are lines in which the freshly discovered images prick the mind into new awareness. In some ways he reminds me of Donne in that the rhythms of his verse at a first reading often seem clumsy and inexpert, but on a closer reading are revealed to be weighed precisely for the sense of what is being said; then, as one reads further, the poems reveal subtleties of assonance, interior rhymes, echoes and cadences that give an added purely linguistic satisfaction that is proper to all good poetry. Also, like Donne, his love poems are the love poems of a real human being and not idealistic troubadour confections. His 'Three Voices' is marvellously tender.

We talk a lot nowadays about why does the poet not speak to the man in the street and only too often when a poet tries he starts to write ominously bad verse. I don't think Dannie Abse tries; he is a poet writing poetry. But I believe his work, and this latest book, as well as being admired by other poets, has a great deal to offer the ordinary reader, which means all of us.

From: *The Poetry Review* Autumn 1962

Fleur Adcock reviews Dannie Abse
Poet on Poet – Collected Poems 1948-1976

Last year in New Zealand I was talking with an old friend about poetry we liked. He suddenly began praising Dannie Abse, and seized my notebook to write him a message of thanks and admiration for me to deliver. Funny, I thought – twelve years ago in London, after he'd met Dannie briefly and read his work, he told me sadly that although he liked the man he really couldn't get at all excited by his poetry.

What had changed: my friend's taste or Dannie Abse's poetry? Looking now at the *Collected Poems*, I'd say the latter. Not that there isn't a consistent personality running through the entire work, and also an identifiable flavour to the style, even while individual elements come and go; but from about the 1960s his poems have a greater depth and solidity and look more directly at reality, with less reliance on fable, allegory and technical tricks. His statements are more lucid and at the same time his language opens out, the tone surer and the rhythms more natural and less obtrusive. His achievement begins to look very substantial.

The poems reveal the basic facts about the man: that he's Welsh, Jewish, a doctor, a family man, politically concerned, humane, and vulnerable. The Welshness, regularly present in the subject-matter, is an element also of the style, particularly in a few of the early poems (too much Dylan Thomas? – but far more, I suspect, in the 'apprentice work' now omitted from the canon.) Welsh characters crop up in some of the later poems – as also, hilariously, in Dannie Abse's prose works which this is not the place to consider.

The Jewish element is, inevitably, more complicated. There are painful poems on Jewish themes, some of which ('No more Mozart' and, in a lower key, 'Postmark') work and some of which, I feel, don't quite. It's hard to judge the effect of certain intensities of tone: too easy to hear a shrill note where the language itself is merely factual, to suspect that words like 'Auschwitz' are being used for push-button results. Also Dannie Abse is himself ambiguous in his attitudes – a non-practising Jew with however a deep commitment; and he is in the later poems subtle, sensitive and sometimes funny when writing about Jewish characters: 'Uncle Isadore' has all these qualities, and they are distributed over the four 'Tales of Shatz', the first being a good joke and the fourth poignant in a way that leaves an odd lingering echo. One must also take into account the completely undenominational religious sensibility apparent in many of the poems, from first to last; and the irony – but it is something more delicate than irony – of 'Portrait of the Artist as a Middle-aged Man' (3.30 a.m., January 1st):

Pure Xmas card below – street under snow,
under lamplight. My children curl asleep,
my wife also moans from depths too deep
with all her shutters closed and half her life.
And I? I, sober now, come down the stairs
to eat an apple, to taste the snow in it,
to switch the light on at the maudlin time.

Habitual living room, where the apple-flesh
turns brown after the bite, oh half my life
has gone to pot. And, now, too tired for sleep,
I count up the Xmas cards childishly,
assessing, *Jesus*, how many friends I've got!

The words 'Jesus' and 'Xmas' (and the spelling of the latter) work interestingly with and against the apple symbol and the images of coldness, snow and death.

From time to time Dr Abse appears wearing his white coat. Medical subjects – hospitals, illness, pain, death – are a gift to poets; the danger is that they can become too easy an option, the mere bleak presentation of the facts acting as an alternative to any actual work by the poet, even when the latter is physician rather than patient or observer. In Dr Abse's case I find that scenes from the ward or the consulting-room, however dramatic or moving, come across less effectively than more muted poems where his combination of clinical clearsightedness and anguished compassion is focused on personal experiences – in 'Miracles', for example, which is about faith, or in the beautiful short poem 'Peachstone':

> I do not visit his grave. He is not there.
> Out of hearing, out of reach. I miss him here,
> seeing hair grease at the back of a chair
> near a firegrate where his spit sizzled,
> or noting, in the cut-glass bowl, a peach.
>
> For that night his wife brought him a peach,
> his favourite fruit, while the sick light glowed,
> and his slack, dry mouth sucked, sucked, sucked,
> with dying eyes closed – perhaps for her sake –
> till bright as blood the peachstone showed.

These, for me, last better than some of the instant-impact pieces such as the horror story 'In the Theatre' or the rather meandering meditation 'The smile was'.

And here I cannot avoid an aspect of Dannie Abse's work which rather worries me: the effect on it of the poetry-reading industry, a temptation to write for the stage rather than the page. He is a good reader, relaxed and unpretentious, and there must be many people who first encountered his poetry when they heard him read it and continue to hear his speaking voice in everything he writes. Nothing wrong with that, of course, nor with the conversational tone of much of his recent work – indeed, I see it as a positive virtue. (There is a connection here too with his experience of writing plays; I don't propose to discuss his successful career as a dramatist except to say that the techniques learnt from it come over into his poems as an ability to shape a scene, sketch characters, and present dialogue.) But I am less happy about the diluting effect on his style of such devices as repetition, loosely-wrapped bundles of phrases, sentences without verbs in otherwise conventionally-structured poems, and the general slackening which can result from writing for immediate aural consumption: 'The smile was', for example, is a performance-poem which doesn't entirely stand up to scrutiny in its printed form. And yet it is one which admirers of his readings will expect to find published, and it should therefore be available for them. Dannie himself seemed aware of this problem when he gave his early 'Emperors of the Island' the subtitle 'A political parable to be read aloud' – one kind of compromise, but there's no easy solution.

A body of work covering nearly thirty years includes, of course, a number of styles. This *Collected Poems* is not comprehensive: it omits, as I've said, much early work which the poet now rejects. But because it is selective it is fair to assume that author wants us to take seriously what he's chosen to retain. So what do we find? The first half of the book is, as one would expect, more 'lyrical' than the mature work, tending to songs, allegories, political ballads (these often predictably Audenesque, in contrast to his mature work which has no discernible influences and in which the political attitudes are more complex without being less honourable.) There are poems on mythological themes, such as the attractively rhythmical 'The victim of Aulis', where the varied singing tone and the vivid description don't obscure the tension of the events. The young Abse's control of rhythms and forms tends to be uneven, but his gift for visual description is constant – often striking, and occasionally deployed for sinister purposes, as in 'The second coming', a grisly fable set in a cornfield. And of course there are personal poems, pieces of social observation, little stories in verse – the range is wide, and continues to be so. Later, though, there is less sense of contrivance, less ornate and rhetorical language, and a higher proportion of colloquial pieces presenting real situations. The formal construction of the poems becomes, on the whole, looser, but there is an underlying sense of structure and an assurance in tone and vocabulary. There is often, though, something a little knobbly, unshaven, unpolished in these poems, as if the poet wished to avoid too smooth a perfection, and sometimes they seem in fact to be pulled out of shape by the strength of feeling in their content; they are, if I may use the word, masculine in style. He is a very honest poet.

Not that this implies worthy dullness. He can be both witty (as in 'A note left on the mantelpiece', which uses the imagery of the race-course to say things about competition, success and failure) and very funny, as in 'Florida' and 'The death of Aunt Alice'. The latter begins:

> Aunt Alice's funeral was orderly,
> each mourner correct, dressed in decent black,
> not one balding relative berserk with an axe.
> Poor Alice, where's your opera-ending?
> For alive you relished high catastrophe,
> your bible Page One of a newspaper.
>
> You talked of typhoid when we sat to eat;
> Fords on the M4, mangled, upside down,
> just when we were going for a spin;
> and, at London airport, as you waved us off,
> how you fatigued us with 'metal fatigue',
> vague shapes of Boeings bubbling under seas.

And there is often humour of a gentle or wry kind mixed in with other moods. 'As I was saying' begins:

> Yes, madam, as a poet I *do* take myself seriously,
> and, since I have a young, questioning family, I suppose
> I should know something about English wild flowers: ...

and ends, after some verbal fun with plant-names:

> But no! Done for in the ignorant suburb,
> I'll drink Scotch, neurotically stare through glass
> at the rainy lawn, at green stuff, nameless birds,
> and let my daughter, madam, go to nature class.
> I'll not compete with those nature poets you advance,
> some in country dialect, and some in dialogue
> with the country – few as calm as their words:
> Wordsworth, Barnes, sad John Clare who ate grass.

He also falls occasionally into a style which is best described by comparing it to Chagall's paintings – bittersweet, slightly surreal, full of dreamlike displacements, and involving such images as magicians, fiddle-players, angels and clouds. Much of the long sequence

'Funland' is in this mode, making it pictorially memorable as well as a vehicle for social satire; and see 'Ghosts, angels, unicorns' for a rather different treatment of this type of material. Here his descriptive talent is still vividly in evidence; and he can still, when he chooses, bring off a lyrical *tour de force*, as in 'A faithful wife', a poem set in ancient Egypt which has something of the resonance of classical Chinese poetry.

For the classical Abse poem, however, I think I would refer new readers to the sequence 'Car journeys'. In this I find all his virtues without the faults I may seem to have been niggling about, and it embodies several of his characteristic themes. It is in four parts, each describing a journey. In the first, 'Down the M4', he is driving to Wales to visit his mother, who is nearly ninety; there is this flashback:

> Then the Tawe ran fluent and trout-coloured over stones stonier,
> more genuine; then Annabella, my mother's mother, spoke Welsh
> with such an accent the village said, 'Tell the truth, fach,
> you're no Jewess. *They're* from the Bible. *You're* from Patagonia!'

And the poem ends:

> ... I whistle
> no hymn but an old Yiddish tune my mother knows.
> It won't keep.

The next poem in the sequence, 'Incident on a summer night', is both fantasy and actual event: the poet is driving along a country lane 'not even in the A.A. book'...

> then, soon, fabulous in the ghastly wash
> of headlights, a naked man approached
> crying without inhibition, one hand to his face,
> his somehow familiar mouth agape.

Later the word 'Paradise' drops into a line, but we have already identified the figure of Adam expelled from the garden, as in the Masaccio fresco.

The third poem has more generalised images – an Asian child on a rubbish heap, an old man 'mouthing a forgotten language', and a feeling of heat, oppression and doom. And in the final poem 'Driving home', the poet passes the scene of an accident and drives cautiously and anxiously back to his family: where all is well and "the eyes of my youngest child / flicker dreamily, and are full of television." Full circle, from the old mother to the young son; but there is nothing heavily obvious or over-emphasised about the structure of the sequence or the significance of elements in it. Dannie Abse doesn't preach or rant; his best poems make their points naturally and with an unobtrusive skill, and reveal further layers and levels on each re-reading. He says in his introduction 'I hope this is only Volume One of a *Collected Poems.*' I look forward to the next, but this one will do well for now.

From: *Ambit* 70, 1977

Tony Curtis
Ask the Bloody Horse

First published in 1948, Dannie Abse has written steadily and with a consistency of quality matched only by R.S. Thomas in Wales, and by virtually no-one else in Britain. Every five years, it seems, we are to be treated to a new collection of his work. His output is substantial rather than enormous, his style flexible, accomplished with an unmistakable quiver of passion working below a surface urbanity. Dannie Abse addresses the human predicament in a unique way. His poetry is at once accessible and complex, entertaining and disturbing by turns.

Ask the Bloody Horse has a pacing and range almost identical to that of the previous collection *Way Out in the Centre*, published in 1981. The banal and the predictable events in the life of this self-styled "fortunate man" can splinter into the bizarre and surreal:

> Abruptly tipped off by MI5,
> what spirits vacated the fountains
> of Trafalgar Square, quit
> the fussy trees in Hyde Park?
> Who, in Harley St, requested
> a prescription for ambrosia?
>
> 'AWOL'

'Ceilings' threaten rather than shelter –

> The alarm-clock hopped around the room surprised,
> flowers of the wallpaper
> poured forth illicit perfume.

It is us if the world refuses to be stable, susceptible to classification. This goes beyond the pathetic fallacy: Abse wants us to believe in the independent life of things, to be wide-eyed and celebratory.

There are a number of humorous pieces, though the rabbis of the previous book and their wry wisdom are, with one exception, replaced by the secular concerns of, for example, putting up with unwelcome guests – 'A Welcome in the Wolds', and by a literary joke at the expense of Craig Raine 'A Translation from the Martian', which pays regard to Raine by out-Martianing the man. There is too, its tortuously oblique pub conversation overheard 'In the Pelican'.

Apart from the 'Martian' piece, there are literary influences acknowledged in a warm address to Peter Porter and a translation from one of Dannie Abse's earliest models, Rilke.

In his two recent readings during the Cardiff Literature Festival Dannie Abse selected almost exclusively from this new book, proving just how well judged is the voice in these poems. 'Hotel Nights' – contrasting experiences 'In the Angel Hotel', 'In the Royal Hotel' and 'In the Holiday Inn' – was particularly well received in performance. Where that other Welsh connoisseur of hotels, John Tripp, glimpsed a social milieu and gained insight into a former age through the brief luxuries of being on the road as a performing poet, Dannie Abse characteristically extends the possibilities suggested by the combination of ease and constriction which a hotel room offers. The central heating of the Holiday Inn leads him to biblical excesses –

> I was King David dancing before the Lord.
> Outside it was snowing but inside it was Israel.
>
> I danced six cubits this way, six cubits that.
> Now at dawn I'm hotter than the spices of Sheba.

Always treading a humanitarian path between religious heights, Dannie Abse celebrates the world with awe and an incisive wit. 'The Abandoned' which, the poet has explained, is a poem he has worked on, abandoned, and re-worked over a number of years, is now one of his most accomplished pieces. It is in two parts, prefaced by lines from both the Talmud and George Herbert*. The first section establishes the necessary part which the existence of man plays in the existence of God, the second is a fine villanelle developed around the key couplet:

> Dear God in the end you had to go,
> we keep the bread and wine for show.

Hear Dannie Abse read this poem and you'll have it haunting you. Hear him read it twice, as did many of us at the Cardiff Literature Festival, and, drunk or sober, you'll be quoting those lines at apposite stages of future theological wrangles into the small hours.

Ask the Bloody Horse is as well constructed as any of Abse's previous collections, poems drawing on, qualifying or extending the possibilities of preceding poems. Thus 'The Abandoned' follows 'Quests', 'The Message' and 'The Vow' and precedes 'Horizon' and the strangely effective 'Encounter at a Greyhound Bus Station' in which the poet encounters a "...kabbalist with eyes closed..." whose cryptic advocacy leads Abse into further considerations of his agnostic stance –

> And what could I, secular, say to that?
> That I'm deaf to God but not in combat?

Despite his unbelief, Dannie Abse is drawn again and again to the possibility of God and to account for the power of the *idea* if not the *fact* of God in both his Jewish and Welsh heritages. Unconvinced by the professional veneer of his colleagues in the medical profession – 'Millie's Date' and 'Case History' contribute further to the canon of his medical poems – Dannie Abse is attracted by the mystery of faith, the triumph of imagination in the context of medical enquiry and its all too limited victories. Indeed, 'The Sacred Disease'

> Else some old quack, a colleague in my art,
> would prescribe blood of a red-haired woman,
> young vulture's brain, young cormorant's heart.

and 'Tuberculosis' build on 'The Doctor' (*Way Out in the Centre*) in their underlining of the necessary conjunction of illness and inspiring vision. Having said that, however, 'Exit' emphasises again the deep sense of futility that Dr. Abse carries from the final year of his mother's life –

And as my colleague extracts the needle
from her vein, the temgesic acts
till the bruised exit's negotiated.
Then how victoriously
you hold the left passive hand
of the dummy in the bed
while I continue uselessly
to hold the other.

This, together with 'Last Visit to 198 Cathedral Road', add to the elegiac work of 'X-ray' and 'Last Winter' from his previous collection. When these poems are considered with the two which conclude this present collection – 'Apology' and 'Somewhere' – it strikes me that one could begin to argue a case for Dannie Abse's place alongside R.S. Thomas, not only as a poet in the first rank of Anglo-Welsh writers, but also in the first rank of our religious poets. Dannie Abse is a concerned, perhaps even a reluctant agnostic, winning from his background of Welsh nonconformity and Jewish nonconformity a body of poems, fertile and eclectic in their imagery, and as distinctly-voiced as any currently appearing in the British Isles.

From: *Poetry Wales* 13.2 (October 1977)

★ 'The Abandoned' has been revised yet again, see *New and Selected Poems*, Hutchinson 2009

Richard Poole
White Coat, Purple Coat – Collected Poems 1948-1988

This second edition of Dannie Abse's *Collected Poems* follows twelve years after the first. Give or take a handful of poems, allow for some regrouping of poems, and it consists of the contents of that earlier volume together with those from *Way Out in the Centre* (1981) and *Ask the Bloody Horse* (1986). There is one new poem, 'Carnal Knowledge'.

'Song for Pythagoras', which closes the book, is the best gloss upon its title:

> White coat and purple coat
> a sleeve from both he sews.
> That white is always stained with blood,
> that purple by the rose.
>
> And phantom rose and blood most real
> compose a hybrid style;
> white coat and purple coat
> few men can reconcile.
>
> White coat and purple coat
> can each be worn in turn
> but in the white a man will freeze
> and in the purple burn.

From quite early on this book worries away at the problem of identity. The semi-doggerel couplets of 'The trial' satirise society's unease at a man who, convinced that his given face did not represent his inner self, did away with it. In 'Duality' the poet declares that he has two faces and that *both* of them are "masks". He calls upon Christ to take away one of them "and leave me all / lest four tears from two eyes fall": lest, that is, he comes in for double the suffering that uncomplicated sensibilities have to endure. It is debatable, however, whether a split or fragmented identity is necessarily a bad thing for a poet. It may on the contrary be the making of him (or her), the condition, for example, of a negative capability which enables its possessor to construct from the jostling bubbles of a natural pluralism a number of different personae. 'A faithful wife' demonstrates that Dannie Abse can write splendidly in persona. He is, of course, a novelist and a playwright as well as poet, and in both of these callings the ability of the shape-changer is essential. By the time of writing of the poem 'Funland' and the play *Pythagoras* based upon it (to which the 'Song' quoted above is a lyrical coda), he had come up with a formula for expressing a divided identity which he obviously felt illuminated his own creative situation. 'White coat, purple coat' implies a series of contraries: intellect and feeling, reason and imagination, ice and fire – to go no further; in Dannie Abse's case these might be thought to come together in the vocations of doctor and poet, man of science and man of art.

In the long poem 'Funland', white-coated scientists and black-garbed priests, specialists in body and soul respectively, "confer and dally", apparently finding no difficulty in getting along with each other. The unidentified narrator (seemingly a patient in this asylum-world, world-asylum) sees an "old smelly magician" clad in a "mothy purple cloak" rise up from the ground in a coffin to wave his wand and cause scientists and priests to cavort in the sky. It is, however, a dream or a vision. No more substantial than the outsider-magician is the outsider-poet. He, wearer of a purple coat made of plastic, is a windy phoney whom the inmates fail to recognise for what he is. This comic treatment implies that Dr Abse's tolerance for prestidigitators and vatic rhetoricians is strictly limited. It is to the point to note that in 'A sea-shell for Vernon Watkins' (the most critical elegy – if that is what it is – I've ever read) Watkins is described as "unreal, unearthed" and a "relentless romantic" who "big-talked / how the dead resume the silence of God". Dannie Abse, then, refuses the gaudy, unblemished purple of the sonorous word-magician. His are the poems of a sceptic whose rationalism makes him doubt all religions and their trappings (saints, miracles, superstitions), leaving him with nothing to set against the gross reality of death but a strug-gling humanism. When, in the early 'The second coming', Christ pokes his head through the earth's crust, it is promptly lopped off by a harvesting machine. Less truculently cavalier is the fairly recent villanelle, 'The abandoned', which begins:

> Dear God in the end you had to go.
> Dismissing you, your absence made us sane.
> We keep the bread and wine for show.

The first line is packed with ambiguities that suggest that losses and gains might in this matter cancel each other out. "Dear", the mode of address of the letter-writer, conveys both the expense and value of having a God, while the rest of the line simultaneously suggests that God withdrew of his own volition and that man got rid of him. The tone of the poem vacillates between the sardonic and the wistful.

An urban poet (but infrequently an urbane one), Dannie Abse is notable for his lack of interest in nature and landscape. He is content to be ignorant of the names of wild flowers and is constitutionally incapable of writing about animals (thank goodness – there are enough poets doing it; see the delightful 'Florida'). His positives are human ones – in the fine 'The smile was' the identical expressions on the faces of women who have just given birth; in 'Smile please' the image of marriage – agreeably free from any Larkinesque patina of vulgarity. Such poems as these represent mature Abse at his most "purple"; and with few exceptions his celebratory poems succeed in avoiding the trap of sentimentality and in keeping their lyrical feet on the earth. Firm and sane though these pieces are, however, they are for me outweighed by those which face away from the light. For it is plain that this writer is a death-haunted man. What the white coat of reason seems above all to require of Dannie Abse, Jew and doctor, is a freezing gaze, an unremitting gaze, not only into death's face but into its stripped innards. Repeatedly this subject brings out the best in him (as in greater, but certainly not less honest poets): in clinical, or self-lacerating, or even horrific poetry. And it is on this ground that, doctor and poet, he reconciles – and reconciles triumphantly and memorably – white coat and purple coat. 'Song for Pythagoras' may claim that the style born of such a reconciliation must be "a hybrid", but it is untrue of Dannie Abse's writing. Only in a few early poems, in fact, does his style strike me as uncertain. Characteristically plain and colloquial, eschewing rhetoric and verbal dazzle, the richness of a sensualist or the complexity of a symbolist, it is perfectly suited to its job. In, for instance, 'Pathology of colours', 'In the theatre', 'Case history', 'Exit' and 'Carnal knowledge' Dannie Abse demonstrates conclusively the fiery qualities of ice.

From: *Poetry Wales*, 25.1 (June 1989)

Tony Curtis
Remembrance of Crimes Past

In the introduction to his *Collected Poems 1948-1976* Dannie Abse
uses the image of water refraction to try and explain his approach to
writing poetry. He says,

> For some time now my ambition has been to write poems which appear
> translucent but are in fact deceptions. I would have the reader enter them,
> be deceived he could see through them like sea-water, and be puzzled when
> he can not quite touch bottom.

He goes on to say,

> Perhaps without repetition there would be no character, no style.

I think these are illuminating remarks for Dannie Abse's work as a
whole; they are certainly to be remembered when approaching this
book, his ninth collection of his new poetry. Dannie does repeat
himself; there are incidents in novels which, with a twist of perspective form the basis of a poem; and anecdote emerges fully grown into
a poem; a poem casts another, quite different light on that character
in the autobiography. Underpinning the wide range of his writing is,
always, the character of the man himself. And the range of the
writing is as narrow and universal as the experiences and sympathies
of the man.

To react to *Remembrance of Crimes Past* by cataloguing the
predictability of the subject matter, or of the persona of many of the
poems of personal experience would be to miss the point and to
exhibit a total lack of understanding of Dannie Abse's stated and
longstanding aesthetic. This was done in a sour and myopic review in
The Independent on Sunday by Alan Jenkins who attacked this collection and Dannie Abse. Jenkins is the *TLS* worker who in recent years
has chosen the poems for that journal. As if that were not bad enough,
he has also worked himself into the MorRaineMotion group of those
who would determine the state of British (English) poetry and letters.
I shall be reviewing his first collection in a future issue of *The New
Welsh Review*. As Jenkins points out, Dannie Abse's ninth collection
has many of the concerns which he has shown in the previous eight.

And I am delighted to report it. He also balances the now-typical Abse persona and voice with the folky narrative style which began to appear two or three collections back. And I am delighted to report that too.

Dannie Abse has always been fascinated by dualities and has characterised himself and his life in terms of elements and givens which are sometimes resolved, sometimes constructively held as polarities in his writings. So, in the present book

> When the hospital priest, Father Jerome,
> remarked, "The Devil made the lower parts
> of a man's body, God the upper,"
> I said, "Father, it's the other way round."

and when, in the final poem he describes the great, ornate doors of the Baptistery in Florence as 'The Gates of Paradise', he inverts Michaelangelo's assertion that they were as close to the reality of 'the entrance to Paradise' as anyone might achieve; not so, says the poet, for

> Besides, sunstruck, the animate street's outside;
> so turn these great shut doors around, front to back
> that their name, one perfect day, be accurate.

Consistently, predictably, Dannie Abse has questioned the world, found it wanting, but renewed his faith in the fact of that world, here and now, as *our* world, the only world in which by our actions and beliefs we may play any part in determining dilemmas of existence and morality. In 'A Prescription' he describes the young poet ascending Cadair Idris, from whence one "comes back in dawn's light / lately mad or a great poet." Dannie waits for him "In this dull room of urine- / flask, weighing machine, / examination-couch, x-ray screen". Poets may well be scholars, but, essentially, finally, it is life in the world which determines inspiration. The war-time autopsy corpse who is addressed in 'Carnal Knowledge' exists now only in the poet's mind and his words. The twig that scrapes against the bathroom window is no more than a shadow of the departed spirit while

> Soon I shall climb the stairs, Gratefully,
> I shall wind up the usual clock at bedtime
> (the steam vanishing from the bathroom mirror)
> with my hand, my living hand.

Of course, in order to exemplify the urgency and drama of the here and now a number of Dannie Abse's poems over the years have occupied the banalities of the suburban, the apparently mundane. In 'Anti-Clockwise (2)' the sight of "Des, our grey-haired neighbour, / conspicuous in vest and shorts" leads to a wry meditation on the despair of ageing and desperate attempts to stave off the inevitable that takes in Abishag the Shunammite and Hermann Boerhaave, the thirteenth-century Dutch physician. There are two poems entitled 'Magnolia, Golders Hill Park' which, each in their way take off from the specific plant and location to images of threat,

> with the tree's white blossom
> wildly scattered on the ground,
> a little blood-stained.

and celebration,

> The magnolia soulangeana,
> the umbrella, the sweet bay,
> the magnolia grandflora
> or bull bay,
> and yulan, the Chinese magnolia

That botanical litany is representative of this poet's continuing fascination with language itself. In 'Dulciana' he wakes in an uneasy mood, feeling that there are so many words which he, even he as a writer, has not used, has no knowledge of, even.

> and yes, there are so many
> so many words in the dictionary
> I have never used –
> some undiscovered,
> some half-remembered or half-heard,
> like the distant, honeyless
> buzz of prayer.

Until those last two lines the poem could have been John Tripp in his 'Sandeman' mode. Dannie is a more enduring poet though, because he has avoided the rhetorical nationalist posturing of some of his contemporaries, because he has retained a balance between the accessible voice and the musicality of poetry. John Tripp eschewed form and musicality in favour of the persona of the suffering journalist. He, like John Ormond and Leslie Norris and others, was forced to turn away from the heat of Dylan Thomas's rhetoric. Much that occurred (and did not occur) in the Fifties and Sixties, and even into the Seventies in English poetry in Wales, can be explained by the overwhelming need of a generation of writers to escape the influence of Dylan. Dannie rarely acknowledges his own first collection, accepted when he was still a medical student and published when Dylan Thomas was still astride the literary London of the late Forties. *After Every Green Thing* announces its roots and its inspiration by its Dylanic title. That generation of Welsh writers, more than any since, had the urgent and difficult task of establishing new voices and strategies. I think that the writers of Wales in the 1990s would do well to hold Dannie Abse as a model, as well as R.S. Thomas. Dannie has a commitment to life and, in the long (and all too short) run, that is more important than and not necessarily the same thing as a commitment to Wales. I'm afraid that the featured writer in this year's Cardiff Literature Festival got it wrong. Sing for life, or shut your trap, all the rest's a load of crap.

From: *Poetry Wales* 26.3 (January 1991)

Daniel Weissbort – 'Startled by the Visible'
Selected Poems

When asked to review 1994s generous offering of Dannie Abse's poetry, I accepted almost with alacrity. It seemed to me the piece must write itself. After all he had been around as long as I had been conscious of a "literary world"; for me he belonged to the older-brother generation, i.e. he was "family". Should I say "mishpokhe"? Probably not because, though my parents' generation was rooted in Poland and continental Europe, little of the heritage was passed on: I grew up, the only member of the family born in England, identifying for all my formative years with imperial and then post-imperial British culture, in particular early post-war socialist aspirations, including, it is true, an excursion into socialist Zionism. Abse, on the other hand, born in Cardiff to Welsh-born parents, whose maternal grandmother spoke Welsh (even if with a Patagonian accent!), would seem to have had relatively ready access also to the Jewish, the Yiddish side of his heritage.

As for radicalism, his father was a determined secularist, one older brother became a famous Labour MP. There appears, in any case, to be less of a chasm between his world and the world of his parents than there is for someone like myself. He is a Welsh Jew, or even a Jewish Welshman, whereas I, in spite of the posturing, never became – or never felt myself to be – even an English Jew, let alone a Jewish Englishman (and I certainly was no Pole). Of course, this may have to do with the camouflaged colonial status of Wales, so much more analogous to the grievous condition of the Jews throughout history up to the mid-twentieth century.

Still, at the time, Abse did seem "family", along with the likes of Michael Hamburger, Bernard Kops, Emanuel Litivinoff, Arthur Boyars, Jon Silkin etc. But what were his particular virtues? He was strikingly intelligent and inventively intelligible, witty or more often funny, urban and urbane. He was a man richly of and in this world, that is our world. At the same time, he glanced off, as did we, into other less tangible states of being, capturing those glimpses in lucidly descriptive writing. In short, I read Abse anticipating pleasure – David Wright is quoted as saying of him that it is "nothing less than pleasure" which we get from his poems – the pleasure of recognition, of companionship, of affirmative, older-brother mentorship. He was reliable, a sure, cheerful but not blandly optimistic guide, precisely because he did not pass judgement, did not set out to be a guide. He never lectured, preached or cajoled. He was simply there, in the same place and predicament as us, if a little ahead, and we were glad of it.

The question for me is whether the above picture represents an immature idealisation or a more solid perception of Abse the poet. Perusing this most recent collection reminded me that I had read very little Abse over the last three or four disruptive decades. It took me a while to re-adjust to his eclecticism, his smorgasbord approach. I found myself wondering just how he had managed, in our forgetful times, to survive as well as he had authorially, since he had nothing particularly sensational on offer, or if he had – for instance, his terrifying "medical" poems, such as the much anthologised 'In the

Theatre' – his work was in no way limited or defined by it.

What can a reviewer, looking for striking angles, say about a poet who gives you a bit of everything? Just that? Well, references to Abse's humanism do abound. He sees the extraordinary in the ordinary; starting, as he notes in 'Mysteries' (p. 75), with the visible, he is "startled by the visible". As a doctor, he probably encountered a wider range of folk, heard more odd tales, than your ordinary member of the literary intelligentsia. Furthermore, if I began by suggesting that Abse *belongs* – to Welshness, to Jewishness – it is at least as true that he is poised *between* them, as he also is between medicine, the scientific approach, and poetry, the work of the imagination. (Of course, as that other scientist/poet, the Czech Miroslav Holub, has often said, these two need not, or should not, be seen as mutually exclusive.)

This *betweenness* is memorably expressed in poems like 'Odd' (p. 37) from *Poems Golders Green* (1962), attesting to his divergence from the bohemian norm of his friends in Soho, as much as from the suburban one of his respectable neighbours in Golders Green. Noteworthy is his not entirely untroubled acceptance of this "oddness". That is, he claims no special privilege, aspires to no special status on its account. It pleases me to speculate that, in straddling two worlds which rarely meet, he might be bringing them minimally closer together, materially (insofar as a poem can do this) affecting the balance of power between them. In 'Even' (p. 59), his secularism comes to the fore. "I don't like them, I don't like them" expresses his elemental aversion for the religious Jews he sees on their way to the synagogue on Saturday morning. He questions this: "could it be I am another / tormented anti-semite Jew?" The answer is not, as it would be with so many, "yes", since the next day he sees Christians similarly engaged. His conclusion, "All God's robots lose their charm / who carry prayer books, wear a hat. I don't like them. I don't like them, / and feel less guilty think-ing that." Abse is both of and apart, the balance, to my mind, well nigh perfect, hence the sweet – though it is often bittersweet – sanity that pervades his work. It is, I think, his very rootedness, his affectionate appreciation of his own origins, that permits him to remain suspended so clearsightedly in apparent ambivalence. I am reminded of the injunction that he who aspires to the mystical life (even if we are not here speaking specifically of mysticism) should have strong family ties!

The new Penguin *Selected Poems* is surely the best introduction to Abse's poetry, since it is frugally and discriminatingly drawn from eight of his ten previous volumes, including a handful of early poems. The volume is best read through, I think, from beginning to end, after which, with the landscape of his work in mind, one may return to individual poems or trace the evolution of different themes. As I began by saying, the latter are unusually varied. Abse lives first and writes later, the ensuing thematic multiplicity dissipating any tendency there might have been – this is common enough, after all – to obsessiveness. So, what do we find here? A short list (with much overlapping) would include the large group of poems issuing from his experiences as a doctor (the discursive 'Carnal Knowledge', p. 195, for my money, having it even over the eerie, celebrated 'In the Theatre', p. 95); poems of memory, encapsulations of happenings more comprehensively treated in his fine prose memoirs and memoiristic stories; inventively tender love poems, in the traditional celebratory genre; poems of political or social commentary (his verses against the Vietnam War have worn better than most); clear-eyed but humane portraits of people, especially family; persona poems (he is, dare I say, as good a ventriloquist as Pound, e.g. the "imaginary letter written by an Egyptian lady, during the reign of Amenhotep 111, about 1385 BCE", p. 90); anecdotal poems drawing on Jewish or other legends, sometimes midrashically elaborated; haunting dream-poems.

It is soon apparent that, through it all, Abse is a gifted storyteller. For a start, he is interested in others, quite as much, it seems, as in himself! In his enthralling recent collection of fictionalised memoirs, *There Was a Young Man from Cardiff* – perhaps I am wrong about this, but that's how I read it – his storytelling gifts are engagingly displayed, including an almost Solzhenitsyn-like ability to invest authenticated historical situations with verisimilitude: the suicide of the assimilated Dr Egon Friedell (Friedman) in 1938 Vienna; the youth Grynszpan's assassination, also in 1938, of German Paris embassy official Ernst Vom Rath (actually in *Ash on a Young Man's Sleeve*, Hutchinson 1954, Penguin 1982); security chief Beria at Stalin's deathbed in 1953. The admirable balance maintained by Abse between imaginative flight and grasp of the earthbound actuality is here exemplified. (If he is not a novelist, in the professional sense, it is surely only because he is above all a poet.) He is interested also in the stories that have come down to us, and draws confidently on the different traditions to which he has access, though increasingly on the Judaic one.

I mentioned above the Midrashic characteristic of some of his elaborations, non-biblical as well as biblical. The linearity of this art, its explorative open-ended quality obviously suits Abse's relaxed undogmatic (anti-dogmatic?) nature. This easefulness is apparent not only in the inclusiveness of his storytelling but also in a prosody which employs traditional forms somehow without being beholden to them. Almost cavalierly he breaks or bends the "rules" – and, one has to say, is better when he does. Yet for the most part he does not abandon metre and rhyme for vers-libre. His is workmanlike versification which can occasionally achieve surprising lyric intensity. (The lyric impulse, when it arises, finds him receptive and able, as in the exquisite plain-song 'Joan', p. 137, the visionary evocation of his father on his deathbed, 'Peachstone', p. 81.) This is not, then, simply the art of catchas-catch-can; his is far too disciplined an intellect for that, his tall-story tendencies, for instance, being well leavened by paradox and aphorism, if not by irony and satire. Actually, he seems to me too good humoured to be a satirist, even if he is not above venting his indignation from time to time.

A significant measure of Dannie Abse's achievement is surely his capacity to engage the dark side, the unnameable (though, in his attentive, circumstantial descriptiveness he comes close to concretizing it), the time-conscious angst of the human condition, the apprehension of a voracious, invasive void, the agonising bewilderment to which we are heir amidst all our knowledge, our science. As suggested above, it is perhaps his rootedness, his basic happiness, if you like, that enables him to explore these regions with such intrepidity. He is not – as was John Betjeman, for instance; whose fearful morbidity produced many terrifying ditties – a tormented spirit, his gaze is not helplessly riveted to what horrifies him. But, as with the lyrical impulse, when the vision becomes real, he recognises it, accepts it properly, as something integral, that is without subjecting it to interrogation, to analysis, or any other such familiar diversionary procedure. A perhaps not quite typical example is the bleak 'A Night Out' (p. 56) where he and his wife go to see a recommended Polish film set in Auschwitz. A few bare notations follow: "Afterwards, at a loss, we sipped coffee / in a bored espresso bar nearby / saying very little". Finally they return home, assuring themselves that the children are alright, go to bed and make love (that is, life is affirmed, because what is the alternative?). Nothing more. The poem teeters on the edge of triteness, which given the subject it was bound to do. But, Abse, at his distance from the events, manages nevertheless to utter something rather than succumbing to silence. He manages because he absolutely eschews commentary (even implicit commentary, I think, of the kind suggested by my parenthetic remark above). In 'The Weeping' (p. 120) he recounts a near-dream or protodream, not attempting to interpret or even characterise it so much as, again, simply to realise the experience of it as it was, leaving in the reader's mind a rich after-effect which, whatever it elucidates, does so within a far larger context than any interpretation might have provided. There are more sinister, ominous dream narrations or evocations than that but my point is that Abse's tactful literalism, as it were, makes him the ideal transmitter of such material. I am tempted to ask (simplistic as this must appear and probably is) whether what we are hearing is the scientist, needing to establish the facts first, or the Jew, approaching problematical material in a curiously direct, intimate way – such being characteristic, we are often told, of his transactions with The Almighty as well. Fancifully perhaps, I catch echoes of an ancient dialogue or artfulness though Abse, as ever, deploys this alongside a thoroughly modern apprehension of reality and of the means at a writer's disposal.

From: *The Jewish Quarterly* (Autumn 1994)

Katie Gramich
Selected Poems

Dannie Abse's poems usually prompt critics to reach for their genial adjectives: liberal, humane, compassionate, sane, civilised, and so on. All of these are undoubtedly applicable to Abse's work, as it is displayed in this generous *Selected Poems*, but none does justice to the distinctiveness and the complexity of his poetic voice. Abse is a poet who manages to be both popular and erudite, often in the same poem, a poet who has you reaching for your dictionary (or medical textbook) one minute and laughing out loud the next. He's a poet whose complexities stem from the variety of his own identities: as Jew, Welshman, doctor, poet; the tensions generated among these identities energise the poetry in a Yeatsian fashion. Abse offers different, often surprising, perspectives which frustrate readerly expectations: a poem with the title 'Of Two Languages' for example, sets up certain expectations in the Welsh reader which are deflected when the poem turns out to be about Hebrew and Yiddish. Like Yeats and Edward Thomas, Abse exploits his multiple identities or masks in his poetry, often making them explicitly the subject of his texts, as in 'Song for Pythagoras' and in 'Duality', the latter of which is reminiscent of Edward Thomas's poem, 'The Other'.

Fundamentally lyrical in tone, Abse's poems nevertheless contain a refreshing directness of utterance, a transparent crispness which is often colloquial. Sometimes, it must be admitted, the expression lapses into mawkishness, as in the penultimate stanza of 'Duality'. The poet takes risks with a vernacular idiom which on occasion comes dose to doggerel, for instance in 'The Trial', but he is also capable of transforming the even texture of a poem with vivid, arresting images, as in 'Elegy for Dylan Thomas':

> At the dear last, the yolk broke in his head,
> blood of his soul's egg in a splash of bright voices
> and now he is dead.

or in 'In Llandough Hospital':

> Here comes the night with all its stars,
> bright butchers' hooks for man and meat.

There is a strong element of humour in Abse's work, which certainly adds to its popular appeal, but the humour is often bizarre or macabre. Meic Stephens has alluded to Abse's penchant for the eccentric in human nature, and this is one of the sources of the Absean comedy, as in 'The Death of Aunt Alice'.

There is aesthetic pleasure to be gained from the neat, composed formality of his verse, often in quatrains or rhyming couplets, whose naturalness and unobtrusiveness bespeak the utter competence of the poetic craftsman. Emotionally, the poems are frequently moving in their honest chronicling of pain and impotence, as found in the poems about Vietnam, the Holocaust, and on the death of mother and father. Many of the poems here seem to stem directly from Abse's experience as a doctor and these are, for me, among the most affecting and poignant, particularly because of their lack of sentimentality. Memorably, in the late poem 'Carnal Knowledge', the speaker addresses the corpse which he is dissecting:

> You, corpse, I pried into your bloodless meat
> without the morbid curiosity of Vesalius...
> I dug deep into your stale formaldehyde
> unaware of Pope Boniface's decree
> but, as instructed, violated you –
> the reek of you in my eyes, my nostrils,
> clothes, in the kisses of my girlfriends.
> You, anonymous. Who were you, mister?
> Your thin mouth could not reply, 'Absent, sir,'
> or utter with inquisitionary rage.

The second person, 'you', is one of the most favoured voices in the selection, and Abse handles the direct address with skill and ease, unsettling the reader with what appears to be an intimate appeal or accusation. The most common voice of all, though, is the first person speaker and perhaps this congenial, confessional voice is one of the most appealing aspects of the poetry, reminiscent of the autobiographical prose works for which Abse is also renowned. It is this voice which so often elicits from us, as readers, the direct human response, the recognition of a mood, an experience, which is common and hitherto unarticulated in this way:

> And I? I, sober now, come down the stairs
> to eat an apple, to taste the snow in it,

to switch the light on at the maudlin time.
Habitual living room, where the apple-flesh
turns brown after the bite, oh half my life
has gone to pot. And, now, too tired for sleep,
I count up the Xmas cards childishly,
assessing, *Jesus*, how many friends I've got!

'Portrait of the Artist as a Middle-Aged Man'

Abse is in a sense a very masculine poet, celebrating the man's experience of marriage in the early 'Epithalamion' in a beautifully sculpted, lyrical form. In the selection from *Journals from the Ant-Heap* recently published in *The New Welsh Review* (no. 22, Autumn 1993) for instance, Abse takes it for granted that poets are by definition men and that wives are useful as sympathetic readers of their work! Nevertheless, there are a number of poems in this selection which deal sensitively with women's experiences, such as 'Portrait of a Marriage' and 'The Smile Was'. I have some reservations about the latter, which celebrates women as mothers and looks upon their experience of childbirth from the male doctor's point of view. It seems carping to be negative about this tribute to women and yet I do feel that it tends to essentialise women and conflate them into one Great Mother: *das ewig Weibliche!* There is, by the way, an undertone of anti-German feeling in the poems which I find distasteful, especially as it sometimes manifests itself as cartoon-Nazi expletives: *Sieg Heil!* actually appears in more than one poem!

On the whole, though, this is a selection which reasserts Abse's position as one of the most individual and worthwhile poets writing in English today. The emphasis of this volume is, quite properly, on the poet's later work, but the reader will find some startling and marvellous poems from all periods of Abse's poetic career. One of my favourites is 'A Sea-shell for Vernon Watkins', which I think captures Abse's characteristically melancholic tone while exhibiting his formal dexterity and his command of the appropriate image:

A stage moon and you, too, unreal, unearthed.
Then two shadows athletic down the cliffs
of Pennard near the nightshift of the sea.
You spoke of Yeats and Dylan, your sonorous
pin-ups. I thought, *relentless romantic!*

Darkness stayed in a cave and I lifted
a sea-shell from your shadow when you
   big-talked
how the dead resume the silence of God.

The bank calls in its debts and all are earthed.
Only one shadow at Pennard today
and listening to another sea-shell I found,
startled, its phantom sea utterly silent
– the shell's cochlea scooped out. Yet
   appropriate
that small void, that interruption of sound,
for what should be heard in a shell at Pennard
but the stopped breath of a poet who once sang
   loud?

From: *Poetry Wales* 30.2 (September 1994)

John Lucas
New and Collected Poems

I first came across the name of Dannie Abse in 1957, when, with
Howard Sergeant, he coedited an anthology of contemporary
poetry called *Mavericks*. *Mavericks* was intended as a riposte to
Robert Conquest's *New Lines*, which had appeared a year earlier
and which soon became identified as the anthology that brought the
Movement to public attention. Not only that. What were perceived
to be the Movement's virtues (or vices) threatened to usurp the little
realm of poetry. Plain speaking, shapeliness, modesty, wit, were
pitted against 'filthy Mozart', 'the myth kitty', 'foreign places', and
the poet as bard, bohemian and boozing braggadocio. When George
MacBeth gave a reading at the South Place Ethical Society in the
autumn of 1958, he wore a belted mackintosh and bicycle clips. This
was no doubt intended as parody but the poem he read about
feeling guilt at drowning wasps in a water-filled jam jar was, if not
pure Movement, certainly *proxime accessit*. And Charles Tomlinson,

who had no love for the Movement – the poems he had sent Conquest were rejected (he took his revenge in a swingeing review of *New Lines* in the journal, *Essays in Criticism*) – was, if anything, even more ferocious in his denunciation of what he called "Gamin contemporary / With Gosse... dressed / in the skin of a Welsh lion."

Tomlinson's sneer at the maverick Dylan Thomas, bereft of the Oxbridge education that had been undergone by all followers along *New Lines*, was par for the course. I imagine most readers of this review will be on the side of the world's mavericks. But there is a problem. In a letter to Sergeant that forms his share of the Introduction to their anthology, Dannie Abse remarks of the Movement poets that "they distrust the image and seem to fear primary Dionysian excitement: it is as if they're afraid of the mystery conversing with the mystery – or to put it into contemporary jargon – the depth mind talking to the depth mind". ("Too reasonable, too truthful," Yeats said, when he rejected James Reeves from his *Oxford Book of Modern Verse*, "We poets should be gay, warty lads".) Combative stuff, and I notice that in the generous review of his *Collected* in the *Guardian* (15.3.03), the reviewer, Nicholas Wroe, reports that Abse was "a leading protagonist in the main literary row of the decade" – i.e. *Mavericks* versus *New Lines*. This is about as sensible as claiming that the major political row of 2003 is over Prince Charles's treatment of his servants. Not only were there infinitely more important literary arguments during the 1950s than this minor spat, more significantly most of the nine poets in *Mavericks* could as easily have fitted into *New Lines*. (Which also featured the work of nine poets.) Only Jon Silkin – and perhaps David Wright – is markedly different.

And Dannie Abse, surely? But no, not really. Of the five poems he contributed, three have made it into his *New and Collected*. True, in all there are echoes of Thomas: "I am that man twice upon this time: / my two voices sing to make one rhyme" ('Duality'), "when we lie down under the same earth / in a dry, silly box" ('Letter to *The Times*'), "Oh nightly something secret breathes and moves" ('Looking at a Map' – oh, oh, those fatal ohs); but these all feel to be stylistic borrowings rather than the sharing of a vision: dutiful as opposed to – well, Dionysian. Besides, there has been some lowering of the rhetorical temperature since 1957. The voices in 'Duality' that cry "all his raving days / until they die on his double-crossed head" survive into the book under review, but in the concluding invocation "Oh Christ, take this one and leave me all", "Time" has replaced "Christ."

A good thing, too. For Abse's virtues have very little to do with the "peculiar rant" on behalf of which he took up cudgels in *Mavericks*. Accordingly, when, years later, in 1989, he came to edit the *Hutchinson Book of British Post-War Poets*, he there remarks that "the pitch, tone, strategy, bias of the Movement poets has predominated, with modifications, to the present day." Whether this assessment is accurate matters less than that it is essentially true of Abse's own work, the best as well as the worst. So much so, indeed, that he called one collection, *A Small Desperation* and another *Way Out in the Centre*. This last is, in truth, a not very sensible title, but the collection itself contains a number of fine poems. To say that these characteristically recognise or testify to a humanist position, while undeniable, is not to scant what seems to this reader a yearning for certainties that have to be repudiated. And it is the tension between the two poles that makes for much that is best – most imaginatively and intellectually scrupulous – in the poems. The title comes from the last line of a poem to Donald Davie, that man of extremes and, like Dryden's Zimri, "So over violent or over-civil / That man with him was either God or Devil", and Abse establishes his own template in the collection's short, opening 'Joan's', with its equivocal registering of evening cold on the spring crocus, "snow melts falling", and, indoors, piano music from which "one note's gone", leaving, though, other notes: "Also the left background. / Their rejoicing, lamenting, candid sound." Abse isn't an especially gifted rhymer, but here the closing rhyme, firm but unemphatic, rather beautifully acknowledges a consonance in which rejoicing and lamenting are held in equipoise.

A different kind of balance is struck in 'The Doctor' who "does not always like his patients", and who has to shush "Cerberus! Soon enough you'll have a bone / or two." Out of context there is an almost brutal flippancy about that enjambment, but the poem as a whole steers its way with great tact between various tones, each of which courts the parodic in order to defeat the simplifications of unguarded absolutes.

Or, as variation, there is a dark, deep humour. (Abse can be a very funny poet.) 'Of Itzig and his Dog' is, literally, a shaggy dog story, and Itzig himself is a character who turns up in several later individual collections, in all instances a kind of droll, Jewish holy fool. Jewishness is, it goes without saying, crucially important in the poems, from first to last.

Among the most telling examples is 'Case History' (from *Ask the Bloody Horse*), which reports the words of a patient who first of all tells Dr Abse that "Most Welshmen are worthless, / an inferior breed", and then goes on to praise "the architects / of the German death-camps". Yet, the doctor poet reports, "I prescribed for him / as if he were my brother." The poem ends:

> Later that night I must have slept
> on my arm: momentarily
> my right hand lost its cunning.

This laconicism, which increasingly characterises the note of Abse's poems, is a much-encompassing strategy or, it may be more proper to say, habit of mind – hard won, no doubt – that makes possible his best work. At the end of his lovely poem 'A Salute on the Way', which is dedicated to Peter Porter, he says "Friend, let's not hurry. Who believes / these days in a second edition?" The wry, humanist scepticism of this, a world away from the Dionysian, is not without its astringent pleasures. Such pleasures abound for any reader of this *New and Collected*.

From: *Poetry Wales* 39.1 (Spring 2003)

William Oxley – 'Undiminished Powers'
Running Late

All the old skill with words and features of style of this poet are here, and as subtly vigorous as ever. It is a pleasure to hear so distinct a voice, like a friend heard in the next room immediately recognisable by tone and arrangement of speech. Like Graves, like Larkin, like Ken Smith, Dannie Abse has an inimitable, always recognisable style. I will try to demonstrate this later. But one thing has to be recorded first, and that is the utter poignancy which hangs over this volume – which includes some dedicated love poems – because of the death of the poet's wife, Joan Abse, in a car crash last year. Especially for those who knew the Abses, a terrible and unfair irony seeps from these last love poems to Joan. Not the irony of Hardy's 'too late I have loved thee' poems to Emma, his deceased wife; rather the irony of the reader knowing the shattering blow to follow the almost serene uxory of Abse's late poems to his wife.

The characteristic of Abse's style, which makes it most genuinely a thing of poetry, is his command of surprising imagery. In the one poem which refers back to the poet's childhood, he says, in answer to the Catholic Brother teacher in the school he attended, 'All I believe in, Brother, is wonder'. It has been his constant faith, wonder; and it is why his imagery and his apercus so often surprise, 'Between the black tree trunks / the snow, white as a frightened eye'; his gift of being able to compress a whole mythology into a single line, as the one that ends this quote:

> Names have destinies. Write your own. Do not forge
> a known sculptor's in Sleep's Visiting Book.
>
> Else boulders will crash down. Like wood, malice of stone:
> wood once took revenge on a carpenter's son.

Truly, the powerful compression of that last line startles. Poetry is surely the newest possible way of expressing the known and the unknown.

If, as Shakespeare says, 'Brevity is the soul of wit', then clearly it is a lesson Abse has well learned. And not just an imagist brevity, but by having honed and pared his anecdotal impulse as a beautiful, even elegant underpinning structure to so many of his poems. There are some fine anecdotal poems in this volume – two of which I particularly commend. The first, 'A Welsh Peace Offering', which, I surmise, is based on some folk tale of the Cymri. Not only does it encompass a story in a mere 35 lines but it is also a developed paradigm of universal human nature. Similarly, if differently, 'The Jeweller', arising from a comment made by a man, seemingly a jeweller by trade, chauffeuring the poet home after a poetry reading, in shorter compass still, develops a sudden illumination to the point of creating that artistic synthesis of thought and feeling, that state of mind both Blake and Keats spoke of and the latter called 'negative capability', or moment of detachment that enables us to perceive a truth most clearly. In the very small compass of this poem there is sudden mental development – a noetic moment of revelation and change.

A life spent devoted to another profession as well as poetry – in Abse's case, medicine – means that the poet runs the risk of a fatal prejudicing, because any profession or discipline of necessity takes a specialised view of reality. To his credit, Abse has struggled against this tendency towards a one-view-of-reality mind-set and the conflict between science and magic: his 'white coat versus purple coat' has shaped his poetry decisively in both style and content. John Heath-Stubbs once described himself as 'a classical romantic'; and I once described Ken Smith as a 'romantic realist'. Abse is a romantic pragmatist with an occasional sweet and an occasional harsh string to his lyre:

> Religion is beyond belief!
> And it's no use shaking a fist
> at the sky when a star falls.
> > ('A Postcard to Oneself')

and:

> And how's your life? Static too? Do you wait,
> as I do, numb, for something to happen
> until it happens? If so, join the queue.
> It stretches all the way to the Old People's Home.
> > ('At the Concert')

but:

> Hurrah, though, I say whenever two dare to marry.
> It's such a brisk signal of optimism, isn't it?
> Like Eve saying Au revoir on leaving Paradise.
>   ('Letter to Stanley Moss')

There is so much else I could quote from this marvellous book of poetry but space denies it. Let me just give two further thoughts on its making – the poetry I mean. The wit expressed is that famed element of Jewish humour that has been thoroughly Englished. The 18th century needed no Jewish input: its wit, which often ran to acres of print in Pope and Charles Churchill, nevertheless invented the briefest and sharpest of instruments: the heroic and satiric couplet. Jewish humour in the hands of Abse and other Jews has made wit far less impersonal and more personally anecdotal. And, finally, in Abse's poetry we have clear traces of that Welsh passion – the same that animated Dylan Thomas – but put over on not so loud a lyre, but quietly, tensely effective as Edward Thomas played.

This is an excellent new book of poems from an octogenarian poet whose powers are still undiminished.

From: *The London Magazine* (June/July 2006)

7. Essays

Jeremy Robson – 'Dannie Abse in Focus'

Both as a poet and as an editor Dannie Abse has always shown a healthy indifference to prevailing literary fashions. In the early 1950s, as editor of the magazine *Poetry and Poverty*, he published many young poets who today are well-known, and in his editorials adopted a generally critical attitude to the rather flat, neutral poetry then in vogue – the poetry of the so-called Movement Poets. Indeed, when in 1957 he co-edited with Howard Sergeant the anthology *Mavericks*, it was largely in order to present the work of some of the good poets who had been excluded from the recently published, Movement-dominated *New Lines* anthology. In an introductory note to *Mavericks* Dannie Abse wrote: 'Language, the Movement believes, should be straight and unadorned. It would be all right if they were just anti-rhetorical. But the Lucky Jim attitude is – apart from anything else – fundamentally anti-poetic... With the Movement Poets one hardly ever gets the impression that the poem has seized the poet and that a struggle has ensued between the poem and the poet, between the nameless, amorphous, Dionysian material and the conscious, law-abiding, articulating craftsman.'

By this time two books of Abse's own poems had appeared, and a third, *Tenants of the House*, was about to come out. When it did, it showed clearly that he, for one, was writing outside the Movement tradition, and what's more was prepared to take risks and look beyond his own back garden for his subject matter. The best poems in *Tenants of the House* are eloquent without being rhetorical ('Letter to the Times'), dramatic without being vulgar ('Duality', 'The Trial', lyrical without being sweet ('Anniversary'). The achievement was summed up by the *Listener*'s poetry critic: 'Dr. Abse's admirable new book of poems shows that while the rest of us have been spending our time being smart or angry or whatever, he has quietly consolidated his position as one of the most satisfying and genuine of contemporary poets, with things to say that matter and the power to say them forcefully and originally.' The success of the volume was all the more surprising when seen within the context of Abse's earlier work, which was too inexact, too bound up with its own music and conceits (and with the music and conceits of others) to be of enduring value – though there were exceptions: the much anthologised

'Letter to Alex Comfort', for example, and the lyrical 'Epithalamion'. That Abse himself recognises the flaws is perhaps evidenced by the fact that he included only four of the early poems in his recently published *Selected Poems*.

Abse brings to his work a wide range of experience. Born in Cardiff in 1923, he is in fact a medical doctor. Although he has lived in London more or less since qualifying, Wales in general (and Cardiff in particular) has remained important to him. This is shown clearly in poems like 'Return to Cardiff', and in his autobiographical novel *Ash On a Young Man's Sleeve*, in which he recreates vividly the Welsh-Jewish experiences of his childhood, setting them against the general troubled backcloth of the times – unemployment, the rise of Hitler and Mussolini, the Spanish Civil War, and so on. He has always had a predilection for the dramatic, and it is not surprising that quite early on he was drawn to write for the theatre. (Out of one of the less successful poems in *Tenants of the House* – 'The Meeting' – evolved a play, *House of Cowards*, which won the Charles Henry Foyle Award.) There is also in his poetry, as well as in later plays such as *Gone*, or his recent novel *O. Jones, O. Jones*, a strong element of humour, always underpinned by an accurate observation of the strange, the ludicrous, the human.

This relationship to the real world has become an important anchor in Dannie Abse's more recent work. Whereas *Tenants of the House* displays a metaphysical approach to its various themes, his next book, *Poems, Golders Green* (1962) is deeply rooted in a specific environment – the city, or more specifically suburbia. The poems in this volume are generally more direct than hitherto, and the strong impact they have had on audiences when read aloud is hardly surprising. They are very much the poems of an outsider living in an 'in' community, and the theme of alienation, of oddity, runs through the book. One poem, 'Odd', is in many ways characteristic of the volume, contrasting the writer's inability to fit into 'nice, quiet, religious' Golders Green with his inability to fit into 'nice, dirty, irreligious' Soho. In both places he wants 'to scream' and thus 'by the neighbours' then 'by Soho friends' is considered 'odd'.

In Golders Green, of course, one's neighbours may well be Jewish, which gives this particular suburb an added dimension. In the volume there is a handful of poems touching on Jewish themes – ranging from the lyrical 'Song of a Hebrew' to the eloquent 'After the

Release of Ezra Pound'. Commenting on this in the Poetry Book Society's Bulletin (the book was their Spring Choice), Abse wrote: 'Hitler made me more of a Jew than Moses'. Such 'Jewishness' as there is in the volume – and it would be wrong to dwell overlong on it – is often symbolic. Abse certainly recognises this, for when asked in an interview whether Jewish notes entered his work, he replied: 'Sometimes, yes; and often in an obscure or arcane way. Without conscious design on my part, I find myself working, for example, on a poem about the remnant of a tree that has previously been struck by lightning. In short, a misfit of a tree rather than say, a tall, straight, beautiful elm. Or I take as subject matter a shunter – you know those slow, slave-like engines you see on railway tracks – rather than an express train. That I choose one subject rather than another, even if not consciously, seems to me to have something to do with the fact that I am a Jew living in the 20th century; and therefore someone who must be aware of the situational predicament of the Jew in a special, close way.' Certainly there is a powerful emotional charge behind these particular poems, as there is in a new poem, 'No More Mozart', included here:

> The German streets tonight
> are soaped in moonlight.
> The streets of Germany are clean
> like the hands of Lady MacBeth...

Throughout *Poems, Golders Green* the symbols of earlier poems recur – the mask is one favourite. There is also a sequence of lyrically haunting love poems ('Three Voices') which harks back to earlier volumes – only now the voice is sure and economical. This sureness is perhaps most striking in 'The Water Diviner', a mysterious, spiritual poem about the lack of inspiration and the self-doubt which all artists suffer – and not only artists, for the poem is about religious doubt also:

> Repeated desert, recurring drought,
> sometimes hearing water trickle,
> sometimes not, I by doubting first,
> believe; believing, doubt.

By talking about or attempting to outline a poet's themes one is of course distorting, paraphrasing the unparaphrasable. Many of the poems in Dannie Abse's most recent book, *A Small Desperation* (1968) in fact explore those areas of experience which defy articulation. Odours, distant tunes, voices behind the voices that we hear – these appeared obsessively in the earlier poems as *ideas,* never quite inhabiting them. In *A Small Desperation* they return. There are 'inviolate odours in halls', silhouettes 'running across the evening fields, knee deep in mist,' the 'darkness inside a dead man's mouth'. Disturbing images these, but concrete, and organic. And the volume *is* a deeply serious, at times grave one, which contains a number of Abse's most ambitious poems. There is in it a new, at times tragic intensity, an obsession with death, with the inanimate, with the indefinable 'nameless' things which order our existence:

> There is something else that I must do
> for some other thing is crying too
> in chaos, near, without a name.

Although the poems are patently contemporary, they avoid pat answers and glib slogans ('protesting poems, like the plaster angels / are impotent...'). Rather they pose questions, offer ambiguities and unusual correlations. Their range, too, is impressive. There is wit and lyricism, social irony and political self-questioning. Also, there is a new element, for this is the first volume in which Abse draws on his experiences as a doctor, both thematically and as a source of imagery (as he does, too, in his latest play, *The Dogs of Pavlov*). The long last poem of the book ('The Smile Was') draws explicitly and affirmatively on the medical background, taking as its starting point the invariable, wonderful smile of a woman who has just given birth. Roland Mathias commented on this affirmative aspect of Abse's work in the *Anglo-Welsh Review*: 'He is no friend to the wry down turn, to the non-committed fragmentization so fashionable recently, to the ultimate cynicism. In his pages there is such a thing as love and, despite moments of non-communication and despair, there are also spiritual intuitions.... The reader who is not himself unsanguine will from time to time cry "True" with the delighted recognition that one accords to something experienced in life but seldom read in the work of serious modern poets.'

Such affirmations may be unusual in a world of Vietnams, yet they never seem false or merely romantic. On the contrary, as in all Dannie Abse's best work the real experience comes through compellingly –

the strength of the voice, the originality of the observation and the inferences he draws from it, opening up unsuspected areas of response and potentiality in the reader and giving the poems a range and character rarely matched by the work of his contemporaries.

From: *Modern Poets in Focus* (Corgi Books, 1971)

John Tripp – 'Dannie Abse revisited'

'Nothing but the enjoyable and the enlivening deserves pushing under any nose,' Geoffrey Grigson has written, rather superficially and optimistically for so grizzled a veteran. Perhaps now that he is nearer the end than the beginning, he requires a few laughs. I think he might appreciate some of Dannie Abse's *Collected Poems* (Hutchinson, cased £4.95; paperback £2.50), though with crusty old Grigson you never know. They are enjoyable because most of them are well-made, they can be understood at a first or second reading which pleases both the author and his considerable follow- ing; they are enlivening because many of them contain moments of humour, give the same satisfaction as a good short story, and are very much of our time in being framed within recognisable situa- tions; and several of them, the core of Abse's achievement, convey a real feeling of unease, which is what interests me most. There are few contemporary practitioners in English who communicate such a sense of something very nasty continuing, through us and around us – a sort of disquieting apprehension that things are about to fall apart even in the most banal and humdrum circumstances. It is as if he really wishes to celebrate only the spontaneous joys, the hopes and consolations of living, but is overtaken by his knowledge of the dust we each come to. Gently, tenderly, compassionately he reminds us – in sadness and some wonder – of the common fate.

Dannie Abse's is a success story only on the unimportant, surface level: doctor, poet, prose-writer, playwright, editor-critic, dabbler in publishing, radio and television contributor, quality impresario, star at readings all over the place. (I believe the one material ambition he has left is to live at Ninian Park and become manager of Cardiff City, whose fortunes he has followed for many years as they go up and down like a yo-yo between the divisions. His poem 'The game' is his good, sentimental tribute to association football.) If Dylan Thomas was one of the few modern poets to be famous in his own lifetime, then Dannie Abse looks like being another, his fame coming partly from being seen and heard regularly on screen and platform; as opposed to the fame of R.S. Thomas, who most of the time retreats from the limelight and thus gains a widespread reputation for monastic inaccessibility.

On the more important, below-surface level – which is what should really matter to a poet – Abse seems to me to be revealed as one who is quietly but agonisingly aware of our tragic failure to survive (as Philip Larkin wrote: 'Life is first boredom, then fear. / Whether we use it or not, it goes'). His fairly polished and assured manner does not quite disguise the fact that through his experience in medicine and his observation as a poet he is both fascinated and appalled by our slow, pitiful decay. Given this fundamentally grave and sombre view of our predicament, no one should be surprised if the notion is put forward that Abse may attempt to relieve his painful vision by maximum activity, cultivating a persona of outward success, assisted by an instinct for PR, turning a modest dollar (nothing wrong with that) and the glossier side of literary life. He is an influential person who seems to know everyone, and everyone knows him. There is a touch of glamour about Dannie Abse. I can see him now – warm, approachable, that nice, kind face and those sad eyes – and hear his pleasant, persuasive voice reading poems which put a chill through you. Then afterwards, perhaps in conversation, the charm and politeness are broken only by an occasional stinging comment or an expression of slight weariness as an admirer asks yet another inevitable and boring question.

How fortunate, then, to be Dr Abse. Or not? Behind the unruffled front, beneath the veneer of success and the confidence of unhindered progress, I have often detected a rational, benevolent pessimism, a man 'looking upon the world with the eyes of a perpetual convalescent,' as he puts it. One of the walking wounded, in other words, and not necessarily on the mend – though he would have us believe that his use of the word 'convalescent' means merely that he is trying to see life in fresh, 'rinsed' colours. His present volume spans the whole 28-year range of his published work from 'The Uninvited', written in 1948, through *Walking Under Water, Tenants of the House, Poems Golders Green,* and *A Small Desperation* to 'Funland', published in 1972, and also includes a section of 13 new poems which have not appeared in book form. It contains all the work he wishes to preserve. At 53, plus a slice of autobiography *A Poet in the Family,* this looks enough, giving us a total of 114 poems to be going on with until he collects Volume Two in old age, a treat in store which he hopes to be able to deliver. Compared with the outputs of, say, Larkin or Geoffrey Hill, Roland Mathias or John Ormond, Dannie Abse is indeed prolific, even if he happened to be an early starter. (I do not agree, incidentally, with one of his favourite aphorisms in an introductory note to this collection: 'Nothing is, unless another knows it too.' Did not, for instance, Hopkins' early verse exist although no one else knew of it for some years?)

A handful of poems gives Abse his reputation, and this is all he needs. At its lowest, in his more lightweight structures, that reputation has come under attack for its presentation of a confessional, London Welsh Jewish 'victim' who believes that modern, urban, confused, middle-class existence is decent subject-matter for poetry. Rubbish, say these shocked reviewers, who shy away from any aspect of contemporary realism, and accuse Abse of representational modishness. They forget that many of us are already tired of the current preoccupation with myth, old stones, back-to-nature tracts and soliloquies in ancient ruins at the height of a Celtic storm. Their idea of a perfect poem would be the result of a serious practitioner going into the wastes of Northumbria, Mercia or Cambria and there contemplating his navel while meditating deeply on the past – all this eked out in prosy, incomprehensible gobbets. Here and now, in the second half of the twentieth century, one would think that fit subjects for poetry were only to be found in the wilder countryside and mountains, never among the aerials and estates of the suburbs. (*People* live there, you see, and preferably we should have a landscape without figures.) Abse makes his point:

> But no! Done for in the ignorant suburb,
> I'll drink Scotch, neurotically stare through glass
> at the rainy lawn, at green stuff, nameless birds,
> and let my daughter, madam, go to nature class.
> I'll not compete with those nature poets you advance,

some in the country dialect, and some in dialogue
with the country – few as calm as their words:
Wordsworth, Barnes, sad John Clare who ate grass.
(From: 'As I was saying')

It is true that he has put on a fashionable, liberal-radical *New Statesman* shirt (e.g. 'Demo against the Vietnam war, 1968', 'Haloes') too often for some tastes, and slides easily into smartness and throw-away journalistic cliché (parts of 'Miss Book World', 'The death of Aunt Alice', 'Car journeys', 'The bereaved' etc.), though charitably one could say that such technique in these particular cases was almost justified, appropriate to the content and journalistic only in its concision. But these are piffling, secondary elements on the edge of Abse's main effort which, as I said, is concerned with this grave apprehension of disaster and a recognition of the terrifying in the midst of ordinariness. He believes that poetry should be written out of a personal predicament – hopefully reaching beyond itself to shared 'universal' experience – not as an essay turned into neat, civilised verse; and his commitment to the difficulty of doing this is total. He has written about things which appear everyday and commonplace; then he suddenly injects the icy unmentionable, and succeeds in making 'large statements out of small concerns':

> By my wife now, I lie quiet as a
>   thought of how moon and stars might blur,
>   and miles of smoke squirm overhead
>   rising to Man's arbiter;
>
> the grey skin shrivelling from the head,
>   our two skulls in the double bed,
>   leukaemia in the soul of all
>   flowing through the blood instead.
>
> 'No,' I shout, as by her side I sprawl,
>   'No,' again, as I hear my small,
>   dear daughter whimper in her cot,
>   and across the darkness call.

(From: 'Verses at night')

Who wrote in margins hieroglyphic notations,
that obscenity, deleted this imperfect line?
Read by whose hostile eyes, in what bed-sitting rooms,
in which rainy, dejected railway stations?

(From: 'Public library')

Later, late, again, far their echoes rage;
hurt, plaintive whistles; hyphenated trucks;
sexual cries from funnels – all punctuate
the night, a despair beyond language.

(From: 'The Shunters')

I don't know why else an official postmark
should make me think thus. He whom I mourned is
half forgot: a sandpaper chin, a smile, a voice,
and the rest is not silence but dark.

(From: 'Postmark')

Quite suddenly, six mourners appear:
a couple together, then three stout men,
then one more, lagging behind, bare-headed.
Not one of the six looks up at the sky,
and not one of them touches the railings.
They walk on and on remembering days,
yet seem content. They employ the decor.
They use this grey inch of eternity,
and the afternoon, so praised, grows distinct.

(From: 'From a suburban window')

So in the simple blessing of a rainbow,
in the bevelled edge of a sunlit mirror,
I have seen, visible, Death's artifact
like a soldier's ribbon on a tunic tacked.

(From: 'Pathology of colours')

For that night his wife brought him a peach,
his favourite fruit, while the sick light glowed,
and his slack, dry mouth sucked, sucked, sucked,
with dying eyes closed – perhaps for her sake –
till bright as blood the peachstone showed.

(From: 'Peachstone')

There are many other examples: the awful grief at his dying father's bedside in 'At Llandough Hospital'; the cold, depressed backward look in the early hours of a New Year's Day in 'Portrait of the artist as a middle-aged man', before he notes "I count up the Xmas cards child-ishly, / assessing, *Jesus*, how many friends I've got!"; the wry transfer of names and numbers from an old to 'A new diary' ("for all lose, no-one wins, / those in, those out, this at the heart of things."); the sickness at human waste – "So Violence, beery, lonely as an old tune, / lifts his lapel to smell the paper poppy" – in 'Remembrance Day'.

I am not competent to assess the value of Abse's experience as a diagnostic physician in providing material for verse, but the remark-able 'Pathology of colours', 'The smile was' and 'In the theatre' are explicitly medical. His shuddering horror story is 'In the theatre', based on a true incident and headed by a chilling comment from his eldest brother, Wilfred: 'Only a local anaesthetic was given because of the blood pressure problem. The patient, thus, was fully awake throughout the operation. But in those days – in 1938, in Cardiff, when I was Lambert Rogers' dresser – they could not locate a brain tumour with precision. Too much normal brain tissue was destroyed as the surgeon crudely searched for it, before he felt the resistance of it... all somewhat hit and miss. One operation I shall never forget...' It is a skilful poem of considerable power, describing the criminal mess of the operation:

> If items of horror can make a man laugh
> then laugh at this: one hour later, the growth
> still undiscovered, ticking its own wild time;
> more brain mashed because of the probe's braille path; ...
>
> Then, suddenly, the cracked record in the brain,
> a ventriloquist voice that cried, 'You sod,
> leave my soul alone, leave my soul alone,' – ...
>
> that voice so arctic and that cry so odd
> had nowhere else to go – till the antique
> gramophone wound down and the words began
> to blur and slow, ' ... leave... my... soul... alone... '
> to cease at last when something other died.
> And silence matched the silence under snow.

This is plain horror. The couple of times I have read this poem at readings, some of the audience have drawn in their breath or tut-tutted in that way which signifies pity or disbelief, gripped by fear and fascination in this terrible account of botched surgery. Everyone feels it could have been him or her, left vulnerable on a table at the mercy of surgical inefficiency, those crude and imprecise probing instruments. An extraordinary poem.

I see no obvious literary influences on Abse. He likes T.S. Eliot very much, which is evident from two of his book titles, the second having a slight twist – *Tenants of the House* and *Ash on a Young Man's Sleeve*; and a reversal – 'Humankind / cannot bear very much unreality' (from 'A winter convalescence'). The best part of the Eliot influence is textual, in Abse's employment of a cool intellect when stacking up a bank of emotional images that could collapse into bathos; there is seldom any loss of control. He has absorbed the wise lessons in Eliot's criticism, and mentions his debt to him in the savage mental-hospital sequence 'Funland', which he refers to as 'The Waste Land gone mad' – and frankly, I find much of it impenetrable. Perhaps we are meant to find it so. The madness and screaming chaos, the pitiful repression, the sexual graffiti as self-expression, the blanket-ing illogic of existence in a terminal asylum are probably well served by jagged disjointedness, the fragmented and staccato style of writing. Coping with minds at the end of their tether cannot be described in a placid, ordered form. Anyway, Abse does not need to explain the obscurities of 'Funland', to analyse it all away in footnotes or before audiences, as apparently Ted Hughes finds himself doing, increasingly, when reading *Crow* in public. Perhaps, too, I backed-off from this sequence as I did from B.S. Johnson's 'novel' *House Mother Normal* (about crippled geriatrics), as both lie at the siberian extremity of our plight – simply a place I do not wish to visit, even through language, for I think we are already present in some sort of irrational madhouse for most of our days and nights. Abse at least has the courage to face what we call certified lunacy and to write about it. I leave it to other investigators to decide whether or not he has succeeded.

I retain one memorable example of how a good poet with a single poem can affect even the *conduct* of a reader or listener. I once heard Dannie Abse read 'A night out' – about going with his wife to see a harrowing film on Auschwitz and then going home afterwards and making love. Apart from the ending, which tried to make the *point* of life as against the bestiality of the Nazis, I felt sick listening to the content of this fine poem, but it must have been even worse for him, being a Jew, to watch the film. Soon after that reading in London, I heard an insensitive pig in a bar in Richmond say that he agreed with the Final Solution of the Jewish problem and I had a violent argument with him. Most of the customers – decent Englishmen – were on my side and they told the pig to shut up or get out. I doubt whether I would have bothered with that dreadful, misguided human being if Abse's poem had not been still fresh in my memory. (What would the poet himself have said about that bar-room scuffle? 'Forgive him, for the poor sod doesn't know any better'? It says much for the communicable compassion of Abse that, later, I felt a twinge of remorse for wanting to injure the fascist pig.) I consider 'A night out' to be one of his best and most significant poems, showing as it does a sensitive and civilised man's speechless, helpless response to barbaric enormity. Flatly he recounts what he sees on the screen, remembers what he and his wife did ('we munched milk chocolate'), notes little details later ('You took off one glove'), mentions without bitterness 'the au pair girl from Germany', and then, blotting out the images of hate, 'in the marital bed, made love.' Here are the last two stanzas:

> Resenting it, we forgot the barbed wire
> was but a prop and could not scratch an eye;
> those striped victims merely actors like us.
> We saw the Camp orchestra assembled,
> we heard the solemn gaiety of Bach,
> scored by the loud arrival of an engine,
> its impotent cry, and its guttural trucks.
> We watched, as we munched milk chocolate,
> trustful children, no older than our own,
> strolling into the chambers without fuss,
> while smoke, black and curly, oozed from chimneys.
>
> Afterwards, at a loss, we sipped coffee
> in a bored espresso bar nearby
> saying very little. You took off one glove.
> Then to the comfortable suburb swiftly
> where, arriving home, we garaged the car.

We asked the au pair girl from Germany
if anyone had phoned at all, or called,
and, of course if the children had woken.
Reassured, together we climbed the stairs,
undressed together, and naked together,
in the dark, in the marital bed, made love.

(What distress those three little words 'at a loss' conjure up.) Churlish critics might say that the last two lines are facile, pointing up the contrast too glibly. But I doubt if Abse would invent a phoney climax to such an important theme; this 'spotlit drama of our night-mares' could only make a genuine poem. Later on, after a visit to West Germany where he looked at the source of the evil, he wrote these succinct, and honestly unforgiving, lines in 'No more Mozart': 'The German streets tonight / are soaped in moonlight. / The streets of Germany are clean / like the hands of Lady Macbeth.' German responsibility for cruelty on such mind-boggling scale could not be shifted elsewhere or swept under history's greasy mat. Understandably, the poet could not forgive or forget what was done to his race ('Nothing is annulled'); these were six million human beings, not flies.

On the other, Welsh side of Abse's ancestry, there has come down the years a seeping criticism from his compatriots that, like Auden, he has a touch of the slick professional about him, a hint of the main chance or 'poet-on-the-make', guilty of over exposure (again, these are the deceptive outward trappings). He has continually and rather frivo-lously described himself as a 'professional poet and dilettante doctor,' as if he had only a superficial interest in medicine, which is not true. This smart labelling, among other things, does not endear him to some of the stricter mandarins, in Wales or England, who are capable of frightening severity in these matters of the limit to be put on poetic success. However, the demands for his personal appearances have been continuous, and there is no denying the popularity of his readings in the schools, colleges, and amateur 'writers' circles' of Wales, as well as at the heavier literary functions; the combination of reputation, craftsmanship and personality make him more than welcome, and rarely can there have been a distinguished poet who appears so much at ease at a high-powered international reading or on the 'literary lunch' circuit. Unfortunately he is not a known supporter of Welsh nationalism ('narrow as a coffin,' he would describe it, or else he might adapt a line from 'Return to Cardiff': 'Faded torments, self-indulgent pity'). He cannot hear the distant drums. His connection with Welsh aspirations towards self-rule and the struggle for the preservation of a culture is nonexistent. More or less at home with the Anglo-Welsh, among Welsh-language writers he would seem as odd as a streamlined *New Yorker* poet. His work, generally, is of little interest to Welsh-speakers or to those who are steeped in the literature of Wales. He appears to them to be well lost, to have been an exile for too long, residing permanently now among the busy sophisticates of Golders Green and Hampstead. He probably prefers it that way, seeing in South Wales a threat of stifling parochialism to his cosmopolitan outlook. Many blown-away Welshmen of lesser talent would agree with him. But, as Patrick Kavanagh pointed out, there is a fine distinction between the provincial mentality, which does not trust what the eyes see until it receives confirmation from the metropolis, and the parochial, which never has any doubts about the social and artistic validity of its parish.

There is a flippant clue to Abse's split allegiance, if such it can be called (he would, I expect, be embarrassed by anyone thinking in terms of 'allegiances' to explain his spiritual dual nationality) in a poem 'A note left on the mantelpiece', where 'attracted by their winning names / I chose Little Yid and Welsh Bard...' Any lingering nostalgia or hackneyed 'hiraeth' has disappeared. He wrote 'Return to Cardiff' a long time ago, the city 'where the boy I was not and the man I am not / met, hesitated, left double footsteps, then walked on.' It seems there is a residual affection for the place, where a remnant of his friends and his favourite underdog team are based, but not much more. Other duties, other loyalties, other considerations have carried him elsewhere. Yet they say that it takes one Welshman to fully comprehend another, and I still think his 'Elegy for Dylan Thomas' (1953) to be about the best and most moving poem written on that poet, a necessary corrective to being saturated in the biography of scandal by various hands serving the Thomas industry (books as 'inveterate as calamity' as Glyn Jones perfectly puts it). The last two stanzas are memorable:

> But far from the blind country of prose,
> wherever his burst voice goes about you or through you,
> look up in surprise, in a hurt public house
> or in a rain-blown street, and see how
> no fat ghost but a quotation cries.

> Stranger, he is laid to rest
> not in the nightingale dark nor in the canary light.
> At the dear last, the yolk broke in his head,
> blood of his soul's egg in a splash of bright
> voices and now he is dead.

Abse was about 30 when he wrote this, and apart from the prosaic 'laid to rest' it looks to me like a major poem, not only anticipating the cheap sensational journalism to come that would have sorely wounded poor Dylan, but bringing off a stroke of near-genius in 'the yolk broke in his head, / blood of his soul's eggs...' This is the poet-physician thinking and feeling again (as in 'In the theatre'), seeing the random cerebral insult destroying a beautiful mind.

Dannie Abse has said that he is 'almost as happy as possible, to quote Edward Thomas, who was a most melancholy man.' (*Nassau Literary Review* (Princeton University), May 1974). Sometimes he despairs and sometimes he celebrates, which sounds like the usual see-saw of intelligent resignation. There was a period when I thought that the visible bits of his pessimism were based on the natural law that if something can go wrong, it will; a dark streak of sardonic acceptance was uppermost. But now, as he grows older, I think the despair is much deeper than that, and it stems from the unsolved mystery of life, the paramount question which cannot be answered – as in 'Hunt the Thimble':

> Is it like that? Or hours after that even:
> the darkness inside a dead man's mouth?
>
> No, no, I have told you:
> you are cold, and you cannot describe it.

This sounds like the end, the shutters coming down once and for all. Finis. But these lines do not imply a stoic acceptance. The mystery remains, and it prevents a kind of tolerable completeness. God is obviously absent, and the vacuum baffles Abse. The threadbare critical approach to his work, the weekend journals which are too often obsessed with him as secular 'Jewish victim' or whatever, is shallow when compared with his concern at this depth. Certainly, when the poetry of his middle span is considered, it does something to dissipate the damp fog of mediocrity generated by some of his English colleagues.

The short blurb on the back of this book quotes the still-respected and usually accurate *TLS*, like some ultimate seal of approval: 'Dr Abse has made a steady advance to a dry recognisable voice... charming but masculine; a craftsman whose skill does not hobble his integrity, an artist whose unvarnished truths give pleasure.' Charming, indeed! Pleasure! I suppose so, but what is more interesting is that inimitable chill going right through you. Didn't the *TLS* scribe read advanced Abse? He deserves that generous puff and much more, after nearly 30 years of conscientious effort – an intelligent, accomplished poet, a deeply learned person and an unfailingly compassionate one. His later years may yet see him evacuating the frantic metropolitan stage to become an urban recluse or to retire to his nest at Ogmore-by-sea, there to complete the long, difficult metaphysical sequence which he surely has it within him to write – assuming that by then the atmosphere of violence and simmering crisis in our society, which is inimical to poetic contemplation, has not defeated him. Meanwhile, here is the carefully selected, definitive Volume One.

From: *Poetry Wales* 13.2, October 1977

Alan Brownjohn – 'Encounters with Dannie Abse'

It seems to me that it might be possible to write an autobiography in the form of a compendious directory of friends and relations, complete with a system of cross references (incidentally supplying one's personal component of that ever more desirable, so far unattempted, volume, *Who Met Who*). At the head of all the alphabetical entries would necessarily come Dannie Abse. On the bookshelf behind me he is only preceded by the verses of Claude Colleer Abbott, and since that most distinguished Hopkins scholar, and editor of the great volumes of *Letters*, was only the most moderate of poets, that hardly counts. For all practical purposes the slim volumes begin with Dannie's 1948 volume, *After Every Green Thing*.

Does anyone like to have a first book remembered only too vividly?

Certainly not, except possibly when it is done in a spirit of celebration: people's recollections of one's excesses of youthful behaviour or conversation are *just* about tolerable at an old college reunion. I should like to celebrate *After Every Green Thing*, briefly, as one of the first volumes by a living poet which I acquired, and hope that its author will not feel embarrassment. It was prised out of the same second-hand shelves, in the same Oxford bookshop, which yielded Roy Fuller's *The Middle of a War*, Spender's *The Still Centre* and a copy of W.H. Auden's *The Dance of Death* with a neat black-ink signature inscribed in it: *Philip Larkin. After Every Green Thing* was written in the free, humane, romantic spirit of 1940s poetry, and as such it spoke to a post-war undergraduate who wanted to know where he might begin with the poetry of his own time.

The wisdom of hindsight allows the reader of 1983 to go back and pick up the hints of the later Abse in this first book. Most – well, all – of the imagery we would think of as 'apocalyptic' has now gone. Yet the occasional rhetorical expansiveness, the line that comes at you with a sudden dramatic strength, in the later work, is surely owed to the romantic young poet of *After Every Green Thing*, who could write:

> When the heads around the table forget to speak...

> ... They ... who saw the long unfocussed street,
> grinning like a greyhound...

> the piano-lid closed, a coffin of music ...

And a poem like 'Epithalamion', the version from *Walking under Water* – one which the poet still, rightly, acknowledges – comes into fine shape and sense out of the lyric impulse which (perhaps too undiscriminatingly) flooded the first book.

In an oddly barren literary London of 1953 (*Horizon* and *Penguin New Writing* having been killed off, and *Encounter* and the *London Magazine* not yet started) it was possible, apart from the weeklies (Abse was reviewing for *Time and Tide*) only to find poems printed in a handful of smaller literary magazines. Each one had – in retrospect still has – its own kind of fascinating aura. Down in SW2 was *Platform*, brainchild of Frederick Woods: substantial, near, serious, critical. Up in NW6 was John Sankey's *The Window*, broadminded, mildly cosmopolitan, nodding in the direction of the remains of literary Soho, very attractively printed and stitched together. In

SW3, Blackheath in fact, was the early *Stand*, Jon Silkin's first half-a-dozen numbers providing a small riot of lively graphics and talented poetic unknowns. And from NW3 came Dannie Abse's *Poetry and Poverty*. *Poetry and Poverty* was small, compact, relatively plain, sensible in editorial tone, and prestigious. In most magazines it was possible for a new writer to rub shoulders with respected, or envied, peers in one's own age group, as part of a large, loose brotherhood of aspirants. In *Poetry and Poverty* it was sometimes possible to rub shoulders with the distant and the eminent.

There was Jacques Prévert, for example, mellifluously and meticulously translated into English by Paul Dehn; and Paul Celan; and Elias Canetti transcribing an African folk legend – Canetti whose *Auto da Fé* one had been drawn to by a famous commendation of Professor J. Isaacs in a BBC Third Programme lecture, as well as by Stephen Spender's acclaim for a novel he described as a 'long howling crescendo of horror.' All my own copies of *Poetry and Poverty* were borrowed and never returned; the magazine is a rarity now, something no doubt difficult for any editor to believe as he tramps the bookshops of the metropolis distributing small bundles, winning sympathy from some proprietors, weary tolerance from many, contempt and even abuse from a few. My first meeting with Abse, as I recall, was on this kind of pilgrimage. Among the bookshops of the Charing Cross Road, you passed Foyle's, left a few copies of your magazine with the shy, knowledgeable and kindly Ken Fyffe at Better Books, ignored Panzetta's, and stopped with the genial and interested Norman Hart of Zwemmer's before you finished at Collet's. I must have first spoken to Abse when leaving copies of a magazine called *Departure* in Norman's tiny office. He had almost certainly been leaving copies of *Poetry and Poverty*.

It was before the days of the late David Archer's poetry bookshop in Frith Street (a venture which briefly revived the same Parton Press which had first published Dylan Thomas.) It was long before Bernard Stone's Turret bookshops, in Kensington and Covent Garden. There was no London bookshop in which you could unashamedly linger, browse, and not purchase. But you might expect to run into other poets and editors at Better Books and Zwemmer's. How many copies of the little magazines ever sell in the shops (their editors dream of the all-embracing mailing list of subscribers which eliminates the necessity of trudging the streets in the rain, spending

more on tube fares than you receive on sales)? And yet their minia-
ture glamour – and their genuine importance – is out of all
proportion to their circulation. Part of the glamour of *Poetry and
Poverty* was the knowledge that this was a magazine that needed to
make its way in a real world of hard-headed London booksellers, not
an undergraduate world in which sales are assisted and pride is
cushioned by undergraduate esteem. And here was one of the real
London editors and poets, leaving copies of his new number.

Was it through Dannie Abse's suggestion, then or at some later
point, that I first found my way to the contemporary Mecca of most
younger (and a few older) London poets and poetry-readers, virtually the only venue for public readings, the dim, dingy and weirdly
haunting basement of the Ethical Church Hall, Bayswater?

Someone should, long since, have written a definitive memoir
about the readings held under the auspices of the Contemporary
Poetry and Music Circle of the Progressive League, at the Ethical
Church Hall. Their fame had gone before them: had not Roy
Campbell supposedly fought a fist-fight with a famous poet of the
1930s at one reading, had not that and other events been preserved
and embellished in more than one novel? Had not everybody of note
read there at some time? All the same, they were scanty gatherings
(even when after the demolition of the Bayswater hall, they transferred to Stanton Coit House off Kensington High Street, and
brought in the likes of Allen Ginsberg and Gregory Corso for their
first London appearance). Ross Nichols had founded the readings,
Alec Craig and Ashton Burall had continued them, taking respective
responsibility for the poetic and the musical items. Craig and Burall
divided the chairmanship of these monthly occasions between them,
sitting side-by-side in two very high chairs. It was rumoured that they
were not on speaking terms. The events lost money. They were free,
but a collection was invited, and the minimum sum asked for once you
were in your seats seemed unduly, if understandably, large. The atmosphere was correct and well-ordered, the more outrageous and
libertarian material in the programmes being introduced and delivered
with a kind of primness derived from the supposition that the atmosphere of an ethical church ought to emulate that of a religious one.

It would have been at one of these two venues of the Contemporary
Poetry and Music Circle that I first heard Dannie Abse reading his
own work, poems from *Walking Under Water*, and poems which later

went into the collection that followed, *Tenants of the House*. Did he read 'Letter to Alex Comfort', from the first of those two books, on that occasion? Alex Comfort certainly read at Bayswater for Alec Craig, but my memory – perhaps unreliably – puts Abse's reading on another, bitterly cold Monday night late in 1953 when the actor Anthony Jacobs gave a memorial reading of the poems of Dylan Thomas, dead that November. The 'Letter' stayed in my mind from around that time, for the duality it explicitly emphasised in Alex Comfort's concerns – and implicitly suggested in Abse's own:

> You too, I know, have waited for doors to fly open, played
> with your cold chemicals, and written long letters
> to the Press; listened to the truth afraid, and dug deep
> into the wriggling earth for a rainbow with an
> honest spade....

Did Abse read this one in the gloomy depths of the Ethical Church Hall basement, where so many young poets of the time dug for rainbows? I doubt whether he read the poem actually called 'Duality', since that came later, I would guess around 1954 or 1955:

> I am that man twice upon this time:
> my two voices sing to make one rhyme.
> Death I love and Death I hate,
> (I'll be with you soon and late).

Public poetry reading had not yet undergone that huge expansion of the 1960s, when it became utterly necessary, for authenticity's sake, to have the poet read his or her own work. Sometimes the radio poetry programmes of the time dared to bring in the poets themselves, but mostly they used actors. Anthony Jacobs certainly read my own first broadcast poem, in a Third Programme feature compiled by Jon Silkin in 1955 which also included – in the gifted interpretation of the same reader – Dannie Abse's 'The Victim of Aulis'. It may have seemed to Abse (it certainly seemed to others) one of his most ambitiously moving, yes, rhetorical and expansive, yet controlled and subtle, poems to date. Why he could not read it himself is inexplicable, except in terms of the received wisdom of the day, that poets could not (unless they were Dylan Thomas) read their own poems to any effect; the practice gained by poets in the later poetry reading boom put paid to that impression. Abse read his own work then, as now, with a singular clarity and force, enhanced by a quiet, almost informal delivery. I think of him as one of the poets who convincingly proved that poetry *could* be delivered without some kind of special, reverential voice copied from stage performances, or elocution classes. It is possible that many poets owe the courage to relax vocally in front of an audience to the quieter skills of the radio readers – Anthony Jacobs and Mary O'Farrell then, Hugh Dickson, Gary Watson and Elizabeth Proud now (to name only a few) – who knew better than to address a studio microphone as if it was a theatre auditorium. Abse certainly had the gift.

It was the period when the 1950s Movement in poetry was getting off the ground. The first post-war literary magazine of the air, John Lehmann's *New Soundings*, was succeeded, to its editor's not unjustified disappointment, by John Wain's *First Reading*, which immediately replaced the metropolitan emphasis of its predecessor with gestures of provincial literary defiance. Soon to come were the celebrated 'literary editorials' in the *Spectator*, written by Anthony Hartley and encouraged by one of the best editors of that weekly in the post-war years, Brian Inglis. In reaction against what were held to be the romantic excesses of Dylan Thomas and his followers, the rule of the day for the new poetry was to be emotional coolness, strictness of form, academic wit – the story has often been told, and definitively charted in Blake Morrison's *The Movement*. What has not been so oft or so fully described is the character and origins of the romantic backlash which followed the launching of the Movement. There was an inevitable desire to 'get back' at the new young men of the *Spectator*; even a literary warfare among the weeklies (a circulation war conducted by poets and literary editors!) which resulted in counter-claims for its own writers by the long-dead weekly *Truth* (for which wrote the young Alan Brien, Bernard Levin and Philip Oakes). But there was also a conviction that the Movement simply did not represent the bulk, or the best, of the verse being written at the time. Out of that conviction came *Mavericks*.

Mavericks, edited by Dannie Abse and Howard Sergeant, was a counterblast anthology dedicated to proving, with the work of a group of poets parallel in age to the poets of the Movement anthology *New Lines*, that the best writing of the 1950s was not sedate, Augustan, a bit bloodless. Like my original copy of *New Lines*, it was lent years ago and never returned, complete with the marginal notes which went into a lecture on the comparative merits of the two volumes, given to a small literary society in West London. *Mavericks* was a good and timely selection, in which the work of Jon Silkin, Vernon Scannell and Dannie Abse himself leaves the most favourable impression in retrospect: and weren't these, with others like Thomas Blackburn, and the co-editor, Howard Sergeant, editor of *Outposts* poetry magazine, the quintessential members of the London little magazine world in the 1950s, a romantic generation who had refined, with the aid of the urbane voice of W.H. Auden, the craft of Thomas, the cadences of W.B. Yeats and George Barker, the 'apocalyptic' poetry of the 1940s to make romanticism acceptable again? As certain members of the Movement (John Wain, Elizabeth Jennings) returned to their romantic instincts, as the poetry of 'the Group' emerged around the turn of the decade, Ted Hughes achieved a virtually instant celebrity with the publication of *The Hawk in the Rain*, and as Philip Larkin came more and more to seem a poet on whom no easy label could be fixed, so the Movement came to look like an isolated episode (and by this time the *Spectator* had fallen into that bizarre phase when it printed, week after week, only the lyrics of Lord Hailsham). *Mavericks* as well as all the polemic expended in *Truth* and elsewhere, began to seem unnecessary. It had not been so at the time.

But poetry was suddenly emerging from the weeklies and the little literary magazines, and taking to the road. *This* tangled and enthralling stage of literary history undoubtedly requires its annalist, who would be charged with tracing the evolution of poetry in, and as, performance, taking in *New Departures*, Liverpool, the Albert Hall readings of 1965 and 1966 – and 'Poetry and Jazz'. There were about three hundred Poetry and Jazz concerts in the middle 1960s, in programmes organised by Jeremy Robson, a number on behalf of Arnold Wesker's Centre 42, with Michael Garrick's quartet. The three I most clearly remember may perhaps serve as a cross section of the efforts of an amazing enterprise. One bitter and misty afternoon the performers took the train to Birmingham to appear in a vast and handsome Victorian music hall, long since demolished in favour of the architectural felicities of the Bull Ring. It sounded, in the pitch darkness out beyond the lights, about half full, but with enthusiasts. Poems were read in the intervals between jazz items, sometimes with *sotto voce* comments from trumpeter Shake Keane or saxophonist Joe

Harriott (not audible to the audience), as the jazzmen loyally remained on stage. Books, including Abse's small collection in the 'Pocket Poets' series were sold in the interval – Laurie Lee, on stage, held up his, proclaiming it as the 'life's work' of a slow writer. There followed a nightmare return journey, made, for some reason, in a minibus with erratic brakes, in thick motorway fog.

On a second night the wholly untypical venue was the Council Chamber at Southall. It was full, but only with the numbers required to fill it with councillors so that the large-looking audience really consisted of about fifty persons. On a third evening the big Colston Hall in Bristol was filled to capacity, justifying the theory that the different followings, for words and for music, would complement each other and create large popular audiences for the right combination of the two. At this stage – I suppose some time early in 1964 – only one poet had the daring to combine the poetry with the music: Jeremy Robson. But he later persuaded John Smith, Vernon Scannell and even Thomas Blackburn to make the attempt. Jeremy Robson I felt to be the organising spirit behind Poetry and Jazz, Dannie Abse (and with the jazz musician, Michael Garrick, who would expound his latest musical and philosophical theories and hopes late at night in motorway restaurants) the stabilising force, whose calm, and common-sense, held a collection of wayward spirits together through several touring years. As a result, Poetry and Jazz in Concert found – or created – its own very special kind of audience, one which cared to listen to words, celebrate jazz, and connect with the craft in both. I doubt whether this has happened since in the purlieus of popular music. There ought to have been more than just two gramophone records of the group; and some lines on the evocative character of recorded sound, in this case Caruso, in an Abse poem read at some of the concerts, seem to offer an appropriate nostalgia:

> Dear classic, melodic absences
> how stringently debarred, kept out of mind,
> till some genius on a gramophone
> holes defences, breaks all fences.
>
> What lives in a man and calls him back
> and back...?

I first recall hearing many of the poems in Abse's next two volumes, *Poems, Golders Green* and *A Small Desperation* in the various reading venues that had sprung up in the London of the mid-1960s: places like the Crown and Greyhound, Dulwich Village (which had a reputation among poets for somewhat chilling, poker-faced audiences), the Questors Theatre (for which Abse was writing plays), the Regent's Park Library, where Elizabeth Thomas chaired the many *Tribune* readings with unflappable ease and authority, and the numerous pubs, clubs and halls where happened the more short-lived reading-series put together by organisers with rather less stamina or manic enthusiasm. In 1967 there was to be a couple of Arts Council Poets' Tours organised by the present writer; one trio of poets, John Holloway, Patric Dickinson and Edward Lucie-Smith, was to go east from London into Essex and Suffolk, and another westwards, to Oxfordshire and Gloucestershire: Dannie Abse, Vernon Scannell and Elizabeth Jennings. The eastern group suffered nothing worse (though that was bad enough) than the theft of Patric's suitcase in the vicinity of a London public school. Two days before the western group was due to set out, Vernon Scannell – in circumstances described fully in his book *A Proper Gentleman* – was sent to Brixton Prison. The first afternoon in the west, a reading at Cheltenham Ladies College, therefore featured a reading by Dannie Abse, Elizabeth Jennings and Michael Hamburger. I drove Elizabeth Jennings from Oxford to Cheltenham; Dannie Abse drove the trio on, for four days, to places like Gloucester and Bicester, a school to read in, in the afternoons, a library in the evenings.

I think of this tour, or perhaps more exactly this year of 1967, as the time when I first became aware of the poems which went to make Abse's *A Small Desperation*. 'As I was saying' (and indeed 'Not Adlestrop') connects inseparably for me with the landscape of Gloucestershire and the high public library hall where I first heard it, a poem in which the gentler face of 1940s romanticism shades into Edward Thomas and Philip Larkin, suddenly assembling evidence of an English tradition which one hadn't previously noticed in three apparently different poets; the subject is wild flowers:

> which is this one and which that one,
> what honours the high cornfield, what the low water,
> under the slow-pacing clouds and occasional sun
> of England.

Other poems in *A Small Desperation*, not coincidentally in the period of the Vietnam war, have that dimension of unease, of alarm lurking just under the surface, which Abse has continued to explore more and more successfully and movingly. It surfaces overtly in the *Funland* sequence, in the book of that title, and I have to say I like it less in that explicit form than in the more menacing, because more indistinct, form it takes in poems like 'The Sheds', which has haunted me since I first heard it:

> Articulate suffering may be a self-admiring,
> but what of the long sheds where a man could only howl?
> How quickly, then, silhouettes came running
> across the evening fields, knee deep in mist.
>
> Or what of nights when the sheds disappeared,
> fields empty, a night landscape unrhetorical
> until the moon, pale as pain, holed a cloud?
> As if men slept, dreamed, as others touched on lights.

One writes 'heard' almost without thinking. In the 1960s and early 1970s the experience of sharing reading platforms with other poets meant that the new work of friends might be as frequently met in that setting as in print in magazines: heard as you sit wondering what on earth you are going to start with yourself when it is your turn to read, or wondering just what kind of impression you have made when you've just sat down after delivering. These are conditions in which a poem has to possess some unmistakeable, immediately recognisable force in order to 'come through.' 'Hunt the thimble' seemed the genuine article, as did 'Fah', the one about the single, repeated note sounded on a piano:

> that one sound, at first amiable,
> soon touched down on the whole feminine,
> far world of hermetic lamentations.
> You sat there, it seemed, absent, unaware,
> like a child (certainly without menace)
> and fathomed it again and played it again,
> a small desperation this side of death.

Some poems settle into the corners of the memory, tacitly offering their themes for emulation; only after several attempts to write a wholly serious poem about the strangely evocative sound of someone idly fingering a musical instrument did I remember that 'Fah' had done the idea conclusively, and content myself with writing an inferior comic one.

If you engage in the activity of reviewing you find your own encomia coming back at you from the dust-jackets of shiny new volumes, recalling the dash for the deadline, the elimination of printers' solecisms from the proofs, the last-second sub-editing which has reduced an immaculate bit of delicate critical syntax to a half-sentence of terse gibberish. On the back of *Funland* I see that I wrote in the *New Statesman* about Abse's *Selected Poems* that 'Dannie Abse's new volume... (*dot dot dot*: what piece of inspired parenthetical elaboration has been excised?) shows a remarkable unity of theme and method in twenty years' work... (This time my own dots). Abse is talking quietly and persuasively to people who will understand, listen and agree. At his very best he uses this warmth and approachableness to lead the reader on to accept some disquieting, original and memorable effects.' You don't invariably feel, especially after the passage of a few years, as if you want to stand by what you wrote just before the Literary Editor rang to demand his copy. I would certainly stand by that statement from 1973, ten years ago – and take it further if I was asked to write it again. In the 1980s, the dust has settled after the wild, raw, demonstrative, sloganising poetry that made news in the sixties and seventies. But it has settled too much, too solidly, and shaped a consensus that poetry should preferably be a decorative whimsical art, only disquieting if it arbitrarily chooses to invert the ordinary world in which people actually live, work, hope and starve to serve the cause of private fantasies. I like to think that one function of poetry is to lead you quietly and unnervingly towards inescapable human truths. And I dare to believe that Dannie Abse will go on writing poems of that kind.

From: *The Poetry of Dannie Abse*, Robson, ed. Joseph Cohen (1983)

Daniel Hoffman – 'Way Out in the Centre'

The title of Dannie Abse's latest book, *Way Out in the Centre*, is self-descriptive, the poets placing of his own work in relation to both the tradition of English poetry and the counter-tradition of Modernism. The titular phrase occurs in his poem, 'A note to Donald Davie in Tennessee,' so I take it that Abse is defining his position, at least in part, in the context of Donald Davie's adjurations to British poets that they take Basil Bunting, George Oppen, and Louis Zukofsky as their models. These poets work from 'the conviction that a poem is a transaction between the poet and his subject more than it is a transaction between the poet and his readers.' Davie's proposing that the Objectivist method, and particularly the work of Bunting, points to 'where English poetry has got to, and where it may go next (at our hands, if we so choose),' is offered in his essay, 'English and American in Briggflats', which Dannie Abse reprinted in his annual anthology, *Best of the Poetry Year* 6 (London: Robson Books, 1979). In 'A note to Donald Davie in Tennessee', Abse replies to his friend's polemic in a tone characteristically understated, saying, 'Still poets / jog eagerly, each molehill mistaken / for Parnassus,' and, he asks, 'where's the avant-garde when the procession / runs continuously in a closed circle?' Abse concludes with lines that reward our scrutiny:

> I too am a reluctant puritan, feel uneasy
> sometimes as if I travelled without ticket.
> Yet here I am in England way out in the centre.

On reflection one must ask if 'in the centre,' why 'way out' and travelling 'without ticket'? Abse's titular phrase is an oxymoron the contradictions of which extend to the poem it describes. I propose to identify several characteristic themes in Abse's work and, exploring these in one or two poems devoted to each, suggest how this poet is both 'In England' and 'in the centre,' yet 'way out,' travelling 'without ticket.'

Since the Second World War English poetry has been dominated, in turn, by the domestic muse, the scaled-down sense of possibilities, of the Movement and the Group poets; by the vehement rejection of such limitations in the violent primitivism of Ted Hughes; and by the meditative mythopoetics of Geoffrey Hill. The genuineness of Abse's work depends on neither the ironic use of traditional forms and meters, as with Larkin; nor on the wrenching disjunction of syntax or leaps of associative imagery, as with Hughes; nor in the allusive, chthonic probings of Hill. Nor, as may be inferred, does Abse resemble Charles Tomlinson, who more than any of his English contemporaries anticipated Davie's advice and sought models in American modernism. If these poets are indisputably and typically English, then Abse's work is triangulated not near any of the extreme positions each has taken but at a distance from all of them, way out in the centre. Abse's aim, as he says in his preface to *Collected Poems*, is 'to write poems which appear translucent but are in fact deceptions. I would have a reader enter them, be deceived he could see through them like sea-water, and be puzzled when he can not quite touch bottom.' Or, as he writes in a late poem, 'The Test',

> Oh the irreducible strangeness of things
> and the random purposes of dreams.

Or, as in 'Mysteries',

> I should know by now that few octaves can be heard,
> that a vision dies from being too long stared at;
> ....
> ....I start with the visible
> and am startled by the visible.

If such lines indicate a concentration upon perception, others explore the mystery of the perceiver's identity:

> Not for one second, I know,
> can I be the same man twice.
> ('Leaving Cardiff')

> my two voices sing to make one rhyme
> ('Duality')

These quotations introduce several terms recurrent in Abse's work: strangeness, things, dreams, purposes, vision, the visible, and the sense of duality whenever the speaker's identity is defined.

Abse is a skeptical humanist, desiring belief by relying upon the visible – which in turn rewards him with moments 'when small mirrors of reality blaze / into miracles.' Yet in another poem, one entitled 'Miracles', a priest says to him,

A doctor must believe
in miracles, but I, a priest, dare not.

Then my incurable cancer patient,
the priest, sat up in bed, looked to the window,
and peeled his tangerine, silently.

The conversational tone is maintained with such calm and verisimilitude that language and rhetoric seem to do little to heighten tension; yet the meaning, the doubleness of implication, rises, all but imperceptibly, in the reader's awareness. That the doctor must have faith while the priest dares not is a reflexive proposition, since 'faith', in this context, must refer to both assurance of God and hope of being cured. Yet how sever these from one another?

Like the lapsed Christian bicyclist in Larkin's 'Church-Going', Abse is unable to participate in his inherited faith (or any other – see 'Even'), though for him – and this is one of the markers of the distance his central position is way out from those of the other English poets of his generation – the faith in which he cannot believe is not the Church of England, or even chapel, but Judaism. Another marker is the distance, psychological as well as linear, between Cardiff and London, for Dannie Abse is not only Jewish but Welsh. Yet again, as he writes in 'Odd', he is always the odd man out: when at home in his respectable suburb, 'by the neighbours am considered odd'; but when 'From the sensible wastes of Golders Green / I journey to Soho where a job owns me,' in that 'not... respectable place' he is once again 'considered odd.' Not only because divided between bourgeois householder and bohemian poet, but also because the job that 'owns' him is that of medical practitioner. The deeper division is between the scientific objectivity of the physician and the sensibility – introspective, humane – of the poet. Of course the poet's job – which also 'owns' him – is to use both sides of each of these divisions – British/Jewish, English/Welsh, seeker/skeptic, bourgeois/bohemian, poet/doctor – in the poems.

The dichotomies between doctor/poet and skeptic/seeker are dramatised perhaps most memorably in Abse's poem 'In the

Theatre'. The theatre is the operating room, in a teaching hospital, of a brain surgeon over forty years ago (the poem is based on an operation witnessed by the poet's brother, Dr. Wilfred Abse), when the only way to locate a brain tumor was to open the skull and feel for it. The patient is under local anaesthetic and conscious, the physician's fingers, 'rash as a blind man's,' probing, probing, 'the growth / still undiscovered, ticking its own wild time,' until

> ...suddenly, the cracked record in the brain,
> a ventriloquist voice that cried, 'You sod,
> leave my soul alone, leave my soul alone,' –
> the patient's dummy lips moving to that refrain,
> the patient's eyes too wide.

Then, as the shocked surgeon withdraws the probe, 'that voice so arctic and that cry so odd... wound down' like an 'antique gramophone,'

> To cease at last when something other died.
> And silence matched the silence under snow.

Compassion is everywhere evident in Abse's work, as is the way language without strain introduces metaphors riven with implication. While 'In the Theatre' would seem to affirm the reality of the soul, the patient speaks in 'a ventriloquist voice' which, as he dying, 'wound down' like an 'antique gramophone.' These tropes maintain to the end – to the end of life, at any rate – that the body is but a mechanism controlled by physical forces.

In 'The Water Diviner' Abse had explored the symbiosis of faith and doubt: 'Late, I have come to a parched land / doubting my gift, if gift I have...'

> The sun flies on
> arid wastes, barren hells too warm
> and me with a hazel stick!
> ....
> sometimes hearing water trickle,
> sometimes not, I, by doubting first,
> believe: believing, doubt.

In 'The Magician' Abse deals with another figure who possesses, or thinks or pretends he possesses, extraordinary power. The stage magician in the poem is a trope for the artist or poet:

Sometimes, something he cannot understand
happens – atavistic powers stray unleashed,
a raving voice he hardly thought to hear,
the ventriloquist's dummy out of hand.

Here the ventriloquist is the artist-figure, whose dummy may take on a life of its own: an implication which reflects on the use of the same metaphor in the poem about the botched brain surgery. The mysterious 'atavistic' power which the magician 'cannot understand' is dramatised compellingly in Abse's recent play, *Pythagoras* (1979). There, as in 'The Magician', the very existence of such power is both affirmed and doubted; yet we tend to come away from play and poem persuaded that something real has been put before us, whether the poet or reader can define it or not.

The very title of Abse's *Poems, Golders Green* (1961) is another oxymoron, since the two halves seem mutually exclusive. This dichotomy is explored in the poem 'Odd', discussed above, and in others in this and his subsequent collections. The title of this book introduces into Abse's work poems concerning his identity as a Jew. The theme is approached in 'After the release of Ezra Pound,' in which the complexity of Pound's case is acknowledged, as is the difficulty of forgiving him. In 'Red Balloon' Abse explores the source of prejudice in a ballad-like fable about himself as a boy in Cardiff –

'It's a Jew's balloon,' my best friend cried,
'stained with our dear Lord's blood,'
....
'Your red balloon's a Jew's balloon,
let's get it circumcised.'

Then some boys laughed and some boys cursed,
some unsheathed their dirty knives;
some lunged, some clawed at my balloon,
but still it would not burst.

The oddness of the story and the simplicity of the ballad structure make the 'Red Balloon' memorable, all the more so for its evocation of perhaps the oldest literary expression in English poetry of persecution of the Jews. Abse's red balloon surely suggests the ball thrown by Sir Hugh into the Jew's window in 'Sir Hugh, or the Jew's Daughter' (Child 155); that ballad accuses the Jews of ritual murder of the boy (the same motif used by Chaucer's Prioress). Abse's reversal of the story's implications is all the stronger for his allusion to medieval precedents. The lad in his poem is experiencing the history of the Jews.

The theme of Jewish identity recurs in such later poems as 'Night Out' and 'No more Mozart'. In the first of these the poet and his wife see a Polish film about Auschwitz – 'We watched, as we munched milk chocolate, / trustful children, no older than our own, / strolling into the chambers without fuss...' It is hard to make the imaged reality a part of one's own life. But in 'No More Mozart', written after a first visit to Germany.

> The German streets tonight
> are soaped in moonlight.
> The streets of Germany are clean
> like the hands of Lady Macbeth.
> ....
> Now, of course, no more Mozart.
> With eyes closed still
> the body touches itself, takes stock.
> Above the hands the thin wrists
> attached to them; and on the wrists
> the lampshade material...

Now, the speaker sees as did 'twelve million eyes / in six million heads.'

In *Funland* (1972), the new poems in *Collected Poems* (1977), and in *Way Out in the Centre* (1981) the poems with Jewish themes are for the most part either sketches of family members or retellings of Talmudic wisdom literature in which rabbis stand on one leg while delivering *mots justes*. These latter, such as 'Tales of Shatz', 'Of Rabbi Yose', and 'Snake' have the charm of folktales. Perhaps it is with this part of his identity in mind that Abse describes his own journey as one in which he 'feel[s] / uneasy / sometimes as if I travelled without ticket. / Yet here I am in England...'

If the central English tradition since Wordsworth has been concerned with the poet's relationship to nature, then Abse is decidedly 'way out.' He has written his *ars poetica* explicitly in several poems besides 'A note to Donald Davie' (who, far off in 'fugitive' territory, Tennessee, would tell English poets the rules of their art). One of these is 'Not Adlestrop'. Again the title is a key, this one referring to Edward Thomas's poem, 'Adlestrop', which we may take as at the centre of the Georgian tradition. Thomas made a pastoral idyll of a moment at a deserted railway depot; but Abse's moment in such a place is *not* 'Adlestrop'; instead of experiencing among the works of industrial man an epiphany in the presence of songbirds, Abse exchanges a momentary glimpse, from the platform, with a pretty girl on a departing train. Abse's tone is always conversational, for his is a poetry which assumes the presence of a reader to whom the poet's feelings and illuminations are being communicated. Thus the objectivism of Bunting and Oppen, which Davie rightly locates in their alienation from their audience, is as foreign to Abse's purpose as is their tone to his style. In style and purpose, in its relation to its reader, Abse's poem *is* in the mainstream of English verse, though, writing in mid-twentieth century, Abse locates feeling in relation to social experience rather than in his response to the natural world. 'I'll not compete with those nature poets you advance' he tells a woman who questions his seriousness for not doing so ('As I was saying'); 'Urban, I should mug up anew' in a book from W.H. Smith the once-evocative names of wild flowers.

As an urban poet, Abse has responded to the London he lives in, and poems of his, with a quiet eloquence as convincing as the work of any of the Movement poets of the 1950s and '60s, limn the sense of dwindled possibilities which afflicted England in the years after the Second World War. In such poems as 'Public Library' and 'The Shunters' Abse writes of 'bed-sitting rooms,' 'rainy, dejected railway stations,' 'the colour of grief... In the tired afternoon drizzle,' 'a despair beyond language.' At that time, however, Abse had taken a polemical position opposing that of the Movement – or rather, a position opposing the polemics of the Movement, which excluded from a foothill of Parnassus all poets not of like mind with Robert Conquest (*New Lines*, 1956). Abse, together with Howard Sergeant, in 1957 published a rival anthology entitled *Mavericks*, offered, as young poets 'writing from the centre of inner experience,' David Wright, Vernon Scannell, Michael Hamburger, Jon Silkin, several others, and Abse himself. There was doubtless too much smoke and fire on both sides of this controversy, which in some quarters generated ill-will that lasted for years. In fact the Movement proved not really a movement, its poets sharing little besides a general attitude; and the Mavericks also each went their separate ways. The ironic trope in Abse's title *Poems, Golders Green* and the implied reduction of 'primary Dionysian excitement' in his next title, *A Small Desperation,* show him determined to mine his own life, however prosaic its surface reality, for poems 'from the centre of inner experience.'

Characteristically, Abse sees himself not alone in a field of flowers but in relation to others. Growing up in the working class, in Wales, where his elder brother Leo became a prominent M.P., it is not surprising that this poet should have founded a magazine entitled *Poetry and Poverty,* or be concerned with political themes. He has said that it was the reading of Spanish Republican poets like Miguel Hernandez in his youth that opened the possibilities of poetry to him. Yet his outright political poems on specific issues are few, and no more successful than the polemics of others. Abse acknowledges that such direct treatment accomplishes little:

> Righteous the rhetoric of indignation,
> but protesting poems, like the plaster angels,
> are impotent. They commit no crimes,
> they pass no laws; they grant amnesty
> only to those who, in safety, write them.
> ('Remembering Miguel Hernandez')

When Abse's political concerns are merged with his larger humane and liberal sympathies and are expressed in fables, his poems have an amplitude of meaning and an inexorability which makes them memorable. His 'Emperors of the Island' (in *Tenants of the House,* 1956), subtitled 'A Political Parable To Be Read Aloud', has the lilting structure of an incremental nursery rhyme, and the grim determinism of a prophecy.

In 'Funland', the long title poem of his 1972 volume, Abse's political concerns merge with his distrust of scientific rationalism as the basis for the organisation of society. Here the governing metaphor is familiar enough; a madhouse is a world. What is original in Abse's treatment is the way that what begins as a comic turn, becomes more ominous as it becomes more mad and more extensive, so that by the end of his nine-part poem the metaphor is reversed and we have a whole world gone mad. At the same time his inmates – the superintendent, an atheist uncle, Fat Blondie, the poet, and Pythagoras (who 'wanted to found / a Society not a Religion' – and did so by inventing

Thracians, a people who could be excluded) – all these are so individualised that although we know them to be mad, we cannot withhold our sympathies from them. Pythagoras seizes power when the superintendent dies – all are deathly afraid of death.

> Let Pythagoras be
> an example to all Thracian spies
> my tyrant uncle cried

as 'Funland' suddenly and starkly becomes a political fable. It immediately modulates into something more universal:

> Who's next for the icepick?

> Already the severed head of Pythagoras
> transforms the flagpole
> into a singularly
> long white neck.

> It has become a god that cannot see
> how the sun drips its dilutions
> on dumpy snowacres.

Abse has boldly invaded the territory of the satirical novel of the absurd, as though intensifying what Orwell, Golding, or Burgess might have written out in several hundred pages. The transformation of the games of Funland into political conspiracy and murder into tribal ritual is as compelling as the stark rhythms and images in which they are presented. The movement is fragmented, disrupted, while the air echoes with unexpressed implications. Abse himself felt this, for the figure of Pythagoras, invented for 'Funland', arrogated to himself a larger structure in a different form. In 1976 Abse's play, *Pythagoras*, was produced by the Birmingham Repertory Theatre and was published in 1979. Here the setting is still a lunatic asylum, with a couple of doctors representing scientism and official order, while the patients may well stand for the rest of mankind. Among them is Pythagoras, who before incarceration was a stage magician (as in Abse's poem 'The Magician'), and who believes himself the reincarnation of the Greek philosopher whose name he has taken. He is a touching and compelling figure of irrationality, the irreducible individuality, the spiritual independence and imaginative power of the human being. The play is a comic, ironical, and memorable fable in which political implications are subsumed in considerations of order *vs.* freedom, rationalism *vs.* belief, identity *vs.* appearance, the claims of science to understand everything *vs.* the imagination with its mysterious secrets. In short the characteristic complex of themes in Abse's poems.

Abse's poems are indeed at once 'in the centre' of the English tradition, yet 'way out' from the terrain marked out by prominent contemporaries. Feeling himself a man speaking to other men and women, though sometimes 'uneasy', he has been no more tempted than have most other English poets by the modernist sensibility with its isolation from an audience, its radical rejections of conventional rhetoric and its formal innovations. Working from within established traditions, Abse has enlarged the subjects and the range of feelings which he uses these to express. His rhythms are accentual-syllabic, creating the illusion of a conversational voice, a muted music, a continuity of discourse. His tone is quite his own, attractively enticing the reader into the poem before the reader knows where he has been brought, what realisations he must come to. We meet, we watch, we listen, as to his 'Three Street Musicians' who sing and play old tunes,

> And as breadcrumbs thrown
> on the ground charm sparrows down from nowhere,
> now, suddenly, there are too many ghosts about.

From: *The Poetry of Dannie Abse*, Robson Books, 1983

James A. Davies – Introduction to Dannie Abse: *The View from Row G*

Dannie Abse has a distinguished international reputation as a poet. He is well-known as a writer of prose, in particular of the autobiographical novel, *Ash on a Young Man's Sleeve* (1954). Fewer people know that he has had success as a playwright.

His interest in the theatre began in his schooldays in Cardiff. *A Strong Dose of Myself* (1983) has a lively and candid chapter on his early enthusiasms for Bernard Shaw and Eugene O'Neill and his first theatre-going. In a rattling tramcar, en route for *Desire Under the Elms* Abse's recklessly confident admiration of O'Neill drew from his friend Sidney Isaacs "a new, inadvertent admiration. Perhaps he felt that I should be one of those fancy, bitch theatre critics who pronounce in the Sunday papers after they have sat, free-ticketed, proud and pampered, in a gangway seat, row G." A few years later he became a less-grand version of that pampered person: when a medical student in London and reviewing off-West-End plays for a small theatre magazine, he was forever, it seemed, taking his "seat in row G among a sparse audience".

This volume could have been entitled *Three Plays* or *Selected Plays*. Its very different title, Abse's own, makes two points. First, these works are *plays*, written for the stage and for an audience. Second, they are aimed, if not directly at a theatre critic, at a thoughtful, critically-minded theatre-goer, whether in row G, the dress circle, or standing at the back. These are serious plays; they are also gripping, moving and often very funny.

That early enthusiasm for the theatre, sustained by visits to Cardiff's Prince of Wales Theatre and the short stint as minor drama critic, made it inevitable that, sooner or later, Abse would try his hand at play-writing. Following the acceptance by Hutchinson of *After Every Green Thing* (1948), his first book of poems, he dramatised part of Balzac's story, 'El Verdugo' ('The Executioner'), as a poetry-drama called *Fire in Heaven* and offered it to The Questors Theatre in Ealing, the important amateur company often used as a show-case for dramas of ideas.

This, to quote the author, "inept" first attempt became *Is the House Shut?*, produced at The Questors in 1964. Later it was again revised to become *In the Cage*. The theme is the clash between conscience and dreadful orders, in this case to execute one's own family because of the terrorist activities of a single member. As such it is an important precursor of *The Dogs of Pavlov*. Equally important is the continuing link with The Questors Theatre, strengthened through the sequence of revisions and strengthened again in 1962 when *The Joker* and the one-act drama *Gone* were produced there. For apart from its value as a try-out venue The Questors, in John Elsom's words, was a place of "high artistic idealism" that fostered Abse's brand of highminded entertainment.

In 1957, three years after the highly successful *Ash on a Young Man's Sleeve*, Abse published his third volume of poetry, *Tenants of the House: Poems 1951-56*. Included was 'The Meeting', which in 1958 was adapted for the radio in dramatised form. This is a derivative work which has been omitted from *White Coat, Purple Coat: Collected Poems 1948-1988*, Abse's most recent volume of work he wishes to preserve. It is easy to see why: the poem is heavily and prolixly indebted to the Eliot of *Prufrock* and to the social poetry of the 1930s. In a world of problems and broken promises unspecified people move through a 'mean city' to a shabby hall to wait for a 'Speaker' who does not arrive to make real their 'one dream'. From this source came *House of Cowards*, first performed in 1960 to open the Questors' first Festival of New Plays. Directed by John McGrath, it won the 1960 Charles Henry Foyle Award for the best play produced outside the West End and was selected by J.C. Trewin for inclusion in volume 23 of *Plays of the Year*. But, though options were sold, a West End production never materialised and not until 1963 was the play professionally produced. This was, ironically, at Abse's old haunt, Cardiff's Prince of Wales Theatre, where the Welsh Theatre Company, under Warren Jenkins, had its headquarters. The opening coincided with the worst of the hard winter of 1963; in a badly heated theatre that few could reach because of the weather the play died the death.

This was not due wholly to snow and ice. Despite an initial favourable critical response Abse considered that a professional performance had exposed faults, notably the inclination to overstatement in dialogue requiring pruning. A coolly objective view came in 1973, from John Elsom. The Questors' influence, he considered, shows itself in Abse's use of moral allegory, which combines very uneasily with the play's naturalistic detail. In addition the themes are derivative, the stock characters lacking in depth and context. Despite such criticism *House of Cowards* has refused to go quietly. In 1967 it was published in *Three Questor Plays* and, two years later, found itself, with Aeschylus, Shakespeare, Molière, Ibsen, Brecht, and others of the same rank, in *Twelve Great Plays*, published by Harcourt Brace, the editor, Leonard Dean, having seen *House of Cowards* performed at Ealing. Such recognition is strong evidence of the play's continuing ability to fascinate; it is a strange and compelling piece.

Thus it is no great surprise that almost thirty years after the first performance Abse has returned to the play and revised it extensively to take account of his own and, it would seem, Elsom's main objections. The relationship between the allegorical and the naturalistic has been eased by demystifying the Speaker: he is given a name and a history that includes possible links with charismatic religion. The characters have become more complex and believable: the details of Hicks's dishonest past are made more plausible and his relationship with Doris strengthened; Miss Chantry is changed from a stock spinster in lodgings to an interesting and amusing eccentric who juggles lemons, whistles, has studied comparative religion and occasionally drinks too much; George Hicks's selfish obsession with obtaining a ticket for the Speaker's meeting, out of character in the 1960 version, is now seen in relation to a history of feckless, compulsive gambling; Alf Jenkins, a stage Welshman whose only claim to individuality was his dubious sexuality, emerges as a person of sensibility and some shrewdness. The dialogue is tauter, faster, with fewer static, set speeches and with more accessible contemporary references. The result is still a serious play with a distinct lyrical element, but, now, a tighter one, with the ideas more effectively dramatised.

Through the 1960s Abse's versions of *Fire in Heaven*, as has been noted, kept him preoccupied with the "question of obedience to an evil command". Poems like 'Postmark', 'Not Beautiful', and the slightly later 'No More Mozart', bear witness to his abiding concern with the Holocaust. Out of such thinking came *The Dogs of Pavlov*, first performed, once again at The Questors Theatre, in the New Plays Festival of 1969. That such a play came when it did in Abse's career is due to two other stimuli. First, as the author acknowledges, was W.H. Auden's essay, 'The Joker in the Pack', which, mainly in relation to Iago, discusses practical joking and deception as evidence of a need for power and as the expression of contempt for others. Second, crucially, was Abse's discovery of an experiment at Yale University devised by Professor Stanley Milgram. Milgram was interested in "the compulsion to do evil" and sought to test the extent to which men "would obey commands that were in strong conflict with their conscience". He advertised for volunteers to take part, they believed, in an experiment to investigate how punishment furthers learning. One 'volunteer' (in reality an actor or actress) was fastened to an electric chair and given verbal tests. If he or she gave wrong answers another volunteer was ordered to administer electric shocks that increased in intensity to a level that caused great pain and threatened life. In reality, the experiment was faked; the volunteers believed they were administering electric shocks whereas their victim was only simulating discomfort and great pain. Milgram discovered that almost all his volunteers – often invoking the interests of science – were willing to reject the dictates of conscience and pull the levers, no matter what might be the observed effect on the victim.

Abse was disturbed by the implications of the experiment, the unethical nature of the deception as well as the responses of the volunteers. As he writes: "[Many] may feel that in order to demonstrate that subjects may behave like so many Eichmanns the experimenter had to act the part, to some extent, of a Himmler." *The Dogs of Pavlov* is a consequence of such feelings; such feelings give the play its great power.

Certainly it was well received at The Questors: after the first performance the theatre was packed and tickets at a premium. Part was televised on BBC 2. The after-performance discussions – a feature of The Questors' festivals – were exceptionally lively explorations of "power and manipulation, racial prejudice and victimisation, and even scientific experimentation" using human guinea-pigs. From Gary O'Connor, theatre critic of the *Financial Times*, came lavish praise: the play was "a work of exceptional merit, well worthy of transfer. A tragedy of feeling... if not in actual fact...." It was an exploration of the "criminal (Eichmann) mentality... the incipient Nazism in the ordinary man in the street's attitude". The characterisation, O'Connor continued, was "hard and objective", the moments of comedy "hilarious".

But the play did not transfer and to date has not received a single professional production in the United Kingdom. It was given an amateur production at Westminster Hospital. There was some continental interest: it was performed in Paris in a French translation, the German rights were sold though no performance resulted. And in 1973 the play was published with an introductory essay by Abse, entitled 'The Experiment', and two letters from Milgram, the first on the essay, the second on the play.

The essay begins by arguing that only the calamities of recent history are real to us and no-one properly understands the 'psychic devastation' of modern atrocities such as the Holocaust and the dropping of the Atomic Bomb. For Abse, as I have already noted, such events raise disturbing questions about human nature: certainly we cannot be convinced that only Germans were capable, say, of persecuting Jews. Indeed, the history of modern Jewish persecution makes only too clear "the willingness of apparently ordinary people to obey evil commands" in Germany and elsewhere. He devotes a short section to the way people are conditioned to obey: "We are trained by punishment and reward, by threat and promise", and then describes Milgram's experiment and its troubling conclusions. Abse makes much of the fact that the volunteers were "hoaxed, fooled", that all, from the electric chair to the victim who was really an actor, to the ostensible aim of the experiment, "was bullshit, a cover story". What Milgram really wanted to know was "how much, to what degree, you would submit to a respectable, apparently reasonable authority – despite the pain and agony of your 'victim' and your slowly awakening conscience".

The last part of the essay is mainly taken up with ethical considerations regarding the conscious motives of the experimenter, the free consent of the subject experimented on, and whether harm was done to the subject, concluding that the Milgram experiment divested the volunteers of all human dignity. But Abse also notes, crucially for our understanding of his dramas, that some of those who pulled the levers were defiant, in great conflict with their consciences, or actively deceived the experimenter by pretending to administer higher doses. He concludes that in this there is cause for at least some optimism.

The essay and then a copy of the play were sent to Milgram who replied, in two letters written early in 1972, that he considered himself perfectly justified in carrying out the experiments. The volunteers were not guinea-pigs but "individuals confronted with a moral choice". One in particular had his life changed through partic- ipation: his consciousness of a conflict between orders and personal beliefs led him to refuse the Vietnam draft and become a conscien- tious objector. Participants were not necessarily victimised, as Abse seemed to think. Some were liberated. In any case, "only the partici- pant knows whether deception had the character of a demeaning experience".

Since then, *The Dogs of Pavlov* has been premiered in the U.S.A. in a performance directed by Maurice Edwards at New York's Cubiculo Theatre. Attempts to arrange a post-performance debate with Milgram came to nothing, as did a proposal to perform the play at Yale.

The Dogs of Pavlov is a powerful and demanding play that requires a professional standard of performance. Abse's revisions – it has been very extensively revised – have made it an even stronger and more demanding dramatic vehicle. The original three-act structure has been reorganised into two Acts, the first ending, with a fine sense of theatre, with Harley-Hoare taking part in the experiment. Further, in the original version the author suggested that film accompanied by music could be shown between scenes, such film to show the relationship between Sally Parsons and John Allison against a lyrical background. This film was to "assist in bleeding off tension". Nowadays sweeping romantic camera-work in, as Abse suggests, London parks, have become clichés of popular advertising and the author is wise to remove it. Tension is now released by a more inter- esting, semi-dramatic device. Act Two, Scene Two, follows two intensely dramatic scenes: Act One, Scene Five, has Harley-Hoare pulling the levers with Sally as subject; Act Two, Scene One, drama- tises Sally's nightmare. But in Act Two, Scene Two, Doctor Daly lectures on his work, the text of the lecture being, in the main, part of Abse's essay, 'The Experiment'. Not only does this provide the audience with some emotional relief but it also creates, within the play itself, a clear, intellectual context for Daly's experiment.

The revisions, then, clarify central themes. In addition, through extensive pruning and some rewriting of the dialogue both Doctor Daly and Doctor Jones become fuller characters and Sally's roman- tic vulnerability is pointed up. Most importantly, there is an increase in tension between the doctors and between them and Sally, reflect- ing the uneasy nature of the scientific enterprise.

The publication of *The Dogs of Pavlov* in 1973 was preceded by that of *Funland and Other Poems*, Abse's sixth volume of poetry. The title poem is a long sequence in nine sections set in an insane asylum. It is a surrealistic work dramatising the idea of life without central aim or purpose. In 1971 the poem was broadcast on BBC Radio 3 and in introducing it Abse referred to what had become an important theme in his work: "the contemporary white coat of Medicine and the old purple cloak of charismatic Mesmer – their relationship and opposition to each other". This clash between medicine and magic has since been explored in the poem 'Carnal Knowledge' and given prominence as the title of his *Collected Poems 1948-1988*. It is at the heart of *Pythagoras (Smith)*.

Following the broadcast of 'Funland' a dramatised version of the poem-sequence was performed by students of the New College of Speech and Drama. Experiencing this made Abse attempt his own dramatisation and for a first performance he turned yet again to The Questors Theatre, who included it in its New Plays Festival of 1975. As Abse admitted, "It was far from being a success". But its potential was recognised by Gary O'Connor, once more in *The Financial Times*, who saw the character of *Pythagoras* as central to the developing play and suggested that Thomas Mann's short story, 'Mario and the Magician', would indicate dramatic possibilities. "So," wrote Abse in his introduction to the published version of the play,

> I took Mr O'Connor's advice: I re-read the Mann story, I re-remembered my own experience as a medical student and as a visitor to mental hospitals; and keeping in mind Coleridge's dictum that comedy is the blossom of the nettle, wrote 'Pythagoras'.

The play received its first performance at Birmingham Repertory Theatre on 22 September 1976. It was well received: the *Daily Telegraph* reviewer, for example, praised its theatrical effectiveness and its touching humour; Michael Billington, in the *Guardian*, was impressed by "a play that blends intelligence with delight in theatrical effect". A later review of a performance at the Gatehouse Theatre Club was also full of praise for the approachable seriousness and humour of the piece. A broadcast followed in 1978, also well received, and publication in 1979, in a volume that included the 'Funland' poem. Reviews of this volume include that by John Cassidy in *Poetry Review*, citing the "flexible and expressive dialogue" and the effective theatricality of the work, plus the "zany humour, high spirits and very good jokes". Both Alun Rees, in *Poetry Wales*, and Tony Curtis, stress the increased accessibility of the play compared to the poem. Since then it has received numerous performances and won a Welsh Arts Council award.

The text now reprinted is the published version of 1979. The only change is to the title: the plain *Pythagoras* becomes the enigmatic *Pythagoras (Smith)*. The absence of revisions reflects understandable authorial satisfaction: "I've written one very good play," Abse said in a television interview in 1983, "I'm very proud of it – it's called Pythagoras.... I think that's a pretty good play."

Dannie Abse is Welsh, but also Jewish, and this second fact must be kept in mind when reading or watching these three plays. For works that feature, respectively, an eagerly awaited Speaker who will transform unsatisfactory lives, a doctor who tricks volunteers into taking part in experiments during which, invariably, the will to obey overrides conscience, and doctors who impose strict authority on the strange and nonconformist, reflect Abse's Jewishness, as has been briefly suggested, through their disturbing links with aspects of the Holocaust.

In *House of Cowards* the audience is left in no doubt about the connections. Thus, when the Speaker fails to arrive, Alf Jenkins, the ambiguous Welshman lodging with the Hickses, still longs for "a new political prophet". George Hicks retorts: "If it's someone like Hitler you're talking about, some demagogue like that, then you're up the pole." "I didn't mean anyone like that," replies Alf, but he protests slightly too much. During the same scene Bill Hicks lights a cigarette and returns us to the Hitler period and its aftermath by remarking: "Immediately after the war in Germany, in 1945, you could get yourself a woman, so they say, wiv one of these." Such references resonate through the play.

The Dogs of Pavlov is permeated with reminders of the worst excesses of the Third Reich. Ironically, Doctor Daly, who is responsible for the experiment to investigate man's capacity for evil, as a medical student worked in the death camps of 1945. The experience was harrowing:

> ...I can't forget what happened. I can't forget what I saw. I keep thinking how somewhere still, if the register should be called, the answer would come back: "I am Auschwitz, I am Belsen, I am Buchenwald, I am Dachau."

His experiment has convinced him of the capacity for evil of all ordinary people, regardless of race or country. As he says in some of Abse's most affecting lines, later reworked into his poem 'Case History':

> In the course of a single day, after seeing the usual Smiths and Robinsons, have we not listened to the heartbeat of an Eichmann, seen the X-ray of a Hitler, palpated the liver of Goering, read the electroencephalograph of Goebbels?

In the play the links are strengthened by the fact that Kurt is half German, his father dying an unrepentant Nazi, and by Harley Hoare's revelations of wartime blood-lust.

Such explicit references are absent from *Pythagoras* but its main statement, as Abse wrote of 'Funland', that "the earth... is a lunatic asylum whose inmates live out suffering lives of black comedy", plus the play's restating of the 'white coat/purple coat' theme in terms of imposed authority, have all-too-plain Holocaustic relevance.

Yet, though Abse is haunted by that most devastating of atrocities, his great strength is his ability to perceive in it an idea of universal and persisting relevance. For all terrible atrocities in the modern period – the Holocaust, for Jew and non-Jew alike, perhaps most of all – are supreme and salutary examples of the destruction of individual identity. Such identity struggles in vain against being subsumed in the popular movements involving elements of mass hysteria that precede so many acts of general destruction (the plays hint at others beside the Holocaust, such as the consequences of Marxism and the American experience in Vietnam). Such acts are directed against those whose difference from an imposed norm, that is, their persisting individualism, causes them to be isolated as enemies and scapegoats. Put plainly, those whose individual identity has been destroyed hate the sight of it in others and react accordingly.

This loss of identity is the main theme of these three plays. In *House of Cowards* it manifests itself in the dramatising of powerful social norms to which characters feel compelled to relate. One way in which this can be seen is in the characters' obsession with constructing versions of their pasts – for example, Bill Hicks's insistence on the unfairness of his previous employers in dismissing him, and Miss Chantry's tragi-romantic fantasy – as a way, not only of explaining to others the present inadequacies of their lives, but also as a means of continuing to fit in, of being acceptable to a world that values employment and being married. In the same play the use of popular songs makes a similar point – they reflect a *shared* evasive nostalgia – as does Bernard Jay, a journalist on a 1950s tabloid. He is a purveyor of dreams for the masses. It is no accident that he is the publicist for a Speaker, Shemtov, who seeks to bring about, in Jay's words, "transient self-extinction", or, as Miss Chantry puts it, "a temporary annihilation of the self". What this can mean is made only too clear in one of the play's most powerfully theatrical scenes, Act Two, Scene Two, when Nott, who may or may not be the expected Speaker, harangues a crowd desperate for Shemtov's arrival. He tells them that they should not seek to escape from self and present but should "accept even our own terror of ignorance, this here and now, this time, this earth". They should reject the sinister possibilities of what Nott calls – it is one of Abse's most evocative phrases – "the Night's infirmary", the escape into the provided dream. But the latter is what the crowd desires. They grow more menacing and become a chanting, mindless mob. Nott is terrified but to the end clings to his belief in individual responsibility: "When we're all perfect, he will have arrived."

The Dogs of Pavlov is a second exploration of dehumanising tendencies of which S.J. Gordon is exemplar *par excellence*. As harsh employer and racialist he ruthlessly stereotypes. To him Harley-Hoare is a servile skivvy dominated by money, an impression to which the latter does his best to live up; Kurt, Gordon's ward but also his employee, is expected to obey; women are tarts, and coloured people "niggers". In taking little account of personal feelings he is a model for Doctor Daly. For the latter is equally reluctant to recognise individual worth and shares Gordon's capacity for stereotyping. His failure to remember Sally's name is only a small instance of his indifference to the uniqueness of others. Daly regards all as essentially depraved and demonstrates his contempt by deceiving them. Sally is very like him for, as Kurt tells her, she "distrusts everybody and everything". She loathes the volunteers for they are, to her, all one of a kind and she expects them, as indeed, she expects even her lover, Kurt, to ignore her essential humanity. This is a consequence, we learn, of losing her previous lover, the coloured actor, John Allison. He has become an activist with Black Power, yet another cruelly stereotyping group, and is given one of the play's most chilling lines:

there is, he says in a taped interview, "no time for human affection any more".

Sally's nightmare is the climax of *The Dogs of Pavlov* and resembles the mob-scene in *House of Cowards*. A vicious chorus of characters led by Gordon first subdues the vestiges of Kurt's independent spirit, then further subsumes individuality in mass response by shouting racialist slogans as it advances threateningly on the sleeping woman: "Kill the nigger lover. Kill the nigger lover. Trust us."

These are powerful scenes and in *Pythagoras (Smith)* there are more, such as Act One, Scene Five, in which Doctors Aquillus and Green use patients in a demonstration-lecture to students, and the patients' concert in Act Two, Scene Four. The former shows what little regard Doctor Aquillus has for his patients' personal feelings. This has been evident throughout, as when, for example, he wants X to volunteer for the demonstration. He regards X simply as a clinical exhibit and cries for help go unheeded:

> X: My bowels are made of glass.
> Aquillus: Yes, yes.
> X: I feel dead inside.
> Aquillus: We'll talk about that later.

There is humour here, of course, but the audience's edgy laughter increases its awareness of Aquillus's exploitative nature. In the lecture itself, his patronising jokes, his impatient orders, and, in particular, his callous rebuttal of X's claim that he is dead by scratching his arm with a needle, plus his concern to impose psychological theory on all responses, degrade his charges by ignoring them as individuals. This disturbing lack of sympathetic imagination is again evident during the concert. Aquillus is patronising and manipulative, hardly bothering to distinguish between student, staff and patient, let alone with how they might wish to react: as Arthur prepares to recite Aquillus instructs the asylum audience: "But tonight he has agreed to read us a new poem. Please keep your hands in the applauding position..."
The Banchaeri madrigal – a reminder that Abse's sometimes arcane details are invariably significant – in which performers amuse by sounding like animals, indicates to us that the audience within the play views the concert as a chance to be amused by the strange antics of the seemingly sub-human. Significantly the concert becomes another mob-scene (Charlie's rabble-rousing in Act One, Scene

Four, being the first) as all, including us, chant nonsense in order to encourage Marian's strip-tease. She has been reduced to sex-object, Pythagoras to amusing charlatan, and we (students, medical staff, audience) discover how easily individuality is lost and human dignity stripped away.

If this was all that could be said these three plays would be unbearably pessimistic. In fact, they are far from being that; Abse's texts, strengthened by revisions, are full of life, humour and individual gestures against imposed authority. All three plays, *Pythagoras (Smith)* in particular, insist on the strange and unique in human nature. All three plays emphasise eccentric, even if, at times, reprehensibly eccentric, behaviour, such as George's gambling, Bill Hicks's unexpected sexuality, Miss Chantry's interest in jazz, Sally's sloganizing, Kurt's fascination for a green Ming vase, Arthur's singing, Biddy's religious longings, and Pythagoras's belief in his own reincarnation and what seem to be magical powers. The plays hum with life and interest and one repeated detail sums up much. In *House of Cowards* Miss Chantry's ability to juggle is shared with Kurt's father in *The Dogs of Pavlov*. Kurt recalls: "He'd taken three lemons from a bowl on the sideboard... and he's juggling them. To amuse me.... He appears to be utterly happy.... My father's face is uplifted and lit up from within, and he's juggling.... I think of him juggling lemons and happy." That the intense moment of happy, carefree, individualistic activity for which almost all Abse's characters strive is dramatised by an activity at once unusual, skillful and absorbing, yet vulnerable and temporary, shows us how greatly eccentricity is prized. We also experience the sadness underlying these lively texts.

In impressive scenes characters protest directly against external controls, as Nott does so powerfully, as Kurt does when Sally tries to test his essential humanity, and as X does against Aquillus's wish to use him as an example for students. But usually characters protest, as it were implicitly and often unconsciously, by demonstrating their unique imaginative potential through the language they use. We are constantly reminded that these are the plays of a fine poet and have their roots in Abse's early attempts to write poetic drama.

A few examples must serve to explain and illustrate. In *House of Cowards* Miss Chantry recalls attending a religious meeting during her youth: "What that voice said, I don't remember. I can only recall understanding everything at the time and feeling inexplicably jubilant, yet peaceful." The intense, poetic, almost tactile cadence of "inexplicably jubilant, yet peaceful", replacing the flatter, colloquial tones of Miss Chantry's normal mode of speech, indicates her empathetic potential and desire for emotional and personal satisfaction so different from any annihilation of self in a violent mob. Again, from Alf Jenkins in the same play: "I'm so looking forward to hearing Mr Shemtov. I've always enjoyed listening to those with the gift of the gab. I like harmonious cadence, even when it's only for vain amusement." The effect is similar: even Alf, very much a man-in-the-street, in a phrase like "harmonious cadence" is moved to aesthetic yearning. Above all, in *House of Cowards*, Nott, roused by the menacing crowd, cries, in a speech already quoted in part: "No more tell me of the rose's waste. I see our eyes move into a different love. I see our heart forget the Night's infirmary.... What value is the grave bedecked with flowers?" Through this momentary transcendence of naturalism Nott, despite or perhaps because of his unstable mind – a precursor, this, of a theme in *Pythagoras (Smith)* – emerges as the truly imaginative and therefore compassionate man, grasping instinctively the deathliness of the general longing for a Speaker's panacea.

In *The Dogs of Pavlov* there are similar moments, such as Kurt's description of his father juggling and Sally's reaction to Kurt's news of his New York appointment: "You make New York sound idyllic. It isn't. It's on the road to hell. I doubt if you'll ever see a rainbow in the sky over New York. One day a dove will drown on top of the Empire State Building." Even Daly, perpetrator of the experiment, when telling his colleague of the death-camps, or confronting in his lecture reasons for evil behaviour, abandons the dispassionate stance of the scientist for a language better able to do justice to his dark theme:

> The actual survivors tell their terrible stories of gold from teeth, of lampshades from human skin and so the abstract geography of hell becomes concrete: we see the belching smoke of the chimneys, we hear the hiss of the gas and the dying cries of the murdered. We may not be able to hold steady, in the front of our minds, the enormity of the offence for very long. The picture slips away in the silence between two heartbeats.

In finding such language even Daly reveals a compelling capacity for sympathetic imagining.

From *Pythagoras (Smith)* are three examples. The first is Charlie remembering the past:

> **Charlie:** Coming home excited, looking forward to seeing the wife again, the kids, on a windy autumn afternoon, coming home twenty-four hours early, arms full of things – I dunno – luggage, gifts, flowers....
> **Biddy:** Chrysanthemums...
> **Charlie:** ... shutting the front door.
> **Marian:** Too loudly.
> **Ellen:** Using one of your feet because your arms are loaded.
> **Charlie:** An' shouting up the stairs, shouting "Hullo, there".... Nothing. The house empty, the living room empty with a window open.
> **Marian:** That windy autumn afternoon.
> **Charlie:** And the curtains flying, flying.

The second is Arthur's singing, the third Pythagoras's frequent shifts into a non-naturalistic and increasingly exotic mode of speech culminating in his poem, 'White coat and purple coat'.

Pythagoras (Smith), in particular, celebrates the magical, the irrational, the imaginative. Through revealing this last quality, in Abse's work linked closely to the other two, characters remind us of their uniqueness as human beings and are valued for so doing. It is no accident that the two – Nott and Pythagoras – who speak most poetically are the ones who assert themselves most forcibly and hauntingly against conformist and subsuming pressures, and so are the ones with whom the audience most sympathises. Of course we sympathise with Sally, but in a different way: she is a victim first of circumstances then of the stereotyping self that circumstances have made of her. We sympathise more with Nott, driven out for speaking the truth, and most of all with Pythagoras, reduced to Tony Smith and set for a dreary lifetime in this play's suggested equivalent of a Shelley Street lodging house.

In his supra-naturalistic flights, whether via poetic language or ritualistic structures (for example, the stylised sequence of revelations, retractions and resumptions that closes *House of Cowards*), Abse is part of the post-war British dramatic movement, led by Beckett, Arden and Pinter, dedicated to making fine theatre from the poetry of ordinary speech. He has been strongly influenced by Pinter: the sexually provocative moments in *House of Cowards* and the interrogation of Kurt during the nightmare scene in *The Dogs of Pavlov*, let alone a recurring atmosphere of menace at times breaking into violence, look back, in particular, to *The Birthday Party*. To make a different kind of link: the close of *House of Cowards*, when characters hurriedly reject the truth about themselves and re-embrace their fantasies, may well reflect the influence of that earlier classic, Ibsen's *The Wild Duck*.

But such are the inevitable results of a life-time's interest in the theatre. What must be stressed is that Abse has his own distinctive dramatic voice. These are plays rich in ideas, plays in which he explores not only the Holocaustic ideas already described but also other important themes, such as the relationships between fantasy and reality, work and personal desires, the uses of dreams, the nature of idealism and of trust, aspects of sexuality, the need for religion, and the notion of human life as a constant moral dilemma.

The endings – the need for pretence, the wish to die, the victory of the white coat over the purple – are, in themselves, pessimistic. Nevertheless, to repeat, the plays are not. This is partly because, as it experiences the endings, the audience is on humanity's side, and because the plays as wholes, their action, humour, life and vigour, remind us constantly of the value of that humanity in all its diversity. Further, amidst all that diversity we recognise a common desire for love and grasp, what both Nott and Pythagoras know, that the capacity to love guarantees human worth.

Such reminders, such knowledge, may not seem much when set against the black tide of this century's atrocities. To Abse they are all-important, to be treasured because they are all we have. As he puts it in his essay on *The Dogs of Pavlov*:

There is the parable of the three wise men who walk past a dead dog. The first utters, "What a terrible sight!"; the second, "what a terrible smell!"; but the third who was the wisest of all, remarked: "What beautiful white teeth has that dead dog!" We must find our consolations where we can.

From: Dannie Abse: *The View from Row G*, Seren, 1990

Jasmine Donahaye – from '"A dislocation called a blessing": Three Welsh-Jewish Perspectives'

Anti-Semitism is similarly a major concern for Leo Abse's younger brother, the writer Dannie Abse, though his response to Welsh nationalism is less direct. Like Leo Abse, he seems to move from periphery to periphery of several worlds. However, where his brother was politicised by an internationalist ideology, Dannie Abse was, by contrast, politicised by the war and the Holocaust, and his expressed sense of Wales, Jewishness and attitudes to nationalism are informed by a deep dismay at ideology of any kind.

In his autobiography *A Poet in the Family* Dannie Abse echoes his brother in writing that he assents to the sentiment expressed by the Russian writer Ehrenberg that "he was a Jew as long as there was one anti-semite alive" and, in exploring why Jews react so strongly to suggestions of anti-Semitism, he claims that no Jew in the Diaspora, "however much he proclaims to the contrary, is other than a Ghetto Jew in the deepest sense – and this is, above all, because of the wartime destruction of the Jew in Europe".[1] This statement echoes Isaiah Berlin, who observes: "I realised quite early in my life that Jews were a minority everywhere. It seemed to me that there was no Jew in the world who was not, in some degree, socially uneasy".[2] Abse qualifies this deeper sense of his Jewishness by identifying himself explicitly as a *Welsh* Jew, thus reaffirming his position at the periphery of two cultures.[3] If the portrait of the spiritual emptiness of metropolitan Anglo-Jewish life given by Leo Abse in *Margaret* is accurate, this perhaps informs Dannie Abse's self-marginalization in England by his identification with Wales. Nevertheless, within a Welsh context, this identification with Wales affords him no greater ease, and appears instead to result in ambivalence, perhaps even anxiety.

Like Tobias, and his brother Leo, Dannie Abse also responds to the Jewish-Welsh connections, but unlike them he does not cite any encounter with Welsh philosemitism, and instead explores only a literary expression of this connection between the two cultures. Nevertheless, he does so in ironic and skeptical mode. In 'Under the Influence' (1984) he explores what he terms "the relationship of David and Dafydd" and somewhat tongue-in-cheek, posits in place of the Mathias/Garlick construction of the longevity of the tradition of Welsh literature in English, an equally viable construct of Biblical influence, citing in its support such continuity as that which exists between the *Song of Solomon* and Huw Morris's 'In praise of a girl'. "One observes", he concludes, "... that the literary tradition of David and Dafydd are not separate entities. Simply, the older tradition permeates the younger, there is a dialectic, a development. A seepage!".[4] Since he introduces this essay on his literary influences by discussing Tony Conran's critical term "seepage", this conclusion reinforces the inference that this essay is less about the David/Dafydd relationship, and serves more as a critique of the construction of a different tradition – that of Welsh literature in English, and also, by implication, Welsh nationality:

> "Seepage", is the word our scholarly critics bandy about. The seepage "on all cultural levels between the two language groups of Wales" as Anthony Conran puts it.
>
> Certainly it is a somewhat mystic notion that allows an Anglo-Welsh poet, ignorant of Welsh literature, to be most marvellously, most miraculously, affected by it. I do not mock. At least I do not mock with conviction because I know things can exist even when they cannot be invulnerably defined – like the concept of Welsh nationality itself.[5]

To what extent this seepage might be through English via the Biblical permeation of Welsh is not explored – he appears to be less serious about this construct in itself than he is about questioning the idea of Welsh seepage into Welsh poetry in English. Indeed, he seems to prefer to claim, perhaps in a typical contrary style, that his influences are a mixture of Dylan Thomas, Rilke and the Talmud![6]

A more revealing attitude to Welsh poetry in English is expressed in his selection of and introduction to the 1997 publication *Twentieth Century Anglo-Welsh Poetry*, in which he explains: "Those verses imbued with the most *blatant* nationalist valency do not find, for the most part, a place here because platform poems of whatever orientation rarely outlast their season".[7] Nevertheless it is the nationalist platform poems that he states he is choosing to exclude, and one infers both from this statement and from his actual selection that it is a political orientation rather than a poetic style that he has censured.

Abse's aversion to platform poems is explained in a *Jewish Quarterly* article entitled 'Finding a Voice of My Own' in which he writes that "a voice shouting loses its distinctive quality. The voice of, say, John Smith speaking is his own but John Smith shouting becomes the raised voice of anonymous humanity".[8] Nevertheless, Abse's own poems sometimes fall prey to this very problem. 'Assimilation', which appeared in *Welsh Retrospective* (1997) could be viewed as one kind of platform poem:

> Even the Sodomites, I said, would allow
> distraught refugees into their desert city,
> provide them with a Sodom-made bed.
>
> But strangers too tall, it must be admitted,
> had their legs chopped off; and nationalist Sods
> heaved at heads and feet of those too small
> till beds and bodies beautifully fitted.[9]

The political content, or even perhaps the intent, of this poem is not so much the problem with it as is the quality of its language – the rhythm is as ungainly as the lines' enforced breaks and rhymes, and the language is flat. His poem 'Altercation in Splott'[10] is of the same genre, and fails in a similar way to overcome the overt political message about racism, but 'Case History', which could also be deemed a platform poem against Neo-nazism, overcomes these limitations in its luminous last stanza. The first stanza employs a similar dullness of language, containing such rote expressions as "architects of the German death-camps" or the prosaic line "and continued to invent curses", and the second stanza is hectoring in its irony:

> When I palpated his liver
> I felt the soft liver of Goering;
> when I lifted my stethoscope
> I heard the heartbeats of Himmler;
> when I read his encephalograph
> I thought, 'Sieg heil, mein Führer'.

But after the doctor-narrator considers the poisons in his dispensary, and prescribes, nevertheless, as if he were his patient's brother, the last three-line stanza transcends the polemic:

> Later that night I must have slept
> on my arm: momentarily
> my right hand lost its cunning.[11]

These lines evoke the Hebrew prayer "if I forgot thee oh Jerusalem may my right hand forget its cunning" and in that evocation lies Abse's profound dilemma as a doctor, a secular Jew, and a humanist, which he conveys in subtle, resonant language.

Both *Welsh Retrospective*, which collects Abse's poems that concern Wales, and his editorship of *Twentieth Century Anglo-Welsh Poetry* indicate something of an alienation from contemporary Welsh affairs and from Welsh culture, and yet they both reinforce the centrality of Wales to his identity as a poet. In the introduction to *Welsh Retrospective*, Cary Archard distinguishes Abse's work as being free of the "occasionally strident nationalism" of some of the other English-language poets' work, but he claims that the book is important "for what it reveals of Dannie Abse's indebtedness to Welsh language forms and Welsh literature and history". Abse, he writes, "replays the tunes of earlier Welsh poets," and the "*Retrospective* contributes to a particularly *Welsh* tradition".[12]

Despite this claim, Abse's approach to that cultural tradition is, unlike his brother's and aunt's certitude, ambivalent. In a letter to *Modern Poetry in Translation* (1995) addressing the editor's question as to why he does not write in Welsh,[13] he evidently excludes himself from the "existential anomie" he attributes to many Welsh poets, whose experiences of the huge change in culture, language and landscape in Wales, he claims, have led to "uncertainty about identity which, in turn, have prompted many to assert their Welshness as if their very core of being had been challenged".[14] It is as an outsider also that his narrative voice is heard in his *Welsh Retrospective* poem 'A Heritage', which describes the end of coalmining:

Above, on the brutalised,
unstitched side of a Welsh mountain,
it has to be someone from somewhere else
who will sing solo....

Only someone uncommitted,
someone from somewhere else,
panorama high on a coal-tip,
may jubilantly laud
the re-entry of the exiled god
into his shadowless kingdom.[15]

In this poem Abse is typically ambivalent: he simultaneously identi-
fies himself as that "someone outside" and "someone uncommitted"
by his very writing of the poem, but is enough of an insider to under-
mine his own "jubilant lauding" by imaging the coal god brandishing
a man's femur, and concluding with the decidedly un-jubilant image
of "blood-stained black roses". This see-saw between engagement
with and self-exclusion from Welsh identity and experience is also
captured in his poem 'Down the M4', which evokes his grandmother
and the world of Lily Tobias:

> Then the Tawe ran fluent and trout-coloured over stones stonier,
> more genuine; then Annabella, my mother's mother, spoke Welsh
> with such an accent the village said, 'Tell the truth, fach,
> you're no Jewess. *They're* from the Bible. *You're* from Patagonia!'
>
> ...Ystalyfera is farther
> than smoke and God further than all distance known. I whistle
> no hymn but an old Yiddish tune my mother knows. It won't keep.[16]

That past, either Jewish or Welsh, won't keep him, nor yet will the
metropolitan Anglo-Jewish world of Golders Green.[17] This deliberate
multiplicity of not-belonging is underscored by his "autobiographical fiction". In his Author's Note to his second such book, he notes
that its earlier companion piece was mistakenly identified as autobiography but that, with *There Was a Young Man from Cardiff*, once
more he has deleted his past and, "despite approximate resemblances, substituted it with artifice". He adds: "If I am disbelieved, so
much the better".[18] Abse's very use of the term "autobiographical
fiction" for this genre of writing reflects what M. Wynn Thomas has
called his "cultivation of non-alignment as an art form".[19] According
to Thomas, Abse has "thrived on a carefully fostered image of being
the eternal outsider" and has created "a living space for his imagination by constantly playing one of his identities off against another."[20]
The poems collected in *Welsh Retrospective* and Abse's several autobiographies and fictional autobiographies demonstrate this cultivated
position on the periphery. Unlike Tobias, however, for whom such a
position resulted in deep, if separatist, sympathy, or Leo Abse, for
whom such a position led to clear alignments and considerable, if
selective, critical detachment, Dannie Abse's embrace of his dislocation has not so much resulted in non-alignment as in ambivalence.

That ambivalence or social uneasiness is perhaps more familiar and easier to accommodate than Leo Abse's rhetorical absolutism or the naïve optimism of Tobias's idealistic romantic nationalism. Nevertheless, despite their varied and often historically dubious political or cultural positions, the writing of all three is marked by a deep humanism and it is evident that this humanism arises not only from their experience of dislocation, but also from the overlooked but profoundly resonant interaction of the two cultures on whose peripheries they stand.

NOTES

1. Dannie Abse, *A Poet in the Family* (London: Hutchinson & Co., 1974), p. 78. Leo Abse cites Ehrenberg in *Margaret, Daughter of Beatrice: A Politician's Psycho-biography of Margaret Thatcher* (London: Cape, 1989), p. 200.

2. Isaiah Berlin and Ramin Jahanbegloo, *Recollections of a Historian of Ideas: Conversations with Isaiah Berlin* (New York: Scribner, 1991), p. 85.

3. *A Poet in the Family*, pp. 78-80.

4. Dannie Abse, *Journals From the Ant-heap* (London: Hutchinson, 1986), p. 147.

5. *Journals From the Ant-heap*, p. 145.

6. *Journals From the Ant-heap*, pp. 150-61.

7. Dannie Abse, ed., *Twentieth Century Anglo-Welsh Poetry* (Bridgend: Seren, 1997), p. 15.

8. Dannie Abse, "Finding a Voice of My Own", *Jewish Quarterly* 26.3-4 (Autumn-Winter, 1978-79), p. 86.

9. Dannie Abse, *Welsh Retrospective* (Bridgend: Seren, 1997), p. 36.

10. *Welsh Retrospective*, p. 34.

11. *Welsh Retrospective*, p. 42.

12. *Welsh Retrospective*, p. 8.

13. "A Letter from Dannie Abse", *Modern Poetry in Translation*, ns 7 (1995), pp. 217-19.

14. *Modern Poetry in Translation*, p. 218.

15. *Welsh Retrospective*, p. 32.

16. *Welsh Retrospective*, p. 19.

17. Dannie Abse, *Poet in the Family*, pp. 162-69.

18. Dannie Abse, *There Was a Young Man from Cardiff* (London: Hutchinson, 1991) n. pag.

19. M. Wynn Thomas, "Prints of Wales: Contemporary Welsh poetry in English", *Poetry in the British Isles: Non-Metropolitan Perspectives*, ed. Hans-

Werner Ludwig and Lothar Fietz (Cardiff: U. of Wales P., 1995), p. 101.
20. M. Wynn Thomas, p. 101.

From: *Welsh Writing in English* vol.7, 2001-2

James A. Davies – *"In a different place / changed"*: *Dannie Abse, Dylan Thomas, T.S. Eliot and Wales'*

After Every Green Thing (1949), Dannie Abse's first volume of poetry, rarely appears in his own lists of previous publications. Of that volume's poems only 'The Uninvited' has survived the cut for his three subsequent volumes titled *Collected Poems*.[1] One other poem, 'The Yellow Bird', has re-emerged, rewritten, in the 2003 *Collected Poems*. Abse has explained this calculated neglect: *After Every Green Thing* was 'immature. I was immature. I caught like an infection, the neo-romantic fashionable mode of the time'.[2] Dominating Neo-Romanticism, though never confined by it, was Dylan Thomas, then at the height of his fame.[3]

"Dylan Thomas's poems powerfully engaged me," Abse stated in his 1984 Gwyn Jones lecture, " – too much so, for a number of my own poems which can be discovered in my first volume, *After Every Green Thing*, are touched by his manner." He offers two examples, which "sound like Dylan's cast-offs: 'harp of sabbaths', 'choir of wounds'"[4]. There are many others, including 'vowelled birds', 'hands tick', 'fugue of birds on fire', plus a distant echo of 'After the Funeral' in 'Poem to a Younger Poet' ('how, when the spade rings, should my ghost protest') and, not so distant, of 'The force that through the green fuse' in 'Psychosis' ('and I am dumb to tell her angels and her visions'). Abse's language throughout this volume is lushly Thomasian, even to the use of the apostrophic or exclamatory 'O', sometimes, oddly, printed in lower-case. Ideas can also be derivative, one example being writing as shedding blood: 'you will expectorate a red star / of blood upon the white panic of a blank page' he informs that much-advised 'Younger Poet' who is also offered a hint of 'process' in 'the timeless flood of blood / that circles the street-ways beneath your flesh'. Elsewhere, with the poet still in sanguinary mode, 'the blood in the virgin's scream', in 'The Journey', in recalling 'The tombstone told when she died', suggests a Thomasian proclivity for sex and violence hardly typical of Abse's work.

After such knowledge there is an understandable drawing-down of blinds. Though Abse's second volume, *Walking Under Water* (1952), has similar moments – Ann Jones's 'fountain heart' in 'A Posy for Summer', for instance, and such Dylanesque flourishes as '[t]oday measure pain with a clock' and 'all the tall dead rise to break the crust of the imperative earth' – the influence is not so pervasive. The same can be said of *Ash on a Young Man's Sleeve* (1954), Abse's famous autobiographical novel. This has a general, perhaps unavoidable, affinity with *Portrait of the Artist as a Young Dog* (1940): less episodic, though a series of significant moments, but centred on home, park, seaside and so forth, to explore a journey into adolescence. There are echoes of 'Fern Hill': 'All day it was lovely' (42), for example, and, again more distantly, 'emperor of my eighteen years, king of the tall fading trees' (197). Here, however, most of such literary references are ironically deployed.

In *Tenants of the House* (1957) Abse finds a voice of his own. Almost two-thirds of its poems have always been collected; one other, 'Photograph and Yellow Tulips', omitted from the 'collecteds', re-emerges rewritten as 'Photograph and White Tulips', one of eight poems he chose to represent himself in *Twentieth Century Anglo-Welsh Poetry* (1997), his own anthology. In its 'yellow' version the poem is typically Abse's in uniting the conversational with the lyrical, the initially transparent with an ultimate opaqueness. It considers photography as reviving thoughts of a lost occasion and a sense of the past as dead, the camera as a 'little black coffin'. Dylan Thomas's influence has dwindled.

Indeed, the last three poems in *Tenants of the House* comprise a form of exorcism. The first is 'Elegy for Dylan Thomas', written in December 1953, shortly after Thomas's death. Abse writes of Thomas's fame during a life always close to death's 'essential kiss', of his posthumous fame and of his death as poetic loss: 'Suddenly others who sing seem older and lame.' 'Tenants of the House', the volume's penultimate poem, attacks the 'Movement', always hostile to Thomas's work and quick to offer his life and work as salutary examples of destructive excess. Yet, writes Abse, with Thomas dead, '[I]n bowler hats they sing with sharp, flat voices / but no-one dances, nobody rejoices'. The final poem continues this theme. 'Go Home the Act is Over', set in a circus and written in the first person, shows the poet as daring trapeze artist, flying above 'pedestrians who with iambics freeze'. He falls to his death, the circus leaves town, the field is empty. All three poems, as will be seen, though recognising loss, offer distinct reservations about Thomas. All three poems imply closure: the field is clear for Abse's next volume, *Poems, Golders Green 1956-61* (1962), which established him as a leading urban/suburban British poet.

Dylan Thomas is an important but not the only influence on Abse's early work. There are occasional borrowings from other poets, one example being 'the dazzled upturned faces' of 'Autumn', in *After Every Green Thing*, that recalls the 'upturned dreaming faces' of Alun Lewis's 'All Day it has Rained'. The second increasingly dominant influence is T.S. Eliot. From one perspective, that Eliot should replace Dylan Thomas is not surprising. The younger Abse so often looked outwards. He was first drawn to poetry through reading poems about the Spanish Civil War. He moved from Cardiff to London in 1943 to continue his medical studies at King's College and Westminster Hospital. Since then, apart from National Service as a doctor in the RAF, his main home has been in London: he and his wife brought up a family in Golders Green. Until his retirement in 1989 he worked as a doctor in a Soho chest clinic. During this time he has been a prominent figure in literary London. In the immediate post-war period he was part of Swiss Cottage café life, and has written engagingly about the aspiring writers – Bernice Rubens, Peter Vansittart and the Nobel prizewinner Elias Canetti amongst them – with whom he talked and drank coffee during his salad days. Viewed from the parochial Wales of that time, from which, of the serious writers, only Dylan Thomas had broken free into international stardom, this could seem (and perhaps was) like Hemingway's Paris, or Dorothy Parker's Algonquin. As John Tripp once wrote, not wholly tongue-in-cheek, there is 'a touch of glamour about Dannie Abse'.[5] His books, published in London, have sold well; *Ash on a Young Man's Sleeve* (1954) has never been out of print. From 1978 to 1992 he was President of the Poetry Society; in 1983 he was elected a Fellow of the Royal Society of Literature. T.S. Eliot's international ambience and sophistication, the mandarin American thoroughly at home in Europe and a British subject since 1927, fitted nicely into the maturing Abse's sense of the Zeitgeist. His poetic tastes changed. T.S. Eliot apart, he wrote: 'I have grown to like Edward Thomas as much as, if not more than, Dylan Thomas. I have become as attached to the peculiarly modest "English" tradition as to the distinctive, aspiring "European" one.'[6] Immersion in metropolitan literary life took him far away from Anglo-Welsh writing with which, in any case, he had little sympathy. At times he tended to suggest there might be no such thing. Thus, in the Gwyn Jones Lecture he radiated well-mannered scepticism about such ideas as 'seepage' and of praise as being an uniquely Welsh characteristic.[7] In his introduction to *Twentieth Century Anglo-Welsh Poetry* he recalls stating in a 1960s broadcast that 'there is no such thing as a specific Anglo-Welsh style or tone, and the Welshness of an English poem simply depends on what the poem is about'.[8]

Eliot was a great poet, who forced contemporaries and successors to rethink notions of what poetry can do. His influence was inescapable, particularly in the 1940s and early 1950s. But lasting wholehearted enthusiasm for Eliot's writing would have been difficult for a young, Jewish, liberal-left-leaning poet like Abse. Eliot's anti-Semitism would surely have troubled him, even though he has noted, not unsympathetically, that after World War Two Eliot was profoundly contrite.[9] Further, the older poet represented the reactionary right. To quote Jonathan Raban, Eliot 'embodies very exactly a type of right-wing millennialism' that regards modern life as the remnants of 'a once great culture'. Despite his reputation as a modernist, he offers 'a doomed, elegiac celebration of an irretrievable (and nostalgically mythicized) past'. He is 'not... the first great modern poet, but... the last writer at the end of an era'.[10] Again, his essentially religious solutions to the modern world's deficiencies would hardly have appealed to secular Abse.

Yet Eliot's influence on Abse's early work is very strong. In *After Every Green Thing* the poems of *Prufrock and Other Observations* (1917), particularly 'The Love Song of J. Alfred Prufrock', 'Gerontion' (in *Poems*, 1920), *The Waste Land* (1922), *The Hollow Men* (1925) and *Four Quartets*, this last completed in 1942 when Abse was in his formative late teens, affect the volume. Hence, for instance, 'the long unfocused street, / grinning like a greyhound', or 'walking through brown fog with blue hands / against the fractured lamp-posts', or '[f]or I have been here before, / many times and in different places' and 'In the bad yellow light of a yesterday lamppost', or 'And after this Lord, what greater error, what / Wisdom known in the last experience of the last?' and even the insomnia of 'Poem at 4 a.m.'. He argues in verse, in the manner of *Four Quartets*:

> No less because of fear of the partial ecstasy,
> the intimate terrible sadness of knowing God, –
> I do not talk about possession, – but of the hint known,
> the stone deciphered under the water momentarily,
> and then lost again.

In *Walking Under Water*, the title itself suggesting the final lines of Prufrock's 'Love Song', Eliot takes over from Dylan Thomas as the dominant influence. Examples include a hint of *Burnt Norton*'s garden scene in 'The Welcome' ('Who will enter through the gate, who now will enter?'), and such Eliotic echoes as 'we die / with the dead' in 'A Posy for Summer', 'tuned in their own stillness' in 'Conversation', and 'space without sound... space without odour... space without image' in 'The Clock'. 'No lips that kiss whisper my name' in 'Ghost' links Abse's poem with *The Hollow Men*. 'Portrait of a Marriage' catches up both Prufrock's 'Love Song' and 'Portrait of a Lady':

> your artificial smile alone
> that floats between the ceiling and the floor
> like some quiet heartbreak, can almost condone
> what, after all, others too must slow endure[.]

The Prufrockian note is heard again in such poems of urban angst as 'Journeys and Faces' and 'The Descent'. 'Ordinary Heaven' even features a Prufrock lookalike: a 'plump man, now half bald' who might have 'dared, ah dared' to 'question: "Is it worth it, worth it...?"'

Abse's next two books, *Ash on a Young Man's Sleeve* and *Tenants of the House*, have, of course, titles drawn from Eliot's writing. In the former, Abse quotes as epigraph the relevant lines from 'Little Gidding', as follows:

> Ash on an old man's sleeve
> Is all the ash burnt roses leave.

Dust in the air suspended
Marks the place where a story ended.
Dust inbreathed was a house – [11]

The famous first line, here eponymously rewritten, opens section two of 'Little Gidding', the first three stanzas of which describe death as the absolute end, without any sense of spiritual hope. They are followed by the bleak Dantean encounter in Blitzed London of the narrator and the 'familiar compound ghost' who contrasts despairingly secular old age with necessary restoration by 'refining fire'. Abse's title associates such bleakness with youth. Yet the novel is one of hope and essential joy: the ending, the narrator as medical student sitting in the park some years after his friend Keith's death from a German bomb, has its autumnal mood and late-adolescent angst redeemed, as so often in Abse's work, by the narrator's humour and ironic self-awareness.

The line from 'Gerontion' that forms the title of *Tenants of the House* (1957) makes a similar unexpected association. The conclusion of Eliot's poem – 'Tenants of the house, / Thoughts of a dry brain in a dry season' – is all too appropriate for Eliot's deeply pessimistic study of an anti-Semitic old man lamenting both his age and the deficiencies of his past life, but a surprising source of inspiration for a young Jewish writer. We may be further surprised by Eliot's continuing influence elsewhere in the volume. For example, 'The Trial' and 'Duality' can be read as meditations on the Prufrock line, 'prepare a face to meet the faces that you meet'; stanza four of 'Photograph and Yellow Tulips' –

we shall hold it, this most sad witness,
and smile please and come a little nearer
to a time that was never twice, to a place
that could never be thanked enough...

– suggests both Prufrock and *Four Quartets*. 'The Field' opens a recollection of 'Little Gidding': 'Should you stroll this way'.

Yet, to repeat, in this volume Abse finds his own poetic voice. The title requires reinterpretation in terms of Abse's work: the 'tenants' are the poems and the 'house' is his poetic sensibility. The poems include a section entitled 'The identity of Love'; we begin to understand such poems as 'Poem and Message', 'Anniversary' and 'The

Moment' – and the volume titles – as, now, effecting a dialogue with Eliot's sombre influence. These passionately tender explorations of newly married love are absolutely Abse's own. T.S. Eliot, for all his towering poetic gifts, could never write 'blind in the pandemonium / of the kiss', as Abse does in 'Anniversary'.

This is not to say that the mature Abse discards Eliot. Rather, he uses him in a consciously strategic way. Two poems make the point. The first is 'Funland', regarded by some as Abse's masterpiece.[12] Certainly it is one of his finest achievements. The poem is a surrealistic treatment of life in a mental hospital, used here as a metaphor for human society.[13] It explores Abse's abiding concern with the nature and exercise of authority, in particular, its readiness to suppress minorities and to repress and control all variations – poetry; imagination, magic – from a totalitarian ideal. Behind such concern is the fact of the Holocaust, a substantial presence in much of his work, and his secularity: a related theme is the failure of religion. 'Funland' dramatises and universalises such themes, in part through the use of intertextual references, mainly to T.S. Eliot's poetry. Thus the narrator offers a version of a line in 'Ash Wednesday', asking of a reborn magician, 'Why should the aged peacock / stretch his wings?' The hospital's poet is reduced to an *East Coker* lumpen peasant as 'he lifts up and down in slow motion / up and down his heavy feet', before being silenced. The hospital superintendent is 'sullen as a ruined millionaire'. The poem's final line – 'Do not wake us. We may die' – increases even the pessimism of Prufrock lingering 'in the chambers of the sea. / Till human voices wake us, and we drown'. But the main thrust of the poem is to set against Eliot's bleak view of modern social collapse aided by religious sterility, supported by such echoes and the poems they evoke, an insistence that, no matter how cruel and despairing life can be, there are always other possibilities. In particular, man's capacity to love, sustained against so much totalitarian pressure, guarantees human worth.

The second poem is 'Prufrock at the Seaside', a product of Abse's late seventies. An elderly Prufrock is at the seaside. A proposal of marriage having failed long ago, he has lived a bachelor's masturbatory life, full of regrets. He has become a voyeur. Here is a humorous poem concerned to satirise Eliot's angst-laden construct, partly by opposing his romantic generalities with realist detail, whilst never being indifferent to Prufrock's aching unhappiness. The final couplet reads: 'The waves lash on but the sea's in its chains. / The beach becomes desolate. The dog remains.'[14] Enter, or re-enter, Dylan Thomas through the echo of the famous ending of 'Fern Hill' and Thomas's 'young dog'.

The mature Abse's dialectical relationship with T.S. Eliot exists in parallel with his developing engagement with Thomas. This last is evident in the publishing and textual history of those three poems, already mentioned, that close *Tenants of the House*: 'Elegy for Dylan Thomas', 'Tenants of the House', 'Go Home the Act is Over'.

'Elegy for Dylan Thomas', extensively revised, is included in all three 'collecteds'. In 1977, when the first 'collected' appeared, much more was known about Thomas's life and death than in December 1953. Brinnin and Fitzgibbon had published their biographies, with detailed accounts of the careless living that hastened death, the perhaps apocryphal whisky drinking during his last days and the death itself. The scandalous life attracted enormous posthumous interest. Many voyeuristic tourists, often wholly ignorant of literature, let alone Thomas's writing, were drawn to Laugharne, where he was buried not in a tomb but in a simple grave. The new version reflects all this.

Thus, 'tomorrow the unconscious kids will cry in the dandelion fields / and tall tourists inspect his tomb' in the earlier version, becomes 'wrong-again Emily will come to the dandelion yard / and, with rum tourists, inspect his grave'.[15] There is a new realisation that 'Death was his voluntary marriage' ('involuntary' in the *Tenants of the House* version) and that Thomas died because, the poem suggests, 'he rode / the whiskey-meadows of [Death's] breath' ('water-meadows' in the first version). In the revised version Abse is honest and even more compassionate about Thomas's life, hints at neglect (perhaps familial) of the grave and is contemptuous of the ghoulish tourism. And when he rewrites 'without a shadow his free ghost flies' as 'no fat ghost but a quotation cries' he emphasises the penetrating power of Thomas's writing.

'Tenants of the House', in which Dylan Thomas is the unnamed 'famous tenant', was omitted from *Collected Poems 1948-1976* but restored in 1989 and 2003, in more explicit form. The new title is 'Enter the Movement'. The 'strange house' of stanza one is changed to 'the Boat-house'. Thomas's poetry – of which Abse may have never been less than a fan – is now described with a fresh enthusiasm: for 'every light put out' in stanza one, we now have 'half the lights put out'; 'his brute songs' becomes 'his gorgeous music'. The final line of stanza two, 'well, he sang the great passion others lacked', becomes 'well, he sang the Welsh passion others lacked'. The original fourth stanza is as follows:

> Then winter came when whistling beggars freeze.
> He, from inner fires, sang catastrophes
> While neighbours jigged with roaring joy outside
> Until laughing that tragic singer died.

The new one is:

> Then winter came when whistling beggars freeze.
> He, to quench inner fires, drank catastrophes
> while corybants, roaring, jigged with joy outside
> till, delirious, that lyric singer died.

'Quench' stresses Thomas's compulsive necessity to write poetry out of personal tension and trouble, his wild living as escape, while the appearance of 'corybants', and so the shift into mythology – corybants were the fertility goddess Cybele's wild dancers – suggests the universal appeal of Thomas's poetry. In the stanza's final line, for apparent carelessness about life is substituted explanation: Thomas was caught up in and destroyed by wild public acclaim. In the poem's penultimate line, already quoted, '[I]n bowler hats they sing with sharp, flat voices', becomes '[p]roudly English, they sing with sharp, flat voices'. The new poem thinks more of his poetry and is more understanding of his tragic predicament. It trumpets Thomas's poetic virtues in terms of a contrast between Welsh writing in English and *English* writing, as demonstrated by the 'Movement'. In publicly highlighting the difference we mark a sea-change in Abse's attitude to literary Wales.

    'Go Home the Act is Over' was omitted from *Collected Poems 1948-1976*, only to reappear, revised, in *White Coat, Purple Coat* (1989). The first-person case is replaced by the third person singular. The poet is now 'Dionysian'. The earlier line '[a]gainst the roof my two shadows dance' becomes '[t]all against the roof his two shadows dance'. The result is the same: the daring, performing poet falls from his high poetic wire to a death the audience seems to expect, and the circus leaves town. The revisions treat Thomas more favourably, but the two versions of the poem make the same central points: he tended to play to his audience and was destroyed by – money's lure ('but seeing gold, trips and loses balance'). Significantly, this poem is omitted from *New and Collected Poems* (2003).

Abse has always made frequent visits to Wales to see his ageing parents, for instance, or to see Cardiff City play soccer. But, as he put it in 'Return to Cardiff', each visit was 'less a return than a raid / on mislaid identities'. The turning point – the small beginning – in his relationship with Welsh writing could well be dated to 1972, with his purchase of Green Hollows cottage in Ogmore-on-Sea where, as a child, he spent idyllic family holidays. During the three decades since he has strengthened his literary and academic ties with Wales. He was elected a Fellow of the Welsh Academy in 1992 and became its President in 1995. An Honorary Doctorate from the University of Wales in 1989 was followed by one from the University of Glamorgan in 1997 and by an Honorary Fellowship of the University of Wales College of Medicine in 1999. For over twenty years he has given great support to Poetry Wales Press, whose Seren imprint has made it an important poetry publisher. Abse is a director of the firm. In 1997 he published *Welsh Retrospective* and *Twentieth Century Anglo-Welsh Poetry*. The former collects all his poems about Wales. They dramatise a shift from, to use a line from 'Sons', 'the hesitant sense of not belonging quite'. This poem of the 1970s is one that demonstrates how much of an exile Abse has been:

> Strange a London door should slam
> and I think thus, of Cardiff evenings
> trying to rain, of quick dark where raw brick could hide.

His Wales is mainly the past, that country from which all are exiled. He looks into family history, insisting affectionately that 'if this be not true, I never lived'; he recalls his childhood, remembering a piano teacher, a cricketer, footballers, cinema-going and family holidays. Later romantic adventures, racial tension, incidents from his medical career, familial deaths and entrances, the observations of age, are all described with a deceptive, because slightly distancing precision, all too aware of the problems of remembering.

Pressing through these poems is Abse's Jewishness: sometimes overt – his dying father 'thin as Auschwitz' – more often implicit in familial explorations and his sense of history. Pressing with equal strength is a British literary tradition, evident in echoes of Shakespeare, Wordsworth, Tennyson, Arnold, Larkin and others, as well as of T.S. Eliot and Dylan Thomas.

Welsh Retrospective makes three important points about Abse and Wales. Firstly, the greater engagement with place and landscape in some of the later poems – 'At Ogmore-by-Sea this August Evening' and 'A Wall' for instance – succeeds the slightly distanced narration of earlier writing, such as 'Down the M4' and 'Return to Cardiff'. Secondly, Abse includes three versions of medieval Welsh poems – 'Meurig Dafydd to his Mistress', 'The Boasts of Hywel ab Owain Gwynedd' and 'Lament of Heledd' – published in his earlier volumes, and places them immediately before 'Elegy for Dylan Thomas' and 'A Sea-shell for Vernon Watkins', thus suggesting a tradition of Welsh writing that, suitably modified, includes Abse himself. This, plus the actual publishing of this book, the third point, stresses Abse's nationality with a new overtness. Ultimately his work floats free of national or racial limitations – 'I hail / the world within a word', he writes in 'A Letter from Ogmore-by-Sea' – but he is now much concerned to exhibit his Welshness. In a volume published in Wales he demonstrates an increasing sense of national identity.

What he makes of this identity, of Welshness generally, can be gauged from *Twentieth Century Anglo-Welsh Poetry*, the anthology he edited, also for Seren, in 1997. 'Anglo-Welsh' in the title is immediately problematic: two writers as different as Jan Morris and Donald Davie, for example, have used it to describe a person with one Welsh and one English parent. In not using the now usually preferred 'Welsh writing in English' Abse betrays some cultural uncertainty. His editorial principles of selection cause further problems: poets are no longer adjudged Anglo-Welsh because of their subject-matter but on the basis of 'Welsh affiliation', which means ancestry, residence or birth-and-breeding. This leads to inconsistencies: Kingsley Amis out, Jean Earle in, is only one of many examples. And though such eclecticism may reflect a suitably postmodern sense of Welshness as an ever-changing construct, it also creates further problems of definition.

These are not solved by the volume's 'Prologue', a stimulating and controversial collection of statements about Welsh poetry in English. Examples include an insistence on the dependence of Welsh poetry in English on the Welsh language, and on what Jeremy Hooker calls positional 'responsibilities' – Anglo-Welsh poets – sited between

'Welsh language and culture and the Anglicising influences of their medium' – and R.S. Thomas's belief that truly Welsh poetry has compulsory links with 'the true Wales', meaning an oddly timeless rurality. Roland Mathias asserts that 'a Biblical tone is a Welsh quality'. He offers Dylan Thomas as an example but, biblically speaking, could equally well link him to an English tradition that includes Jeremy Taylor, John Donne's *Devotions* and Milton. Abse's own contribution to the 'Prologue' debate is an extract from *A Strong Dose of Myself* (1983), which cites an awareness of the past as an aspect of Welshness and suggests difference from the English does not depend on the Welsh language. This, so far as it goes, is not a great help. Neither is the Prologue: its various quotations merely confuse. All is further complicated by two generalisations in Abse's introduction: that Welsh poets 'side with the losers of history and of life's procession – the underdogs, the outsiders, the downtrodden' and that Welsh poems, in the main, 'aim at the tropopause of feeling'.

His selection of poems makes further points. One is an egalitarian stance, perhaps typically Welsh. The maximum number of poems by any one author is eight; thirteen poets have the full complement. They are Edward Thomas, Wilfred Owen, Jean Earle, R.S. Thomas, Dylan Thomas, Alun Lewis, Leslie Norris, John Ormond, Dannie Abse, Gillian Clarke, Tony Curtis, Sheenagh Pugh and Robert Minhinnick. This is an impressive list. But it is also a list in which some are far more equal than others. Secondly, with few exceptions, the choice of poems reflects the principle of accessibility, the poet speaking to his or her community, a point emphasised in Abse's introduction. Dylan Thomas, for instance, is represented only by immediately accessible poems, in his case the most famous ones. But one welcome consequence of applying the accessibility principle is the inclusion of a substantial amount of humorous verse: A.G. Prys-Jones, Harri Webb, Mercer Simpson, Douglas Houston, John Davies, Christopher Meredith and Abse himself, with 'Welsh Valley Cinema 1930s' and 'Thankyou Note'. They help tweak the introduction's stereotype.

David Jones apart, the token High Modernist, there's not much engagement with the last century's more extreme poetic approaches. Ironically, given Abse's one-time hostility, the main basic influence here is the 'Movement', though there is much that escapes. So many of the poets are uneasy with realism per se, and reach readily for symbolism, historical allegory, rhetorical transformations; from which it could be said that, wherever possible, Abse chooses poets like himself. Further, he is unable to offer a precise, or even a convincingly inclusive, notion of Welshness. He has long recognised the problem: 'Not for one second, I know / can I be the same man twice' he wrote in 'Leaving Cardiff'. The older man who acknowledges the existence of 'Welsh writing in English' is not the same person as the younger self who once rejected its validity. The country where he has a second home is very different from the one he left in 1943. His anthology seeks to make sense of these changes. The result is both stereotyped and blurred, which may be appropriate for the inhabitants of a fractured country.

It is surely significant that 'The Uninvited' is the single surviving poem from *After Every Green Thing*, for it ends with lines that can describe some permanent effects of exile:

> and we are here, in a different place,
> changed and incredibly alone,
> and we did not know, we do not know ever.

Via escape from the Dylan Thomas effect, the establishing of difference from T.S. Eliot, and a renewed appreciation of Dylan Thomas, Abse has come to embrace literary and geographical Welshness. For Wales this is not all gain: its maverick outlook, its cosmopolitan outpost, both lose force and definition. Abse is no longer as much the salutary Other which a small literary world probably needs. His anthology's uncertain stereotyping – perhaps, paradoxically, its most valuable, thought-provoking characteristic – echoes our own confusion. Dylan Thomas also puzzled over Welshness: on the one hand he sought to foster 'the development of Anglo-Welsh poetry',[16] on the other he stated that 'Anglo-Welsh poetry... is an ambiguous compromise'. He ended: 'It's the poetry that counts... not his continent, country, island.'[17] In Dannie Abse's case it counts a lot as an achievement of the first importance, whatever we might think of his thoughts about Wales.

NOTES

1. *Collected Poems 1948-1976* (London: Hutchinson, 1977), p. 1; *White Coat, Purple Coat: Collected Poems 1948-1988* (London: Hutchinson, 1989), p. 3; *New and Collected Poems* (London: Hutchinson, 2003), pp. 3-4.

2. Joseph Cohen, 'Conversations with Dannie Abse', *The Poetry of Dannie Abse*, ed. Joseph Cohen (London: Robson Books, 1983), p. 151.

3. The starting point for all discussions of Abse, Thomas and Eliot is Tony Curtis, *Dannie Abse*, Writers of Wales (Cardiff: University of Wales Press, 1985). The present writer seeks to build on Curtis's useful pages.

4. *Journals from the Ant-Heap* (London: Hutchinson, 1986), p. 151.

5 'Dannie Abse Revisited', *Poetry Wales*, 13.2 (Autumn 1977), p. 19.

6. *A Poet in the Family* (London: Robson Books, 1974), p. 156.

7. *Journals from the Ant-Heap*, pp. 145ff.

8. Dannie Abse (ed.), *Twentieth Century Anglo-Welsh Poetry* (Bridgend: Seren 1997), p. 13.

9. *Intermittent Journals* (Bridgend: Seren, 1994), pp. 180-1.

10. Jonathan Raban, *The Society of the Poem* (London: Harrap, 1971). pp. 11, 15.

11. The second line is often misquoted in editions of *Ash on a Young Man's Sleeve*. It should read 'Is all the ash the burnt roses leave.' The omission of the article makes the line more lyrical but more general, seemingly an unconscious minor mitigation of the older poet's pessimism.

12. Gigliolá Sacerdoti Mariani, 'From Funland to Funland: An Ellipse', *The Poetry of Dannie Abse*, ed. Joseph Cohen, p. 74. The poem is the title poem of *Funland and Other Poems* (London: Hutchinson, 1973).

13. My comments on 'Funland' are, in part, drawn from my article 'dramatising "Funland" ', *New Welsh Review*, 15 (Winter 1991-2), pp. 38-41.

14. *New and Collected Poems* (2003), pp. 414-15.

15. In the revised version (*Collected Poems 1948-1976*, pp. 32-3) these lines, rewritten, are all that survive from the *Tenants of the House* stanza two and replace the last two lines of stanza one. 'Dylan Thomas told the story of how a certain American lady said how much she admired his Hornblower series. When Dylan remarked that C.S. Forester was the author, the lady's husband shouted out "Wrong again, Emily"': Cary Archard, notes on the poems in Dannie Abse, *Welsh Retrospective* (Bridgend: Seren, 1997), p. 65.

16. Dylan Thomas, *The Collected Letters*, new edn, ed. Paul Ferris (London: J.M. Dent, 2000), p. 385.

17. Dylan Thomas, *The Broadcasts*, ed. Ralph Maud (London: J.M. Dent & Sons, 1991), pp. 31-2.

From: *Beyond The Difference – Welsh Literature in Comparative Contexts* (UWP 2004) eds. Alyce von Rothkirch and David Williams

John Pikoulis – 'Abse ab se'

I

Who is Dannie Abse? A simple answer is: the man who left Cardiff in 1943.

> I wait in the evening air.
> Sea-birds drop down to the sea.
> I prepare to sail from where
> the docks' derelictions are.

This is the opening of 'Leaving Cardiff', the first poem to be included in his *Welsh Retrospective*. In a sense, Abse has been travelling ever since, his self (or *se*) being held in suspension. He belongs to no one place and is defined by no one set of affiliations. 'Derelictions', in the fourth line, suggests that his departure was an escape from something that had broken down. He travels in hope as well as necessity.

The sea-birds that drop down to the water grant Abse's passage the logic of migration, an inevitable movement towards a natural end.

> I stand on the deck and stare,
> slack hammocks of waves below,
> while black shapes upon the pier
> make the furthest star seem near

Such standing and staring recall Milton's sonnet upon his blindness:

> ... [God's] state
> Is Kingly. Thousands at his bidding speed
> And post o'er Lands and Ocean without rest:
> They also serve who only stand and wait.

Those who stand and wait are as much part of the divine scheme of things as those, like Abse, who 'post o'er Lands and Ocean'. But his departure carries overtones of both, for he is at once passive ('I wait in the evening air') and active: 'I prepare to sail'. Perhaps that is because his journey is as much predetermined as voluntary. One *se* does, the other is done to.

296

Standing on the deck also brings to mind Felicia Heman's 'Casabianca':

> The boy stood on the burning deck
> Whence all but he had fled;
> The flame that lit the battle's wreck
> Shone round him o'er the dead....

In Abse's time, every schoolboy would have known the story of the boy, Casabianca, who, following his father's orders, remained on the deck of his ship in battle while all others deserted it. When it exploded, he went up with it.

His heroism is echoed in 'hammocks of waves', an allusion to Sir Henry Newbolt's 'Drake's Drum', yet another schoolboy classic. In this poem, Sir Francis Drake appears as a man who is always ready to spring to his country's defence:

> Drake he's in his hammock an' a thousand mile away,
> (Capten, art tha' sleepin' there below?)....
> Drake he's in his hammock till the great Armadas come
> (Capten, art tha sleepin' there below?)
> Slung atween the round shot, listenin' for the drum,
> An' dreamin arl the time o' Plymouth Hoe.
> Call him on the deep sea, call him up the Sound,
> Call him when ye sail to meet the foe;
> Where the old trade's plyin' an' the old flag flyin'
> They shall find him ware an' wakin', as they found him long ago!

Such samples of heroism obviously offer an ironic comment on Abse's tearstained departure from Cardiff, though, somewhat contradictorily, they also lend it a certain weight. At the same time, they paint a portrait of the kind of grammar-school boy he was, one who grew up at the tail end of Empire and enjoyed the kind of education which these texts, in all their earnestness and romance, were a part of. They also imply that his leaving is linked to his emergence as a poet, which in his mind is touched by these examples of maritime derring-do. The point is all the richer when placed in the context of Cardiff's role in the British Empire, with its emphasis on war, trade and the movement of people and ideas.

A further literary/historical lurks, perhaps, in the pier's 'black shapes' which are said to make 'the furthest star seem near' The reference here is to Keats's 'Bright star!' sonnet, once thought to be his last poem and composed at Lulworth Cove while he, too, was 'preparing to sail' for Italy in 1820, four months before his death. The comic disproportion between the two departures suggest Abse's status as an epigone, one who follows, partly in admiration, partly in resistance, the achievement of the older poet.

Even so, his divisions remain much more internal than external.

> Now the funnel's negations blow
> and my eyes, like spaces, fill,
> and the knots of water flow,
> pump to my eyes and spill.

> For what *who* would choose to go
> when *who* sailing made no choice?
> Not for one second, I know,
> can I be the same man twice.

This is Abse's farewell to Cardiff. Yet the '*who*' (or *se*) who leaves has not elected to do so while another '*who*' acknowledges that, once he has left, he can never recapture the '*se*' he used to be (or might have become). The Absean *se* is split, never to be healed again. He is both one who goes and one who resists (or laments) his going; he is both an initiator of movement and its subject, both hero and anti-hero. Henceforth, 'Abse' is the name given to the sum of these fragmented '*se*'s, contingent or historical.

As it happens, 1943, when Abse left Cardiff, coincides with the emergence of the philosophical movement known as existentialism, which emphasised the loss of fixed systems of values. All 'isms' had become 'wasms'. All that was left were individuals and their decisions in the void. It was in 1943 that Jean-Paul Sartre published *l'Etre et le neant* (Being and Nothingness), his examination of the meaning of human freedom in an empty universe. He emphasised the need for individuals to create '*se*'s for themselves, to assume responsibility for their actions rather than seeking to refer them to some preordained value system, be it social or ethical. Nothing in life was fixed; there was only the *se*, shaped in response to altering circumstances and to be followed by others. Such resolutions of the '*se*' might appear spontaneous but operated with the force of destiny. Since there was no essential *se*, only the *se* shaped by free will mattered. That was as much meaning as one could claim in a meaningless universe. First there was life – and then there was the end of life. All one could say was, 'Here am I; this is who I am'.

The contemporary poet who most influenced Abse, T.S. Eliot, wrote a famous poem about his comico-pathetic alter ego, J. Alfred Prufrock, portraying him as a man who nervously confronted a world that mystified him, forcing him 'To prepare a face to meet the faces that you meet'. Prufrock's social comedy hints at a deeper crisis of emptiness that besets him, Sartre's *nausee*. Prufrock's different 'faces' are the different selves that haunted Abse after he left Cardiff.

II

He was to return many years later, an occasion described in 'Return to Cardiff'. The opening word, 'Hometown', is placed in inverted commas, thus queering the concept. For Abse, Cardiff lacks secure identity of its own. (In another poem, 'Sons', he calls it an 'Awkward Anglo-Welsh half town, half countryside'.)

> The journey to Cardiff seemed less a return than a raid
> on mislaid identities....

Returning now allows him to explore the possible '*se*'s that might have developed had he remained. Equally, what was lost then has contributed to his life and to his poetry, which has responded to the shifting identities he contains within himself. There are any number of voices and experiences that come back to him from the past, 'odds and ends', but no one *se*.

> Unable to define anything I can hardly speak,
> and still I love the place for what I wanted it to be
> as much as for what it unashamedly is
> now for me, a city of strangers, alien and bleak.

'Hometown', indeed.

Abse's Cardiff, then, is not a 'was' but an 'is' as well as a 'what I wanted it to be', a real town but also the town of his imagination. It is not, however, the Cardiff of his youth; that has gone, never to be spoken of. Thus sundered from his memories, Abse mourns the what-might-have-been.

> Unable to communicate I'm easily betrayed,
> uneasily diverted by mere sense reflections
> like those anchored waterscapes that wander, alter, in the Taff,
> hour by hour, as light slants down a different shade.

Everything alters in a mutable world; the only reality is the smell of earth.

> No sooner than I'd arrived the other Cardiff had gone,
> smoke in the memory, these but tinned resemblances,
> where the boy I was not and the man I am not
> met, hesitated, left double footsteps, then walked on.

Abse haunts himself. In this ghostly meeting, trapped between past and present, he meets his Other, between one Cardiff and another, between illusion and reality, not the boy he was but the boy he was not, the one who never fathered the man he has become. By the same token, the Abse who returns is not the boy who lived in Cardiff but the man who developed as a result of the split within himself.

But if Abse is neither the boy nor the man, who is he? The short answer might be: the man who left Cardiff, the '*who*' who did not altogether want to leave but had to nevertheless. Had he remained, he might have become something different. No wonder he cannot identify with the boy he used to be. He is the sum of his discontinuous selves.

Such a sense of shifting identity would have seemed shocking to people of Walter Scott or Jane Austen's generation. Today, it is but a commonplace, and not only as proof of a neurotic personality. People accept that they contain different '*se*'s and that these may alter in given circumstances, an alteration that appears both inevitable and natural. As a result, the language they use to describe themselves has had to change. There is no one reality we open our eyes to, only those we construct for ourselves, in the same way that we construct our '*se*'s. Everything has become relative.

III

In 'In Llandough Hospital', Abse expands on this notion of the discontinuity of personality. The poem turns on the approaching death of his father:

> darkness will not come –
> his sunset slow, his first star pain.

Once again, as in 'Leaving Cardiff', it is evening and, once again, a departure is being prepared for, his father's life nearing its end as once his own moved in a different direction. And once again a star appears to highlight the void into which his father's life slips. The afterlife is no life at all.

It is this waiting void, this existencelessness or nothingness, that touches off memories of the Holocaust. By another striking coincidence, it was at the Wannsee Conference in 1942 that the Nazis settled on their 'final solution' of the Jewish question and initiated a programme of mass extermination in death camps, a trauma that now returns to haunt Abse's father's dying:

> Now, since death makes victims of us all,
> he's thin as Auschwitz in that bed.

No-one but a Jew could have written these lines – and then only about another Jew. Sylvia Plath's exploitation of Jewish suffering is well-known but leaves some readers queasy. Certainly, the results were vivid but, by metaphorising the Holocaust, she appears to diminish it. Her inner anguish was such as to make her feel that she, too, was a camp victim but, by appropriating the historical parallel to subserve her own, she opens up a gap between image and fact, her psychosis and the historical suffering of the Jews.

'In Llandough Hospital' is equally bold but more convincing. His father's approaching death reveals the fact that human beings are victims of a greater horror than the Nazis' – the world's emptiness. The comparison with Auschwitz and 'the camps of death' turns death into a kind of extermination. The Nazi experience points to a yet deeper chasm.

In 'In Llandough Hospital', new identities emerge to add to the ones I have already mentioned. There is Abse the doctor who, at the beginning pleads with another doctor to hasten his father's demise. Then there is Abse the Jew as well as Abse the Welshman, a duality familiar to readers of Abse's poetry. At the end, however, he speaks more simply as a man:

> here comes the night with all its stars,
> bright butchers' hooks for man and meat.

– a shocking image, both in its comparison of people to carcasses and for transforming the stars into butchers' hooks on which they are slung. 'Here comes the night' recalls the 'Oranges and Lemons' (especially the choppers that come to chop off your head) while the stars recall 'Twinkle, twinkle little star', whose diamond-like sparkle fill children with wonder and now shed their light on the dying man.

> I grasp his hand so fine, so mild,
> which still is warm surprisingly,
> not a handshake either, father,
> but as I used to when a child.

Here is another new '*se*': Abse, the son. He is not the least problematical of the personae we have been examining since, as we have seen, he has in effect mislaid his childhood. In this poem, he begins to rediscover it and only the drama of his father's death allows him to do so. The significance of the moment is emphasised in the third line of my quotation above when Abse directly addresses his father, at that moment converting the poem from one about his father to one spoken to him, memories of childhood and nursery rhymes easing the way.

In this fascinating poem, Abse's selves multiply, meet and conjoin: doctor, son, Jew, Welshman, boy, man, poet. Perhaps the child is even more significant than the Jew, just as the Jew predominates over the doctor and the doctor over the Welshman.

> And as a child can't comprehend
> what germinates philosophy,
> so like a child I question why
> night with stars, then night without end.

Abse questions the meaning of existence overshadowed by – determined by – death and whacking the traditional consolations of 'philosophy', be they natural or religious. The poem ends by contemplating an end that is no end at all and has no termination, aim or purpose.

Such is the account Abse gives of himself, Abse by Abse (*ab se*).

IV

Another Ab/*se* emerges in 'Case History', his description of his medical examination of a patient who makes disparaging references to the Welsh while praising 'the architects / of the German death-camps', adding a side-swipe at liberals ('White blacks'). By implication, Abse is one of these, too.

> When I palpated his liver
> I felt the soft liver of Goering;
> when I lifted my stethoscope
> I heard the heartbeats of Himmler;
> when I read his encephalograph
> I thought, '*Sieg heil, mein Führer*'

In reminding Abse of the Nazis, the patient activates in him a sense of revenge all the stronger for its association with their putting medicine to evil use. The patient's soft liver and heartbeats are at his mercy while poisons which could easily be administered lie near to hand.

> Yet I prescribed for him
> as if he were my brother.

No doubt, a very liberal – or Welsh or Jewish – thing to do. Abse loves his brother, even though his brother is so unlovable. Briefly, however, he has experienced in himself the black heart of history.

> Later that night I must have slept
> on my arm: momentarily
> my right hand lost its cunning.

The reference is to a line from Psalm 137 which, in the King James Bible, reads: 'If I forget you, O Jerusalem, let my right hand forget her cunning' (in the sense of 'skill' or 'ability'). In resisting the impulse to act against his patient, Abse has 'forgotten' or neglected his Jewishness. In this instance, Jew and doctor are set against each other.

That is an inevitable consequence of the dispersal of his '*se*'s triggered by his departure from Wales in 1943 and their relation to the Holocaust and the broader theme of the existential emptiness of life only adds to his quandary. In 'Last Visit to 198 Cathedral Road', Abse's father is dead and he now returns to the family home like a burglar, his pocket-torch picking out such details as a table, a vase or a curtain in the dark.

> Omnipotent, I returned them to the dark,
> sat sightless in the room that was out
> of breath and listened, that summer night,
> to Nothing.

'Omnipotent' is what God once was; now, the word ironically denotes no more than Abse's ability to return the rooms' furnishings to the dark with a flick of his switch. As Genesis does not say, let there be no light. The room in which he stands is described as 'out of breath', denoting the tension of the occasion and its variance with the summer setting.

'Nothing', at the end of the verse quoted above, is as revealing a word as 'Omnipotent', playing on the world's nothingness and Abse's inability to concentrate on any subject but his father's death.

> Not a fly the Z side of the windowpane,
> not one, comforting, diminutive sound
> when the silence calmed, became profound.

Nothing slides into silence as stillness covers everything. No life is to be found here, not one jot of it. The poet poises deep over sorrow as his *se* nears extinction.

V

Trapped thus between insecure adulthood and unmemoried youth and adrift in a city lacking a fixed historical identity, moving between different cultural and professional affiliations, Abse resists final definition. Rather, he is the product of the conflict between them: too Welsh/young to be London/old, too savage to be tame, too one thing to be another. Is he Welsh? Sort of; a Londoner? Up to a point; a doctor? Some of the time; a Jew? Of a sort; a son? No longer. Who, then, is he? One who lives 'At the frontier of Nowhere', a place where 'order and chaos clash', the very embodiment of the 20th century nightmare.

> Goodbye, 20th Century.
> What shall I mourn?
> Hiroshima? Auschwitz?
> Our friend, Carmi, said,
> 'Thank forgetfulness else
> we could not live;
> thank memory
> else we'd have no life'.

This, from 'A Letter from Ogmore', is addressed to Abse's wife, and the point is significant, for in tenderising the emotion Abse reveals another *se*, the husband and lover. Once again, the poem ponders the survival of humane values in the present world.

And, again, various ghosts gather – from his past, from his dead family and friends and from those who perished in World War II. Contending with them, a final '*se*' appears: the priest or seer charged with interpreting the blank 'unrolling / holy scrolls of the sea' at Ogmore-by-sea.

> ....The enigma is alive
> and, for the Present, I boast,
> thumbs in lapels, I survive.

He has become a survivor himself – not yet dead, still sexually active, still capable of appreciating art, music, literature and the 'Present', whether that signifies the passing moment or the gift of life itself.

Like another Glamorgan poet, Iolo Morganwg, Abse surveys the sea. But where Iolo would have detected seven sails when there was one, he gazes with a stricter eye, shoring his fragments against history's ruin.

> Goodbye, 20th Century,
> your trumpets and your drums,
> your war-wounds still unhealed....
> Has the Past always a future?

Has the future, too, died?

> Now secular strangers come
> sealed in Fords and Nissans,
> a congregation of cars,
> to this opening estuary
> so various, so beautiful, so old.
> The tide *is* out.
> And from the sleeping reeled-
> in sea – not from
> the human mind's vexed fathoms –
> the eternal, murderous,
> fanged Tusker Rock is revealed.

The fright of that last line is very great. Like Yeats, Abse adopts a prophetic stance here, one which derives from Matthew Arnold, whose mantle he deliberately assumes as he confronts the dangers that lie before him.

In particular, he refers to 'Dover Beach' and the death of faith that Arnold detected in the 'long, withdrawing roar' of the retreating tide. That tide is now fully out and humanity prepares itself against an even greater threat, one which, like Arnold's,

> Hath really neither joy, nor love, nor light,
> Nor certitude, nor peace, nor help for any pain;
> And we are here as on a darkling plain
> Swept with confused alarms of struggle and flight
> Where ignorant armies clash by night.

Those armies might portend the armies waiting to be released with such devastating effect in the 20th century.

What Arnold foresaw in his euphonious way, Abse locates in Tusker Rock. In that image lurks the geology of the absurd world – not the rock on which the church was built but the one on which it foundered. The bloody, predatory implications of the image appear with fearful energy. Perhaps the future has yet to die; even so, something is waiting which could destroy it.

But then that is what life always was: the struggle of the survivor against the murderous fangs poised against him, the being and then the not-being. The existential agony is the primeval one, after all.

Laura Wainright – 'Spatializing Memory in Dannie Abse's Poetry'

'Memory', Walter Benjamin suggests in 'A Berlin Chronicle' (1932), 'is not an instrument for exploring the past but its theatre. It is the medium of past experience, as the ground is the medium in which dead cities lie interred'.[1] Benjamin's spatial conceptualisation of memory as theatre and terrain, as well as his likening of former experiences to buried cities, are appropriate to his overall project in this essay of recalling – or excavating – the Berlin of his own childhood and youth, of what he calls his 'topographical route'[2] into his past. Moreover, Benjamin's analogies and approach often also resonate with many of the poems in Dannie Abse's *Welsh Retrospective* – a collection in which, as in 'A Berlin Chronicle', the nexus between space and memory is persistently conveyed and explored.

Several of the poems in *Welsh Retrospective*, in fact, take the city in which Abse grew up as their subject – 'Return to Cardiff', for example, which begins:

'Hometown'; well, most of us admit to an affection for a city:
grey, tangled streets I cycled on to school, my first
    cigarette
in the back lane, and, fool, my first botched love affair.
First everything. Faded torments; self-indulgent pity.[3]

These opening lines call to mind Benjamin's metaphor, as well as Primo Levi's later description, of 'the little theatre of memory';[4] it is as if we are hearing the thoughts or internal monologue of a speaker who is witnessing the dramatisation of his past experiences on stage, as he comments for example: 'my first / cigarette / [...] and, fool, my first botched love affair.' Indeed, the stressed word in this last line, 'fool', has distinctly thespian connotations, evoking the stock character in English Renaissance drama; and this connection is reinforced, both in the following stanza through Abse's reference to Cardiff Castle as 'a joker's toy façade' (l. 10) – an analogy which I discuss more fully below – and in another poem from *Welsh Retrospective*, 'The Game', where a football match at Ninian Park, the home of Cardiff City, metamorphoses into an Elizabethan-inspired 'theatre of memory':

The white ball smacked the crossbar. Satan rose
Higher than the others in the smoked brown gloom
to sink on grass in a ballet dancer's pose.
Again, it seems, we hear a familiar tune
not quite identifiable. A distant whistle blows.

Memory of faded games, the discarded years;
talk of Aston Villa, Orient, and the Swans.
Half-time, the band played the same military airs
as when the Bluebirds were champions.
Round touchlines the same cripples in their chairs.

Mephistopheles had his joke...[5]

As Abse reveals in his *Intermittent Journals*:

> I was nine [...] when I went to Ninian Park for the first time on my own. I
> watched a game between Cardiff City and Torquay United. Cardiff were
> floundering near the bottom of Division 3 [...]. No matter; the spruce
> military band [...] played the Bluebirds' inappropriate signature, 'Happy
> Days are Here Again' as the City team ran down the dark tunnel.[6]

In 'The Game', Christopher Marlowe's *Dr Faustus* (1604), in which
the tragic hero, Faustus, makes a pact with Satan after summoning a
demon, Mephistopheles, acts as a 'medium' for this past experience.
On one level, Abse seems to be invoking Marlowe's play in order to
suggest that a football match briefly renders the world more compre-
hensible and epistemologically certain, like a world where the
existence of God and the Devil, Heaven and Hell, has been proved;
as the speaker suggests, 'Here all is simplified, and we are partisan
who cheer the Good, / hiss at passing Evil. Was Lucifer offside?' Yet
this theatrical dimension also has further, more subtle implications,
creating a sense of the essentially staged or subjectively reconstructed
nature of 'remembrance' – of an activity that, as Benjamin proposes
in 'A Berlin Chronicle', 'is [after all, arguably] really the capacity for
endless interpolations into what has been'.[7]

In 'Return to Cardiff', memory is spatially located, in a literal
sense, not at Ninian Park, but in a Cardiff 'back lane' and on the 'grey
tangled streets' of the city that the speaker 'cycled on to school'; and
Abse's distinctly 'topographical route' into his past in this poem is
marked out more clearly in the second stanza:

> The journey to Cardiff seemed less a return than a raid
> on mislaid identities. Of course the whole locus smaller:
> the mile-wide Taff now a stream, the castle not as in
>   some black,
> gothic dream, but a decent sprawl, a joker's toy façade.

(ll. 6-10)

Here, childhood memories are distilled through a physical 'return' to Cardiff, and communicated by means of a distinctly spatial and topographical vocabulary exemplified in the speaker's references to the smaller 'locus' and 'the mile-wide Taff now a stream'. Moreover, Abse seems to be articulating, and attempting to comprehend, in spatial terms what Katie Gramich has described as the 'duality [...] between past and present selves'.[8] The visions of Cardiff Castle as sublime ('as in / some black, / gothic dream) and as 'decent' Victorian pastiche – the realisation of the fantasies of the Marquess of Bute ('a joker's toy façade') – as seen by the child and adult respectively, also register this process. Abse's conflation of self (or selves) and locale is apparent too in the speaker's description of his return as 'a raid on mislaid identities' – a 'raid' connoting a surprise attack on, or invasion of, a particular space, especially an urban building.

The returning 'self' of Abse's poem does indeed appear a kind of interloper in the space of contemporary Cardiff. The speaker perceives

> Unfocused voices in the wind, associations, clues,
> odds and ends, fringes caught, as when, after the doctor
>   quit,
> a door opened and I glimpsed the white, enormous face
> of my grandfather, suddenly aghast with certain news.
>
> Unable to define anything I can hardly speak,
> and still I love the place for what I wanted it to be
> as much as for what it unashamedly is
> now for me, a city of strangers, alien and bleak.

(ll. 11-19)

In these lines Cardiff becomes an almost Eliotic 'Unreal City':[9] a space that, like the ghostly, defamiliarised urban environment of T.S. Eliot's 1917 poem, 'Rhapsody on a Windy Night', seems momentarily to 'Dissolve the floors of memory / And all its clear relations / its divisions and precisions'.[10] The voices of the people, carried and snatched away by the wind, elicit an early memory of an, at the time, similarly half-understood, yet also, in this context, remote and dislocated moment – the appearance of the speaker's grandfather in a doorway, 'aghast with certain news'. Once again, there is a sense here of memory as 'the staging of the past'.[11] While ostensibly emulating a child's perception of an adult's shock, the speaker's recollection of a 'suddenly aghast', 'white, enormous face' also chimes with the earlier references to a 'fool' and a 'joker', and has a distinctly melodramatic quality. But this moment also evokes Benjamin's approach to memory in the sense that the speaker seems to be excavating his past from the disorder of his present environment 'like a man digging', and unearthing 'images, severed from all earlier associations, that stand – like precious fragments [...] – in the prosaic rooms of [his] later understanding.'[12]

In 'Return to Cardiff', then, Abse explores memory and selfhood through 'talking', as Benjamin does, 'of a space, of moments and discontinuities';[13] and this is similarly apparent in the penultimate stanza in which the speaker concedes:

> Illusory, too, that lost dark playground after rain,
> the noise of trams, gunshots in what they once called
> Tiger Bay...

(ll. 25-27)

Abse's use of 'they' in this second 'moment', rather than 'I' or 'we', emphasises the speaker's double-estrangement – his sense of distance, not only from the Cardiff of the present, but also, increasingly, from the Cardiff of the past. Like the 'Unreal city' that contemporary Cardiff has become, the Cardiff of the past is now similarly 'illusory', leaving the speaker to inhabit an intermediary psychological territory between past and present selves – a position that is spatially enacted in the closing stanza:

> No sooner than I'd arrived the other Cardiff had gone,
> smoke in the memory, these but tinned resemblances,
> where the boy I was not and the man I am not
> met, hesitated, left double footsteps, then walked on.

(ll. 31-34)

This act of 'walking' in a city – what Benjamin aptly, in this context, suggests might be called 'the art' of 'losing oneself' or 'straying'[14] – is only explicitly mentioned in these final lines of 'Return to Cardiff'. Nevertheless, it is often implicit in the text, and this idea of wandering through a particular space and into the past also forms the basis of 'On the Coast Road':

> Soon the roofs of Ogmore recede out of sight
> as I walk on awake in the wrong weather...
>
> Tons of air! And nobody on this coast road,
> and nobody on the beach below where
> the thaumaturge sea thrashes the rocks
> and hey-hey presto, fakes fountains of snow.
>
> Down there, on that rock's pulpit, my father fished
> till his days grew shorter. Now, briefly,
> this road leads to the Past. Is it the scolding wind
> that makes my teeth ache and my eyes water?
>
> At the old, shut farmhouse, I meet a boozy gang
> in fancy dress. The man in a white sheet
> holds up, on a pole, the skull of a horse.
> The Mari Lwyd? I blink. They vanish of course
>
> and the graffito I, as a boy, once chalked
> on the ruined barn beyond this farmhouse
> has vanished too: STRAIGHT ON TO THE FUTURE....[15]

In this poem a walk along the coast road at Ogmore-by-Sea, a location that Abse visited frequently as a child and where he now has a home,[16] leads the speaker into his 'Past' – the capitalisation of 'past', as if it were a physical place, recalling the way in which memory is spatialized in 'Return to Cardiff'. Also echoing 'Return to Cardiff', we see the externalised or spatial evocation of the speaker's feeling of suspension between past and present selves. Just as the Cardiff of the past and present appeared, suddenly, similarly 'illusory' in that poem, in 'On the Coast Road' contemporary Ogmore has a 'thaumaturge sea' that 'hey-hey presto, fakes fountains of snow', while the Ogmore of the past (encountered, once again, as 'images' of a 'gang / in fancy dress' led by a man holding up 'the skull of a horse' on a pole,[17] and a graffito that the speaker chalked on the wall of an old barn) repeatedly materialises and 'vanishes' in a way that makes it seem a part of the same disorientating magic show. In the case of the speaker's 'graffito', the conjuring trick is formally and typographically performed and inverted – the revelation that 'the graffito has vanished too' being directly followed by the reappearance, 'hey-presto', of, presumably, those very words: 'STRAIGHT ON TO THE FUTURE'. The similarly miraculous appearance and disappearance of 'the Mari Lwyd' – a Welsh folk rite that dramatises the encounter between the dead and the living, as well as the old year and the new – underscores the confluence of past and present in Abse's poem, recalling Vernon Watkins's Prologue to his 1947 'Ballad of the Mari Lwyd':

> It is New Year's Night.
> Midnight is burning like a taper. In an hour, in less than an hour, it will
> be blown out.
> It is the moment of conscience.
> The living moment.
> The dead moment.
> Listen.[18]

The magic theatre that Abse associates with the process of remembering in 'On the Coast Road' also creates a sense of the mysterious spontaneity of memory; but equally, as in 'The Game' and 'Return to Cardiff', the theme of performance hints at its constructed and even deceptive nature. This, in turn, foregrounds the malleability and indefiniteness of the notions of self that memory inevitably informs – an idea that re-emerges throughout *Welsh Retrospective*. In 'Leaving Cardiff' for example, Abse writes:

> For what *who* would choose to go
> when *who* sailing made no choice?
> Not for one second, I know,
> can I be the same man twice.[19]

It is not only walking, however, that facilitates Abse's spatial exploration of memory and self in this collection. In 'Down the M4', a car journey along the motorway into South Wales also 'leads', as in 'On the Coast Road', both 'TO THE FUTURE' and into 'the Past':

> Me! dutiful son going back to South Wales, this time
>   afraid
> to hear my mother's news...
>
> Each visit she tells me the monotonous story of clocks.
> 'Oh dear,' I say, or 'how funny,' till I feel my hair
>   turning grey
> for I've heard that perishable one two hundred times
>   before...
>
> Then the Tawe ran fluent and trout-coloured over
>   stones stonier,
> more genuine; then Annabella, my mother's mother,
>   spoke Welsh
> with such an accent the village said, 'Tell the truth,
>   fach,
> you're no Jewess. *They're* from the Bible. *You're* from
>   Patagonia!'
>
> I'm driving down the M4 again under bridges that leap
> over me, then shrink in my side mirror. Ystalyfera is
>   farther
> than smoke and God further than all distance known.
>   I whistle
> no hymn but an old Yiddish tune my mother knows.
>   It won't keep.[20]

Like 'On the Coast Road', this poem uses movement through space as a means of foregrounding the elusive and constructed nature of memory. As the speaker drives down the M4 towards South Wales, he simultaneously travels into memories of his previous visits to his mother's home in Ystalyfera, and, in turn, into her own remembrances. Paralleling the drive 'down the M4', both the speaker's and his mother's memories have become formulaic and almost rehearsed. The speaker's memories have coalesced into a generalised recollection of the repetitiveness of his mother's stories – an effect emphasised through Abse's use of the present tense ('Oh dear', I say, or 'how funny' [...] / [...] / for I've heard that perishable one two hundred times / before'). Within this ironic poetic voice we also hear that of the speaker's mother, both retrospectively romanticising the Ystalyfera of the past – 'Then, the [river] Tawe ran fluent and trout-coloured / over stones stonier, more genuine' – and privileging a particular past event: a naïve local reaction to her own mother's Welsh-Jewish origins. The emphasis on the partiality of memory here simultaneously reinforces its elusiveness – a quality that, once again, finds spatial expression through the speaker's description of the 'bridges that leap / over' his car and 'shrink in [his] side mirror'.

The fluidity which, as in 'On the Coast Road', Abse's portrayal of – or journey into – memory affords the self in 'Down the M4' has a particular significance. The poem, of course, dramatises Abse's own mixed Welsh and Jewish heritage[21] – his complex and conflicting sense of identity which, M. Wynn Thomas argues, has informed his 'long-standing cultivation of non-alignment as an art form',[22] or, as Jasmine Donahaye calls it, his 'deliberate multiplicity of not-belonging'.[23] In representing the memories of his Welshness and Jewishness as elusive, partial and constructed, Abse subtly presents the notion of identity shaped by those memories as mutable and insubstantial. This effect is encapsulated in the speaker's assertion that Ystalyfera is 'further than all distance known' – a statement that simultaneously suggests geographical, temporal and personal remoteness from Wales – and in the final lines of the poem: 'I whistle / no hymn but an old Yiddish tune my mother knows / It won't keep.' On the one hand, the speaker's insistence that the song is 'no hymn' distances him further from Welsh culture, yet there is also a strange conviction in his comment that the Yiddish tune 'won't keep' – a willing acceptance that it will inevitably be caught up in, and concealed or worn away by, the selective processes of memory. What is clear from this poem, and indeed from many of the poems in *Welsh Retrospective*, is that, like Benjamin, Abse uses particular spaces as areas in which to embrace or 'abandon [himself] to [both] the shifting currents of [...] memories'[24] and the shifting sense of identity that they create.

NOTES

1. Walter Benjamin, 'A Berlin Chronicle', in *One-Way Street and Other Writings*, translated by Edmund Jephcott and Kingsley Shorter, 2nd edn (London and New York: Verso, 1997), pp. 293-346 (p. 315).
2. Ibid., p. 306.

3. Dannie Abse, 'Return to Cardiff', in *Welsh Retrospective*, 2nd edn (Bridgend: Seren, 2008), p. 20, ll. 1-5. All further references to Abse's poems are to this edition.
4. Primo Levi, 'The Little Theatre of Memory', in *The Voice of Memory: Interviews 1961-87*, ed. Marco Belpolti and Robert Gordon, translated by Robert Gordon (Cambridge: Polity, 2001) pp. 47-56 (p. 47).
5. Dannie Abse, 'The Game', pp. 21-22, ll. 16-26.
6. Dannie Abse, *Intermittent Journals* (Bridgend: Seren, 1994), pp. 199-120.
7. Benjamin, p. 316.
8. Katie Gramich, 'Both In and Out of the Game: Welsh Writers and the British Dimension', in *A Guide to Welsh Literature: Welsh Writing in English* VII, ed. M. Wynn Thomas (Cardiff: University of Wales Press, 2003), pp. 255-277 (p. 258).
9. T.S. Eliot, 'The Waste Land', in *T.S. Eliot: Selected Poems* (London: Faber and Faber, 1961), p. 42, l. 60. All further references to Eliot's poems are to this edition.
10. T.S. Eliot, 'Rhapsody on a Windy Night', p. 16, ll. 5-7.
11. Susan Sontag, 'Introduction', in Walter Benjamin, *One-Way Street and Other Writings*, translated by Edmund Jephcott and Kingsley Shorter, 2nd edn (London and New York: Verso, 1997), pp. 7-28 (p. 13).
12. Benjamin, p. 314.
13. Benjamin, p. 316.
14. Ibid., p. 298.
15. Dannie Abse, 'On the Coast Road', p. 73, ll. 1-23.
16. Cary Archard, 'Introduction', in Dannie Abse, *Welsh Retrospective*, 2nd edn (Bridgend: Seren, 2008), pp. 7-9 (p. 7).
17. As Cary Archard notes, '*The Mari Lwyd* refers to a Welsh folk custom which still exists in the area around Maesteg, north of Dannie Abse's home in [Ogmore,] South Wales. The custom centres on a horse's skull carried on a pole which was led from house to house during the Christmas season.' Cary Archard, 'Notes', in Dannie Abse, *Welsh Retrospective*, 2nd edn (Bridgend: Seren, 2008), pp. 81-91 (p. 90).
18. Vernon Watkins, 'Ballad of the Mari Lwyd', in *The Complete Poems of Vernon Watkins* (Ipswich: Golgonooza Press, 1986), p. 41, ll. 17-23.
19. Dannie Abse, 'Leaving Cardiff', p. 11, ll. 15-16.
20. Dannie Abse, 'Down the M4', p. 19, ll. 1-29.
21. As Archard notes, Ystalyfera is 'the village where Dannie Abse's mother was born and grew up, on the River Tawe north of Swansea.' Archard, 'Notes', p. 81.
22. M. Wynn Thomas, 'Prints of Wales: Contemporary Welsh Poetry in English', in *Poetry in the British Isles: Non-Metropolitan Perspectives*, ed. Hans-Werner Ludwig and Lothar Fietz (Cardiff: University of Wales Press, 1995), pp. 97-114 (p. 101).
23. Jasmine Donahaye, '"A dislocation called a blessing": Three Welsh-Jewish Perspectives', in *Welsh Writing in English: A Yearbook of Critical Essays*
24. Benjamin, p. 295.

ACKNOWLEDGEMENTS

The compilation of this Sourcebook would not have been possible without the support and cooperation of Dannie Abse who has been unfailingly generous with his time and advice. Seren is particularly grateful for his permission to reprint the material included in Section A which covers some fifty years of his writing career.

I am also grateful to the following for their kind permission to reprint their essays and reviews: Fleur Adcock, Alan Brownjohn, Tony Curtis, James A. Davies, Jasmine Donahaye, Katie Gramich, Daniel Hoffman, John Lucas, William Oxley, John Pikoulis, Richard Poole, Jeremy Robson, John Smith, Daniel Weissbort. The essays by John Pikoulis and Laura Wainwright were especially commissioned for this book. I am grateful to Carolin Hendschke for compiling the index.

SELECTED BIBLIOGRAPHY

By Dannie Abse

Poetry

After Every Green Thing (London: Hutchinson, 1948)
Walking under Water (London: Hutchinson, 1952)
Tenants of the House (London: Hutchinson, 1957)
Poems, Golders Green (London: Hutchinson, 1962)
Dannie Abse: Pocket Poets (London: Vista, 1963)
A Small Desperation (London: Hutchinson, 1968)
Selected Poems (London: Hutchinson, 1970)
Funland And Other Poems (London: Hutchinson, 1973)
Penguin Modern Poets: D. Abse, D.J. Enright, M. Longley (London, 1976)
Collected Poems 1948-1976 (London: Hutchinson, 1977)
Way Out in the Centre (London: Hutchinson, 1981)
Ask the Bloody Horse (London: Hutchinson, 1986)
White Coat, Purple Coat: Poems 1948-1988 (London: Hutchinson, 1989)
Remembrances of Crimes Past: Poems 1986-89 (London: Hutchinson, 1990)
Selected Poems (London: Penguin, 1994)
On the Evening Road (London: Hutchinson, 1994)
Welsh Retrospective (Bridgend: Seren, 1997)
Arcadia, One Mile (London: Hutchinson, 1998)
New And Collected Poems (London: Hutchinson, 2003)
Running Late (London: Hutchinson, 2006)
New Selected Poems 1949-2009 (London: Hutchinson, 2009)
Two For Joy (London: Hutchinson, 2010)

Novels

Ash on a Young Man's Sleeve (London: Hutchinson, 1954)
Some Corner of an English Field (London: Hutchinson, 1956)
O. Jones, O. Jones (London: Hutchinson, 1970)
There Was a Young Man from Cardiff (London: Hutchinson, 1991)
The Strange Case of Dr Simmonds And Dr Glas (London: Robson Books, 2002)

Autobiography and other prose

Medicine on Trial (London: Aldus, 1967)
A Poet in the Family (London: Hutchinson, 1974)
A Strong Dose of Myself (London: Hutchinson, 1983)
Journals from the Ant-Heap (London: Hutchinson, 1986)
Intermittent Journals (Bridgend: Seren, 1994)
Goodbye, Twentieth Century (London: Pimlico, 2001)
The Two Roads Taken (London: Enitharmon, 2003)
The Presence (London: Hutchinson, 2007)

Miscellanies

Miscellany One (Bridgend: Poetry Wales Press, 1981)
Touch Wood (Llanrwst: Carreg Gwalch Cyf, 2002)

Plays

Fire in Heaven (London: Hutchinson, 1956)
Three Questor Plays (London: Scorpion, 1967)
The Dogs of Pavlov (London: Valentine Mitchell, 1973)
Pythagoras (London: Hutchinson, 1979)
The View from Row G (Bridgend: Seren, 1990)

Editor

Poetry And Poverty, Nos. 1-7 (London, 1949-1954)
Mavericks: An Anthology (with H. Sergeant) (London: Editions
    Poetry and Poverty, 1957)
Modern European Verse (London: Vista, 1964)
Corgi Modern Poets in Focus (London: Corgi, 1971)
Poetry Dimension Nos. 2-7 (London: Robson Books, 1974-1980)
Wales in Verse (London: Secker, 1983)
Doctors And Patients (Oxford: Small Oxford Books, 1984)
Voices in the Gallery (with Joan Abse) (London: Tate, 1986)
The Music Lover's Literary Companion (with Joan Abse) (London:
    Robson Books, 1988)
The Hutchinson Book of Post-War British Poets (London:
    Hutchinson, 1989)
Twentieth Century Anglo-Welsh Poetry (Bridgend: Seren, 1997)
Homage To Eros (London: Robson Books, 2003)

On Dannie Abse

Books and Articles

Cohen J. (ed): *The Poetry Of Dannie Abse* (London: Robson Books, 1983)

Conran, Tony: 'Funland and the Work of Dannie Abse' in *Frontiers in Anglo-Welsh Poetry* (Cardiff: University Of Wales Press, 1997), pp. 234-248

Curtis, T.: *Dannie Abse*, Writers Of Wales Series (Cardiff: UWP, 1985)

Gramich, Katie: 'Both in And out of the Game: Welsh Writers And the British Dimension' in M. Wynn Thomas (ed): *Welsh Writing in English* (Cardiff: UWP, 2003), pp. 257-261

Hawkes, T.: 'Dannie Abse Selected Poems', *Poetry Wales* 6.2 (Autumn 1970)

Hoffman, D.: 'Doctor and Magus in the Work of Dannie Abse', *Literature and Medicine 3*, (NY, 1984)

Jones, Glyn: *Profiles* (Llandysul: Gomer, 1980), pp. 332-335

Mathias, Roland: 'The Head Still Stuffed with Feathers', *Anglo-Welsh Review* 15.36 (Summer 1966)

Mathias, Roland: 'The One Voice That Is Mine', *AWR* 16.38 (Winter 1967)

Oxley, William: 'Poetry and Pizza', *New Welsh Review* 11.2 (Autumn 1989)

Pikoulis, John: 'Dannie Abse: Predicaments of Otherness', *Poetry Wales* 13.2 (October 1977)

Punter, David: 'Varieties of Defiance', *Straight Lines* 2 (1979)

Sergeant, Howard: 'The Poetry of Dannie Abse', *Books and Bookmen*, (July 1977)

Smith, John: 'The Search for Identity', *Cahiers Franco-Anglais* vol 1 (1967)

Winegarten, Renee: 'Dannie Abse: Vision and Reality', *Jewish Chronicle Literary Supplement* (December 1982)

Wroe, Nicholas: 'Profile', *The Guardian* (March 2003)

Interviews

Poetry Book Society Bulletin, Summer 1962
Jewish Quarterly, Winter 1963-64: *Flame* (University of Essex)
   March 1967
Anglo-Welsh Review, Spring 1974
The Guardian, January 31, 1978
Good Housekeeping, May 1981
The Times, February 28, 1983
New Welsh Review, 11.2 1989
Chiron Review, Spring 2000
New Welsh Review 62, Winter 2003
Sunday Times, November 12, 2006
The Times, August 16, 2008

INDEX

Page references to extracts are shown in bold.

Index

Index